After a Child Dies
Counseling Bereaved Families

Sherry Johnson, R.N., Ph.D., has worked extensively in thanatology over the last 15 years. She is a graduate of North Park College, Chicago, Illinois in nursing and psychology. Dr. Johnson received an M.S. in psychiatric nursing and a Ph.D. in clinical nursing research (thanatology) from the University of Michigan, Ann Arbor. She writes, researches, lectures, teaches, and practices in the areas of loss, death, dying, and bereavement. Currently she is in private practice as a grief therapist at South Shore Pastoral Counseling Associates in Hingham, Massachusetts, where she lives with her husband, Dr. William Soderberg, and their daughter, Britt.

After a Child Dies,
Counseling
Bereaved Families

Sherry E. Johnson, R.N., Ph.D.

SPRINGER PUBLISHING COMPANY
NEW YORK

Springer Publishing Company, Inc.
536 Broadway
New York, NY 10012

88 89 90 91 / 5 4 3 2

Library of Congress Cataloging-in-Publication Data

Johnson, Sherry E.
  After a child dies.

  Bibliography: p.
  Includes index.
  1. Children—Death—Psychological aspects.
2. Bereavement—Psychological aspects. 3. Parents—
Counseling of. I. Title. [DNLM: 1. Attitude to
Death. 2. Counseling. 3. Death—in infancy &
childhood. 4. Grief. BF 575.G7 J69a]
BF575.G7J625   1987   155.9'37   87-16637
ISBN 0-8261-5690-8

Printed in the United States of America

. . . to my best friends, supporters, and loves
Bill and Britt

MALCOLM: Merciful Heaven!
What man! Ne'er pull your hat upon your brows;
Give sorrow Words. The grief that does not speak
Whispers the o'erfraught heart and bids it break.

SHAKESPEARE (*Macbeth*, Act IV, Sc. 3, 204–205)

Contents

Acknowledgments

How does one thank the people who have helped question, develop, and implement such a project? There have been so many people who have brought me to this point: my mentors, my family and friends, those who assisted with editorial and typing tasks, and the families from my research and practice. It is these people I wish to acknowledge.

I have had many mentors and helpers; some of whom may not even be aware of their role. I thank my professors and clinical mentors who helped me learn to think, explore, research, and practice: these include Dr. Maxine Loomis, Dr. Jean Wood, Dr. David J. Stinson, Dr. Jeanne Quint Benoliel, Dr. Eric Bermann, Dr. Samuel Schultz, Dr. Carolyn Aradine, Dr. Marti Hoffman, Dr. Al Cain, Dr. Elisabeth Kübler-Ross, Ms. Delores Johnson (deceased), Ms. Hannah Plaut, Dr. Melvin Sonneson, Rev. Mary Miller, Rev. Herb Freedholm, Dr. Zenos Hawkinson, Mr. David Thorburn, and Dr. Zaffar Rizvi.

I wish to thank abundantly my family, Bill and Britt Soderberg, who were so patient in their help and support. I thank Britt for developing part of the title. I thank my parents, Verna and Russell Johnson, who raised me with love, the quest for knowledge, and a meaningful religious background. To my sister, Sue Lindberg, and her family (Wes, Sally, Jon, and Erik) and my grandmother, Minnie Johnson, I give thanks for continuous encouragement and multiple ways of support.

My cousins (Joann, Paul, Sven, and Lars Gustafson) were also extremely supportive and always helped me find the "truth." I thank Eleanore (my spouse's aunt) and Bob Berguist for always being there for us. Special love goes to our Papa, William A. Soderberg (who died in 1984) and Betty Clapp (our babysitter and supporter) who for eight years kept home life as consistent and pressureless as possible. Their love was more than was expected or deserved.

Much thanks also goes to my dear friends and colleagues: especially my associates at South Shore Pastoral Counseling in Hingham, Massachusetts—Dr. Paul Chaffee, Dr. Norman Pierce, Dr. Ann Webb, Dr. Ron Siegal, Karen Farmer; Keohane Funeral Home; Jane and Darrell Balmer; "The Dirty Dozen"; Dr. Philip and Cathy Sokoloff; Ann Anderson; Beth Eckert; Dr. Dan and Debbie Weinstein; Elizabeth and Ralph Anderson. Some of these and other supportive friends' and relatives' first names appear in this book as pseudonyms for the families presented here.

I offer great appreciation to Nina Leek, in addition to Dr. Adrian Leek, who provided invaluable assistance in editing the manuscript, being supportive, giving food, wine, and hugs. I thank Mark Cahill for his editorial comments and support. I also thank my editor, Ruth Chasek, who made thoughtful and helpful comments on the manuscript.

With gratitude I thank Susan Richards Kilmartin who created artwork to enhance the concepts presented here. Other artwork was done by my clients.

Special gratitude and love to Jane Davies Cahill. Her speedy fingers, editorial comments, willingness, and dedication extended far beyond work hours and human limits, and helped keep my anxiety level at a minimum. I am indebted to Ms. Donna Zweep, who initially typed chapters of this book, as well as the previous research papers. Much thanks goes to Personal Computer Resources (PCR), in Norwell, MA. The staff's computer assistance was very much appreciated.

Sincere gratitude is expressed to the parents in my research and my clients who welcomed me into their lives, shared intimate details and secrets, and helped me to understand their grief more fully. Their sharing of their pain and loss has taught me much, which has been translated to other bereaved families. These people have been my teachers, and I hope will be yours.

Introduction

This book is intended for practitioners who counsel survivors, particularly families who have experienced the death of a child. The qualitative, rather than quantitative approach used stems from my own background in thanatology as a hands-on practitioner of grief therapy.

The stimulus for this book came from a need that evolved from my practice, research, lecturing, and therapy supervision of health professionals in order to provide better care for clients who had faced the death of a loved one. In speaking to professionals around the country, I have been asked continually for more detailed information on how I conduct grief therapy; my framework for treatment in dealing with the assessment of family themes; the individual nature of grief, mourning, and bereavement; and the implementaton of appropriate interventions.

My own interest in working with the dying and bereaved began when I was working on my master's degree in psychiatric nursing at the University of Michigan during the late sixties. Two events in particular began my journey. The first was that I met Elizabeth Kübler-Ross, then unknown, who was coming to the University to interview dying persons. Her book on her experience with dying people was soon to be published. At that time, I thought "Why would anyone want to do that?" (a question I am now often asked myself). I began to realize, however, that I had been socialized *not* to deal with or care for dying persons other than their physical needs. I had been taught, nonverbally, to place the dying person at the end of the hall. When a patient would say something like "I think I'm dying," I would disagree and say "Oh no, you are doing much better today!" I began to realize that I had been taught in my home, church, and schools not to deal with "those folks," even though I was an educated health professional.

The second event occurred during this same period. In addition to coming to the realization of a need for a better understanding of death and dying, a personal crisis occurred that made a lasting and painful impresson upon me. I experienced the first death of a person whom I loved very much: my future mother-in-law, Linnea Soderberg. She had fought a valiant battle with cancer for over 20 years, but she lost the fight for life. In addition to the grief and pain of this loss, I was disturbed by the obvious uneasiness and lack of knowledge shown by the physician, nurses, and hospital in caring for this dying woman and her family. I thought that there had to be a better way to help patients and families cope.

These two critical and important situations started me on my journey in the area of thanatology and led me to my current practice and research. Over the years, it has become more and more apparent that I needed to write about grief, mourning, and bereavement for other therapists and health care professionals as an extension of my therapeutic work with individual clients. The book is for a wide range of health professionals, including nurses, physicians, social workers, psychologists, and clergy, who find themselves working with this population.

Many health professionals often have frequent, although not necessarily structured or intense, emotional contact with families who are grieving. A therapist, on the other hand, enters into a contract in treating and reconstructing the emotional health of clients. I will use the word "counselor" in the book since this term addresses both therapists and the broader group of health professionals who may find themselves in a grief counseling role.

I strongly believe that those in the health professions who have the opportunity and knowledge to conduct early interventions in their counseling can make a difference to the outcome of grief. However, it is important to know one's limits and to know when to refer a person or family to a specialist in grief therapy, because of pathology or the potential for pathology.

The terms grief, mourning, and bereavement are often, and unfortunately, used interchangeably. I regard each term as having a distinct meaning. Grief involves the multiple feelings, physical and emotional reactions, and behaviors surrounding a loss. Bereavement is an all-encompassing term that includes the physical, emotional, social, and cultural responses to the pain of loss. Mourning, on the other hand, is the process of readjustment to one's life with the loss. These terms will be used accordingly throughout this book.

The information presented in this book tends to be qualitative in nature and is based upon hundreds of bereaved parents and families whom I have treated over the past 15 years. Each of these individuals and families has contributed to my data base and are the heroes of this book. Inasmuch as hard numbers and data are usually recognized as the foundation of professional research, a humanistic and qualitative approach is essential in a practice confronting the human pain of dying and bereavement. This "grounded theory" approach has been the basis of my practice and research (Glaser & Strauss, 1967). The development of this data, theory, knowledge, and techniques form the basis of this book.

Although other examples of grief will be shared, including grief of siblings, the primary focus of this book is the painful grief of parents who have had a child die. The theory of grief themes described in this book may be applied to other types of losses and crises, but it seems particularly important to address the special problems of counseling grieving parents.

Parental grief is a unique and special kind of grief because it arouses the cultural taboo of children dying before their parents. It brings to the fore the ultimate issues of powerlessness, guilt, and the fact that as parents they were unable to protect their own child. In addition, after a death of a child, parents often question their own values, roles, and beliefs. There is much potency and pain with such a death.

I most often treat either one or both parents and young siblings for grief. The group that I rarely have the opportunity to treat are adolescents, and this gap is reflected in the book. It is often very difficult for the adolescent to recognize that there is or could be a need for counseling, and consequently be willing to enter into such a therapeutic contract.

Adolescents are not unlike others who hesitate to enter treatment because they fear other people might think they are "crazy" or think they are "weak" because they need help with their problems. Because of this peer pressure, many adolescents are "not ready" to confront their loss(es) until sometime later in adulthood. Many adults who have suffered the death of someone close during childhood and adolescence wish that they had dealt with their grief then because of the pathology that developed from the repression. However, it is difficult to convince adolescents that "anything" could be good for them, including therapy.

In the following pages I will explore the development of a child's concept of death; discuss family methods or "themes" of coping with crises that typically occur after a death; describe grief "symptoms," that is, common reactions, both psychological and physical to bereavement; review the stages of grief in the first, second, and third years of bereavement; and discuss therapeutic interventions. Theory, research, and many clinical examples will be used to explore these issues.

Additionally, I will explore the emotional well-being of the health professional. This is an often overlooked and neglected area. Working in such an intense and sad area provides fertile ground for burnout. It is important for the therapist or counselor to be involved and yet learn to detach her or himself from the sufferings of clients and families. Above all, the counselor must maintain a separate, satisfying, and enjoyable private life.

REFERENCES

Glaser, B., & Strauss, A. L. (1967). *The discovery of grounded theory: Strategies for qualitative research*. Chicago: Aldine Publishing.

CHAPTER I

The Development of A Child's Concept of Death

This chapter will explore how a child develops a concept of death. The development of the concept of death is a complicated and lengthy process whereby the child learns that death is irreversible, permanent, and universal. Clinical, theoretical, and research approaches will be discussed to show the development of concepts in the normal growth and development of a child into adult life. Effects of cultural and socioeconomic influences on this development, as well as changes that take place once a terminal illness has occurred, will also be explored in this chapter. The process of normal development will be presented in sections from infancy to 2 years, 2 to 7 years, 7 to 12 years, adolescence, and adulthood.

This information is the foundation for understanding how the concept of death develops in an infant and influences one's reaction to loss and grief throughout the life span. This chapter provides fundamental concepts in counseling the bereaved at any age.

This discussion should not only assist the professional in understanding how a child develops a concept of death, but also may be helpful in teaching parents and grieving people to understand the necessity of such games as "Peek-a-Boo" and "Hide-and-Seek," and their own regressions in separation anxiety because of a loss.

NORMAL GROWTH AND DEVELOPMENT OF A CHILD'S CONCEPT OF DEATH

Infancy to Two Years

As far as we know, the healthy newborn reacts to any life situation with a stimuli-and-response behavior. The same seems to be true when a life-threatening situation is at hand. There is no evidence that a newborn has any intellectual capacity to understand death. The question then becomes: How does the child learn to understand the concept of death?

As young as 3 months of age, the child begins to experiment with his or her awareness of presence and absence via games like Peek-a-Boo and later Hide-and-Seek. These seemingly unimportant games help the child to develop object and person permanence. These two concepts involve learning that "things" and people exist even though the infant cannot see them. This is a very difficult concept to master. Until approximately age 6 months the child will not know to retrieve an item or person if it is out of sight; this relates to the old saying, "Out of sight—out of mind." Consequently, if the infant cannot see it, it does not exist.

It is also during this time that separation anxiety begins to develop. This is a series of protest responses that occur when a child is removed from the sight of his or her parent and placed with strangers (Schaffer & Emerson, 1964). Separation anxiety begins at about 5 weeks, peaks at about 7 to 10 months, and then levels off at about 18 months.

Once the child "understands" object and person permanence and separation anxiety he or she can distinguish between presence and absence. A child 3 years old or younger, however, probably does not comprehend the difference between absence and death. Separation anxiety and object and person permanence are probably the beginning of the concept and fear of death.

Bowlby's study (1960) of separation anxiety describes three responses to separation: protest, despair, and detachment. Most parents are aware of some of these behaviors: the child protests violently when the parent goes out the door, and then, because object and person permanence has not totally developed, immediately stops crying. This is normal, although the new parent often feels devastated because he or she is not missed. When the child is separated from the parents for long periods of time, as in a hospital situation, the child will appear despairing and eventually become very detached and not respond to human contact. Bowlby's work is important because it indicates that a young child responds to a loss with separation anxiety, long before he or she understands the concept of death.

Some of the responses to separation anxiety are similar to the grief and mourning an adult experiences. Helene Deutsch (1959) suggested that the mature ego (the adult) experiences grief, while the young child experiences separation anxiety. The responses may be similar, but the labels are different. Of course, the cognitive processes and many of the symptoms are different, but basic symptoms such as crying, sadness, or anger are similar.

The question of a child experiencing grief and mourning is controversial. Much of the research on separation anxiety is psychoanalytic in nature. Data were collected during and just after World War II, which itself had an impact on the development of those children's concept of death. Even though the war may have had an effect, the question still remains: can a child under 2 years old experience grief and mourning or is he or she experiencing separation anxiety?

From clinical experience, I believe that until object and person permanence has developed and separation anxiety has decreased, the child is experiencing separation anxiety and not grief. However, through the cognitive learning process of object and person permanence and separation anxiety, the foundation of the concept of death is forming. The child learns that people go away, BUT RETURN. Children need to know that people and objects exist even though they are not in their immediate environment. Death involves NOT RETURNING. It seems inconceivable that the concept of death (not returning) could develop without the preexistence of object and person permanence and separation anxiety. The child cannot comprehend NOT RETURNING unless he or she understands RETURNING.

Two- to Seven-Year-Olds

Taking these concepts into account, at what age does separation anxiety become grief and mourning? The research of Anthony (1940), Steiner (1965), and Koocher (1974) proposes that a child's understanding of death follows Piaget's theory of cognitive development.

Piaget (1965) labels four stages of development (see Table 1-1). The first stage is the prelanguage stage where the basis for future development occurs (e.g., object and person permanence). The second stage, from 2 to 7 years, is the preoperational stage. Skills to interact with the environment, like speaking and walking, are de-

TABLE 1-1. Piaget's Four Stages of Development

Stage	Age
1. Prelanguage	Prespeech
2. Preoperational	2–7 years
3. Logic and reasoning	7–12 years
4. Propositional operations, implications, and logic	13 years and older

veloped. The third stage is concrete operations, which occurs between 7 and 12 years of age. Logic and reasoning predominate this stage. The concerns of the fourth stage, which is attained at the preadolescent and adolescent levels, center on propositional operations, implications, and logic.

The research of Anthony, Steiner, and Koocher in addition to Piaget's work, suggests that the 3- to 6-year-olds tend to mix magic and reality when thinking about the causes of death. They also tend to believe that death is reversible, like the flowers dying in the fall and then blooming again in the spring (see Table 1-2).

This "magical" thinking seems to be supported by cartoons and other media, such as movies and television. For example, the child may see "Wile E. Coyote" falling off a cliff to the bottom of the ocean, exploding but then running alive in the desert.

Another media example that supports a child's belief that death is reversible, and adds to the confusion, would be when a child sees an actress killed on a television show one week and then sees her appearing on another program or in a movie the next. Since the young child is unable to reason logically these life experiences, he or she concludes that people can die, but that they will later return.

Because of the lack of cognitive ability to understand the difference between fantasy and reality, the child often fears that he or she has caused the death of a loved one by some deviant behavior or thought. For example, a 5-year-old boy was referred to me by his school nurse. This child had always had a discipline problem until his mother was killed in a car accident. Soon after her death, his be-

TABLE 1-2. Ages Three to Six

Mix magic and reality
Death is reversible

havior changed dramatically and he became a very compliant child. Although his teacher was very pleased with his new behavior, the school nurse was very perceptive in noticing that something was wrong. The boy's father, too, had difficulty realizing that this change of behavior, for what appeared to be the better, could be a warning sign. The child and father consented to therapy. As we worked in therapy, I began to uncover the secret that was reflected by his change in behavior. He believed that he had caused his mother's death by telling her that he hated her and was going to run away from home after an argument that they had the day she was killed.

Another girl, a 6-year-old, developed a school phobia after her grandmother died. She believed she had killed her grandmother because she did not draw enough pictures for her. It may seem like a silly and trivial reason, but she truly believed this was why her grandmother died. The guilt and the pain were acted out through her school phobia.

Seven- to Eleven-Year-Olds

Between 7 and 11 years of age, children become aware that death is irreversible, permanent, and universal (see Table 1-3). Because of cognitive, emotional, and additional variables they develop a concept of death. They also understand death vocabulary and are able to give specific examples of the causes of death (e.g., "she died of cancer"). This development is consistent with Piaget's third stage of concrete operations. The child can now utilize logic and reason as he or she processes information.

Children at this age are able to give examples of abstract causes of death. ("He was not a very good person and that is why he died.") This type of reasoning makes it difficult to understand a death that does not fit into their abstract logic. ("I don't know why Kelly died. She was so good and *good* people aren't supposed to die so young.")

Adults may also exhibit this childlike type of questioning, when there is no answer. This type of thinking often happens when people have no legitimate or logical reason for the loss. Rabbi Harold S. Kushner's book, *When Bad Things Happen to Good People* (1981) has helped many grieving people to realize that often there are no answers. There are easy answers, but when a child, or adult, is at this fourth level of thinking they attempt to find an answer, even if it means that they shoulder the blame themselves.

With the development of logical thinking about death, fears also become apparent. Children begin to recognize that death will also

TABLE 1-3. Ages Seven to Eleven

Death becomes:
1. Irreversible
2. Permanent
3. Universal
4. They are aware of death vocabulary
5. They can give specific examples of death
6. They have abstract causes of death
7. They express logical thoughts about death
8. They express fears of death

---

happen to them. To cope with these fears, they will often sing well known childhood chants such as

> The worms crawl in,
> The worms crawl out,
> The worms play penuchle on your snout,
> Your stomach turns a slimy green,
> And pus comes out like shaving cream

or practice superstitions such as holding their breath as they pass a graveyard. By making up a game or singing a song children are able to cope with the fear of death, believing that they can control the danger. Children can also cope by identifying with the feared object; for example, during Halloween children dress up as feared objects, such as ghosts, thereby identifying with them.

Adolescence

There is little published research on the adolescent's concept of death. Although 13-year-olds may have an adult attitude toward death, they are not yet adults. There are some differences between adolescent and adult reactions to death, although they are difficult to define fully. The adolescent is continually searching for "self," developing emotional and intellectual tools, and is strongly influenced by cultural mores. Time is extremely important; they live intensely in the present and death is only a remote possibility (see Table 1-4).

Jersild (1978) states that the adolescent fantasizes about death. He believes that if the adolescent is faced with death, he or she would tend to believe it possible to be rescued at the last minute. This belief

TABLE 1-4. Adolescent Concepts

1. Searching for self
2. Developing emotional and intellectual tools
3. Influenced by cultural mores
4. Time urgent
5. Death seems remote

may have some relationship to the high suicide rate among teenagers. They may plan and attempt a suicide, believing that they will be rescued at the last minute.

Kastenbaum (1967) believes that the brighter adolescent thinks a great deal about death, while others shy away from it. One has to take into account the adolescent's socialization regarding death, both at home and in the environment. There are many personal, cultural, socioeconomic, and religious influences that can affect the development of a concept of death for the normal child. Several examples of these influences are the age of one's first experience with death; the degree of attachment to the person who died; how the experience was perceived by the child; and learned cultural ways of behaving, feeling, or thinking about the death.

Adult

By the time a person reaches adulthood, he or she should comprehend that death is universal, irreversible, and permanent and respond with grief feelings and reactions. Although adults may exhibit similar qualities as the adolescent such as time urgency and search for self, age and death experiences often assist in the realization that death is more of a certainty to all.

Although the permanent concept of death should be firm, traumatic death and loss experiences, as well as cultural, social, educational, economic, and religious variables, have evolved to produce often death-denying behaviors within a person or family. Therefore, the concept is understood, but the process, feelings, and reactions denied. This may occur through the development of a conspiracy of silence, denial of grief symptoms and feelings, or avoidance of loss and grief situations. It is the avoidance or distancing maneuvers that adults tend to employ that often cause distress and produce complicated bereavement. The need to deny feelings, reactions, or situations may then be projected onto the child, which then may cause problems in the child's grief resolution. These issues add to the complicated issues of family grief.

CULTURAL, SOCIOECONOMIC, AND RELIGIOUS INFLUENCES

The early studies of the 1930s and 1940s dealt with children's feelings about death that reflected the cultural attitudes of the day. In addition to children's feelings, there was a minimal amount of cultural research which dealt with a developmental approach to a child's concept of death. This research was conducted by Cousinet (1939) in France and Anthony (1940) in England. Although they speak about using a developmental model, these researchers used a contradictory cultural and situational approach based upon the World War II experience.

In 1948, Nagy reported her research with Hungarian children. Her cultural theory drew heavily from developmental processes, but has been advocated by many. The theory utilizes a specific cultural background to understand how the culture influenced the development of a concept of death in children. In my work, I find there are multiple variables, but Nagy was one of the first researchers to look at a specific variable that could influence the development of a concept of death in children. Nagy reported that a child develops a cultural idea about death in three stages (see Table 1-5), which occur from 3 to 10 years of age. Her suggestion was that the concept of death develops and matures as the child grows. The first stage occurs between 3 and 5 years of age and involves a "denial" of death as a regular and final process. I question whether this is true denial or simply reflects the level of cognitive development of the child.

The second stage occurs between 5 and 9 years of age. This stage involves the process where death is personified in the child's mind as a person, such as, "The Boogie Man." The child also realizes that death is irreversible and eventual, but still feels that it occurs outside of "me." Therefore, at this stage the child does not view death as being universal. They may see others die, but believe it will not happen to them.

The third stage occurs around 10 years of age. The child now views death as being permanent and realizes it happens to everyone.

The research of McIntire, Angle, and Struempler (1972) conflicts with Nagy's research. They studied the concept of death in midwestern American children. These children disregarded fantasy and

TABLE 1-5. Nagy's Three Stages of Death Concept Development in Hungarian Children

	Stage	Age
I.	Denial	3–5 years old
II.	Personified Irreversable Eventual "Not me"	5–9 years old
III.	Permanent "Happens to me"	10 years old

focused upon "organic decomposition" as early as 5 to 9 years of age (e.g., "John Brown's body lies a-mold'n in the grave").

Furman (1964) also found that a 2- or 3-year-old is capable of mastering the concept of death and that a 3- or 4-year-old who has developed a concept of death is able to mourn the loss of a loved object. McDonald (1964) found that 3- to 4-year-old children whose mothers had died expressed a loss response that included denial and regression. Consequently, *it is not necessarily the age of the child, but the life experiences and cognitive growth that facilitate the development of the concept of death.*

Since the late 1960s, when Elisabeth Kübler-Ross and others opened the door to discussing this taboo topic, many more adults and children have learned to think, study, and discuss death. I, among others, have given countless seminars for professionals, as well as laypeople. These seminars often stimulate discussion and openness at home. Children are now hearing more about death at a younger age because parents have become more comfortable with the topic.

There are situational factors, such as an accident or the illness or death of grandparents, parents, or friends, which make the child confront the reality of death at an early age. There is not just one variable affecting the development of a child's concept of death, but many.

McIntire, Angle, and Struempler (1972) found socioeconomic status to be an influencing factor in a child's development of a concept of death. The child from an urban, low socioeconomic group was more likely to cite violence as the general and specific cause of death. Middle-class and older children were more likely to cite disease and old age as general causes of death. These conclusions were based upon the assumption that children in the low socioeconomic group have "early and repeated exposure to death, chronic illness, violence, and exploitation; whereas, the middle-class child was already familiar with the death-denying tactics".

Although there isn't much research on the religious influences on the development of a child's concept of death, certainly there is a socialization and philosophical process that occurs. As the child is confronted with death or the concept of death, religious rites, practices, and beliefs are taught. Whatever the religious framework, it becomes a means to make feelings and reactions acceptable and expressible. The religious rituals that develop become a means of working through thoughts and feelings, often provide a framework for personal growth as one struggles through difficult questions that may not have answers, and instill hope.

When evaluating a child's, as well as an adult's, concept of death, one must take into account the effects of culture, media, socioeconomic groups, religious background, and environmental issues such as parental comfort, schooling, and interaction with friends. No research to date has involved all of these variables. However, I find that once a child has been confronted with death, either with a pet, stray animal, or loved one, they learn its permanency very quickly.

DISCUSSING DEATH WITH CHILDREN

As with sex education, it is helpful to answer the questions that the child asks on his or her own level and to give only the information sought. If they need more, they will usually ask. When one talks about death with a child, it is helpful to introduce the idea of hope. Hope becomes the process whereby the person finds something "to live for," and may reflect religious beliefs, values, thoughts, or one's own experiences. Death can be very frightening to children, as well as to adults, and hope allows one to see some light in an otherwise dark and sad subject. Hope may be reflected in such statements, if appropriate, as: "We will see Papa again some day in Heaven;" "We hope that the doctors and nurses can do their very best;" or "I hope you know you did all you could in finding Clover (a dead cat), carrying her home, and preparing a lovely grave for her." This is not false hope, which is wrong, but a true and supportive hope.

Another issue is to demonstrate a realistic feeling of power. In the face of death we often feel very powerless, which may, in the short or long run, decrease our self-concept. People often "give up" not necessarily because of the severity of the situation, but because one feels little effect or power to change the situation. One is not able to change death, but may be able to control aspects of death-related issues (e.g., funeral behavior).

I find it helpful to encourage children, as well as adults, to find what power they can in a powerless situation. This nurtures and supports a positive self-concept, which is often a stabilizing force. The power may come from the process of prayer, rituals, actions, meditation, relaxing, or decision making.

Summary

Although it is very difficult to study how a child develops a concept of death, because of the multiple variables, it is an important issue to pursue. Studies of the "normal" child help the clinician and parent to better understand and help a troubled child. The reported research helps to establish guidelines when working with children. However, one must remember they are only guidelines and exceptions are often found. For example, I have seen a child as young as 7 months presenting all appearances of a grief response to the death of her grandmother. Researchers may deny that a child so young could experience a grief response. Granted, this may have been separation anxiety and now that she is 3 she does not remember it, but it was a response to a loss of a loved one. In future chapters I will report case studies of young children who understood that their sibling, grandparent, parent, or pet had died.

IMPACT OF A TERMINAL ILLNESS ON A CHILD'S CONCEPT OF DEATH

As with the normal newborn, the terminally ill newborn will react to stimuli but does not intellectually know that he or she is struggling for survival. There is a unique feeling when you see a helpless infant fight for survival. This valiant struggling that one often sees in dying infants is described in the literature as a "death agony."

There are numerous and varied studies that address the issue of a child's reaction to death when confronted with a terminal illness. In an early study, Richmond and Waisman (1955) found through observations of fatally ill children that they reacted to their illnesses with an air of passive resignation and acceptance. Rarely were overt concerns about death expressed. Knudson and Natterson (1960) came to a similar conclusion in their studies of hospitalized fatally ill children. One must take into account, however, that these studies were done during a time when death was very much a cultural taboo, which may have had some influence on their findings.

Waechter (1971), using eight picture completions, found that fatally ill children of 6 to 10 years of age could express death themes and fears of body intrusion more overtly than they could explain mutilation or separation. Her study suggests that terminally ill children may be aware that they are dying and are able to express it verbally.

Spinetta, Rigler, and Karon (1973) tested Waechler's findings and found that fatally ill children, who were not aware that their illness was fatal, were more fearful of threats and intrusions into their bodies than they were of death itself. They concluded that fatally ill children are aware of the seriousness of their illness.

Clinically, I find that children, even very young ones, know their illnesses are serious and perhaps fatal. In knowing this, they are still upset when their bodies are invaded, poked, or prodded. I believe the two are separate issues and should not be confused—a child may understand that he or she is going to die, but the fears associated with the death tend to coincide with the age and developmental level that the child has reached. In fact, the child under 3 years of age is more afraid of parental abandonment than of death itself. The 3- to 5-year-old is afraid of mutilation to his or her body. The 5- to 7-year-old views death as a personification of something inhuman, like the Boogie Man. This age group may not see death as permanent, but does know that it is something different than just leaving for a while. Their fears may be expressed in dreams, separation anxiety, or direct or symbolic verbalizations (see Table 1-6).

In my clinical experience, I find that children may not understand death cognitively, but they do realize and often verbalize that something is seriously wrong. They often make vague statements indicating that they are "scared of something" or "something terrible might happen." Even if the child is unaware of the seriousness of his or her illness, he or she may tend to express many suspicions. The clinician

TABLE 1-6. Fears Associated with Death in Dying Children by Age and Developmental Level

Age (yr)	Fear
Under 3	Fear of parental abandonment
3–5	Fear of mutilation
5–7	Personification of something inhuman

or parent who hears these suspicions can encourage their symbolic or direct verbalization.

Vernick (1973) notes that many practitioners believe that the younger child is increasingly aware of his or her impending death. I certainly find this to be true. I was working with a family who had a 2½-year-old with leukemia. All she kept asking for was to go home to die and to ride her tricycle one more time. Her parents still had hopes that she would recover, but finally listened to her wishes. She was able to ride her trike one last time and then she died the next day.

The death of a child for any reason, is probably the worst pain a parent must ever experience. One feels helpless and powerless. One cannot do what a parent "should do," and that is to protect their children from harm. It is this grief, as well as other types of grief and pain, that this book explores.

SUMMARY

This chapter explored the literature, however contradictory, which covers acquisition of a concept of death in healthy and terminally ill children. Cognitive and emotional development are essential to this process. Following infancy, once a child experiences (even second or third hand) a fatal illness or accident, he or she understands the threat of death. Prior to this time, death is not necessarily an issue with young children.

With sick or well children, an honest and caring response is needed when questions are asked regarding dying and death. With this approach there is less regret and guilt in the event of the child's death.

How a child develops a concept of death is very complicated and involves multiple variables. Cognitive and emotional development is extremely important. Other factors such as the media, socioeconomic background, religion, environment, and experiences with death influence a child's understanding.

REFERENCES

Anthony, S. (1940). *The child's discovery of death*. New York: Harcourt, Brace.

Bowlby, J. (1960). Grief and mourning in infancy and early childhood. *Psychoanalytic Study of the Child, 15,* 9–52.

Cousinet, R. (1939). "L'idee de la Mort Chez les Enfants." *Journal Psychiatrie Normale et Pathologique, 36,* 65–76.

Deutsch, H. (1959). A two-year-old boy's first love comes to grief. In L. Jessner & E. Pavenstedt (Eds.), *Dynamics of psychopathology in childhood*. New York: Grune and Stratton.

Furman, R. A. (1964). Death and the young child. In *Psychoanalytic study of the child* (Vol. 19, pp. 321). New York: International Universities Press.

Jersild, A. (1978). *The psychology of adolescence* (3rd ed.). New York: Macmillan (pp. 260–261).

Kastenbaum, R. (1967). The child's understanding of death: How does it develop? In E. Grollman (Ed.), *Explaining death to children*. Boston: Beacon Press (p. 105).

Knudson, A. G., & Natterson, J. M. (1960). Participation of parents in the hospital care of their fatally ill children. *Pediatrics, 26,* 482–490.

Koocher, G. (1974). Talking with children about death. *American Journal of Orthopsychiatry, 44,* (3), 404.

Kushner, H. S. (1981). *When bad things happen to good people.* New York: Avon Books.

McIntire, M., Angle, C., & Struempler, L. (1972, June). The concept of death in midwestern children and youth. *American Journal of the Diseases of Children, 123,* 527–532.

Nagy, M., H. (1948, September). The child's theory concerning death. *Journal of Genetics and Psychology, 73,* 3–27.

Piaget, J. (1965). *The moral judgment of the child.* New York: Free Press.

Richmond, J. B., & Waisman, H. H. (1955). Psychological aspects of management of children and malignant diseases. *American Journal of the Diseases of Children, 89,* 42–47.

Schaffer, H. R., & Emerson, P. (1964). The development of social attachment in infancy. *Monographs of the Society for Research in Child Development,* (Serial No. 94, Vol. 29, 3, pp. 5–77).

Steiner, G. L. (1965). *Children's concepts of life and death: A developmental study.* Unpublished Doctoral dissertation, Columbia University, New York.

Vernick, J. (1973). Meaningful communication with the fatally ill child. In J. Anthony and C. Kaupernik (Eds.), *The child in his family: The impact of disease and death,* (Vol. 2, p. 105). New York: Wiley.

Waechter, E. Y. (1971, June). Children's awareness of fatal illness. *American Journal of Nursing, 71,* 6, 1168–1172.

CHAPTER II

Family Themes in Coping with Death

People have a variety of ways of reacting to and dealing with a death. Everyone grieves in his or her own way: *there is no one way to grieve*. Many authors have developed models for the stages, symptoms, phases, and processes of mourning (Bowlby, 1980; Lindemann, 1944; Parkes, 1970; Schoenberg, Carr, Kutscher, Peretz, & Goldberg, 1974; Westberg, 1961). However, Elisabeth Kübler-Ross (1969) was one of the first to explore the feelings and reactions experienced by the terminally ill themselves. Her participant approach concluded that dying people go through five stages: shock, anger, depression, bargaining, and, acceptance. This progression through "neat" stages, concurrent with the progression of final illness, has been widely accepted. Many of us have found, however, that it is not quite that simple. People are often disappointed that the grief work is so very complicated and not only involves the dying but the family as well as significant others, including health care professionals and people outside the situation.

J. William Worden (1982) developed four primary tasks of mourning: to accept the reality of the loss; to experience the pain of grief; to adjust to an environment in which the deceased is missing; and to withdraw emotional energy from the deceased and reinvest it in another relationship.

Kübler-Ross discussed the process whereby one "felt" or "reacted" to the issue of being terminally ill. Worden, on the other hand, described the tasks one must accomplish in one's grief. In working with survivors, it is imperative to develop a model that includes the family. Such a model should also include the history of the reactions, feelings, and tasks experienced by each person. Grief is so complicated because it involves such multifaceted variables as issues, feelings, and reactions for everyone involved. Therefore, I found it necessary to develop my own model dealing with family grief themes (Johnson-Soderberg, 1981).

Themes are recurring subjects or motifs that have appeared and sometimes reappeared throughout the family's history, without apparent resolution. They are labels that I use to describe the family's behavior during a crisis situation. There are several purposes in utilizing family themes:

- Themes give a historical perspective of key family dynamics that warrant consideration as a means of coping at the time of death.
- Themes provide a broader understanding of the stages or processes of mourning, as defined by Kübler-Ross, Worden, and others.
- Themes provide a basic understanding of how a family is coping so that necessary interventions can be made, thus avoiding destructive physical or emotional deterioration.

In my research and practice, I have found that the most common family themes are scapegoating, conspiracy of silence, detachment, guilt, and masochism. A discussion of each of these themes follows.

SCAPEGOATING

A scapegoat is a race, person, institution, or sex that bears the blame, prejudice, displaced aggression, irrational hostility, or projected feelings of others. It implies a process of singling out one or more persons to bear the brunt of the family's or group's dissatisfaction. A scapegoating situation always requires the existence of a group that is threatened. In this case the group is threatened by death.

If family history is assessed, one will usually find that the family has used scapegoats in the past as a means of coping with a difficult situation. In order for scapegoating to occur, at least three participants are required: one participant projects anger or blame onto another, while a third or more endeavor to validate the "bad" or "evil" of the scapegoat (see Figure 2-1).

Two primary defense mechanisms are utilized: projection and displacement. *Projection* occurs when an attitude or feeling is emo-

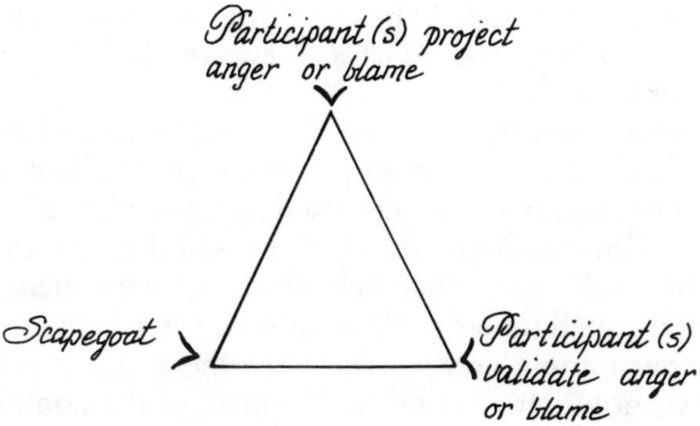

FIGURE 2-1. Scapegoating triangle.

tionally unacceptable in oneself and, therefore, unconsciously rejected and then attributed to another. *Displacement* permits emotions or reactions (e.g., anger, resentment, anxiety) to be transferred from the original object to a more acceptable substitute. The target is then changed from self to the scapegoat.

The scapegoating theme occurs in varying degrees. It can range from simply displacing the anger from a terminally ill family member onto the physician or nurse to a full blown destructive scapegoating process, which can occur over a period of years. This latter type of scapegoating can emotionally or physically destroy a family member or significant other. An excellent clinical example regarding family scapegoating caused by a fear of a father's impending death from heart disease was expounded by Dr. Eric Bermann (1973a,b).

Although nondestructive scapegoating is most usually found, the clinician must be aware of potential hazards that this theme can produce. This theme has the capacity to be very destructive, since one or more persons within a family may be chosen to bear the blame of the death. As the scapegoating process continues, the scapegoated person begins to believe that he or she is "bad" and, in destructive ways, continually "kick" themselves. The following case history illustrates an extreme and tragic case where this hazard of scapegoating occurred.

The Leek family had a 6-year-old son, Oliver, who died in a tragic farm accident. No one was really sure how the accident occurred. At the time there were three other children, one of whom was an infant.

After the accident, the parents chose their two oldest children as scapegoats. The children, along with the father, had been in the farmyard when the accident occurred. The children constantly received messages of: "Why are you alive while your brother is dead?"

and "You are not wanted." These children were made to feel guilty for being alive (existential guilt) and eventually believed that they caused Oliver's death.

Eighteen years after the accident, the daughter came into treatment because of destructive relationships with men. She began to realize that she and her brother had been used as scapegoats all those years. She secretly believed that she had caused her brother's death, although she could not remember what had happened. During an interview performed under sodium amytal, she recalled that she had been in the barn doing needlepoint when the accident occurred. She was the first, however, to find her brother in the combine.

As they became adolescents, the children began to act out that they were bad. This masochistic behavior continued the scapegoating process. The children abused drugs and alcohol and there was a teenage pregnancy. The daughter in particular placed herself in situations where she could be "kicked" so that the scapegoating issue could continue. She married in her teens an alcoholic and abusive young man. She divorced him several years later, only to choose a second spouse of similar character.

Since scapegoating has the potential for being destructive to individuals or an entire group, it is necessary to attempt to prevent it. This is often difficult since clients/families are usually in crisis when the scapegoating theme may begin to develop. In crisis, it is difficult for the health care professional to intervene or provide long-term therapy; any therapy is usually directed toward crisis intervention. If the health care provider can encourage or give permission for people to feel and express their anger appropriately, scapegoating usually will not be displayed or projected. Then scapegoating will possibly not occur.

It is helpful to observe the family to see if there is displaced aggression toward people within or outside the family group. If so, there tends to be a greater chance for scapegoating to occur. For example, I had been called to consult on a case of a new psychiatric admission. Tom was a 52-year-old man who appeared at least 75. He and his wife, Sheri, had married late in life. Throughout their lives each had taken little responsibility for their own behaviors and used projection and displacement to a great extent. Therefore, the defense mechanisms needed for scapegoating were already established. In this crisis, they had mutually scapegoated their parents, friends, and health care providers for what appeared to be a nonverbalized death fear over Tom's recently diagnosed cancer. For Tom, it built to such a proportion that he eventually threatened his parents and wife with a butcher's knife.

I remember well the first time I met with Tom. I had diagnosed a scapegoating process and attempted to get to what I thought would be an underlying death fear. Eventually, the tears were rolling down his cheeks and he said, "I'm so frightened; I'm going to die." Through the scapegoating both Tom and Sheri were attempting to gain power in a powerless situation.

Although Tom gained some insight into their behavior, Sheri was never able to. His cancer metastasized to his brain and he became confused. The scapegoating continued and reached disastrous proportions: they were planning to sue (although ungrounded) the oncologist, the radiologist, the nurses, and the hospice. All potential and actual health care providers were targets for the scapegoating theme. Needless to say, the providers were fearful to treat him.

I tried to halt this theme. The circumstances, however, including the lack of insight and the long history of scapegoating prevented this. (It is a good lesson that although we may do our best, we can't "cure" everyone.)

As providers, we must attempt to be aware of unhealthy defense mechanisms in patients that can lead to the destructive scapegoating process. No one wins in a scapegoating situation.

CONSPIRACY OF SILENCE

Another theme is the conspiracy of silence. It occurs when nobody talks about "IT"—whatever the "IT" may be. Usually the "IT" deals with cancer, terminal illness, funeral planning, death, and survivor issues such as remarriage, managing money and property, and future decisions and goals.

The goal and the behaviors in the conspiracy of silence are to avoid at all costs the topic of death, dying, and surviving. This avoidance is done both verbally and nonverbally. When a couple whose child died from Reye's syndrome were out for dinner for the first time since the death, a brave woman asked how they were "really doing." Before the couple could respond, a diversion was introduced immediately by a man at the table who said, "My, I like your new carpeting." Other people will use body language to show that they are implementing the conspiracy of silence. One man remained at the door of an intensive care room with his arms and legs crossed, shoulders rounded in, and his body rigid. The message was, both verbally and nonverbally, "I don't want to deal with this terminal illness."

There seems to be several reasons for the conspiracy of silence to be initiated. First, since death is still a culturally taboo subject, people have been taught not to talk about it. People think they can discuss death, but when it becomes personalized and one's own family needs to acknowledge it, they retreat to previous coping methods or mechanisms—that of silence relating to threatening topics.

Second, we are socialized not to discuss the "ITs" of life. People may not know what to say to a significant other: "How do I start?" "What should I say?" In social situations I am often avoided because of the fear that the topic of death may arise. I was once asked to leave a hospital where I had been developing a clinical speciality in grief. The reason given for the request was not that my work was inadequate but because "they had no dying patients." Concurrently with my departure, they changed the name of the morgue to the "pathology annex"—a wonderful illustration of the perceived cultural threat of the topic.

Third, family members or significant others are often afraid of emotional reactions like tears or anger so they decide that avoidance is more helpful to all. Finally, people are often frightened or worried about how others will react toward them if they express their feelings or beliefs.

The conspiracy of silence may last only a short period of time or it may continue for years, in which case it becomes pathological and destructive to family relationships. When I initially saw the Leek family (discussed previously regarding scapegoating) I uncovered that their conspiracy of silence continued for 18 years. No one ever mentioned Oliver's death, how it happened, what people remembered, nor their own grief pain. By not dealing directly with the death, the family developed a pathological means of coping through the following themes: scapegoating, conspiracy of silence, and repressed grief symptoms. Very little, if any, outward and "appropriate" grief was expressed individually or as a family. Nina, the mother, did not even know how the accident happened until she was well into treatment.

The reason that the conspiracy of silence ended was that a grandchild had recently died of a cardiac ailment. Nina began grieving in an "exaggerated manner" for this granddaughter. She was brought to my office by her daughter, Elizabeth. She did not know what was wrong with her mother, but since the baby died she would cry hysterically day and night.

In trying to assess a presenting problem, I always determine if there are other situations that might cause an "exaggerated response" (e.g., divorce, returning to work or starting a new job, problems with children or spouse, health problems, and, especially, previous deaths). It is also important to assess whether the person really knows what they are feeling or thinking and whether they are "covering" one feeling with another. People often use one feeling to cover what they are truly feeling but cannot acknowledge or understand. Men, for instance, often react angrily when they are really feeling scared, whereas women often display depression when they are feeling angry.

Nina denied any other stresses in her life, either past or present. In my clinical judgment, "something" had happened, probably in the past, that was triggering this extreme reaction. Finally, with great relief, she admitted that her little Oliver had died 18 years ago. She had never talked about this event; there had been a total family conspiracy of silence. All of Oliver's things had been locked secretly in a drawer that had never been opened, his pictures had been taken off the wall, and stories were never shared about him. The only expression of grief was the blaming or scapegoating of the other children. All the memories and anything that might promote them were locked away, both physically and metaphorically.

But grief cannot be locked away. As you will see in the symptom-formation chapter, the unresolved grief will probably manifest itself somewhere else—either emotionally or physically. Somehow it will be expressed. Nina began to understand that she had been clinically depressed for 18 years. Therefore, the conspiracy of silence is ironic: it is used to prevent dealing with grief, but instead the grief continues and is prolonged and stands ready to raise its ugly head.

Another man that I treated, Wes, had a daughter, Verna, who died at the age of 8 during surgery for a cardiac ailment. Wes had signed the consent form for the surgery. He believed that he had killed his daughter by signing the consent. He refused to allow his family to talk about Verna. Several years later Wes developed his first ulcer. Ulcer surgery became almost a yearly routine until only a small portion of his stomach remained. His family became very concerned when he started sleeping about 21 to 23 hours a day, lost more weight, and refused to talk at all to any of them.

Wes was admitted to our group on the psychiatric unit. Fourteen years after the death of his daughter the conspiracy of silence began to break down. He professed not to remember when Verna died, but I am convinced it was not just coincidence that his ulcer surgery always took place near the anniversary of her death. The conspiracy of silence was such a strong coping mechanism for him that he refused to have a grave marker placed on her grave.

The conspiracy of silence is an umbrella issue (see Figure 2-2). All or several of these feelings or reactions are involved. Not speaking of or acknowledging that the person was alive and now is dead, or one's

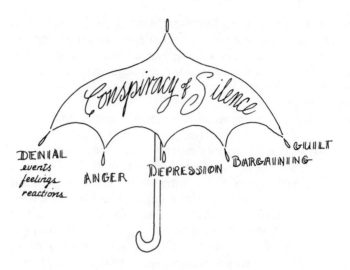

FIGURE 2-2. The conspiracy of silence.

feelings or reactions to that fact, constitutes denial. There is often extreme and inappropriate anger, which is usually aimed indirectly toward other people or other issues. As feelings are redirected from the triggering source, depression usually develops. In addition, I find that these families also use bargaining: "I'll be good, God, and then this will never happen again." The bargaining behavior is a way of structuring life so that no further similar threats will be felt.

After the death of a "significant other," the survivor may turn to a charismatic or fundamentalist religion. In addition, this type of survivor may often utilize bargaining and a conspiracy of silence. In one of my cases, a 45-year-old man named Alden, had had multiple well-known affairs described as "going away with the boys" on golfing vacations. Years after these affairs his 14-year-old son, Bob, committed suicide. Alden became a "born-again" Christian and became "very good," giving large sums of money to television ministries. He chose new friends only among born-again Christians. His old friends felt that he was walking a tightrope.

One can recognize as much pathology from any extreme: being crazy and loose or becoming overly rigid and myopic. Alden was able to continue with his behaviors until his father died, at which time he came to me. The conspiracy was then broken and he was able to talk about his son's suicide as well as express his "true" feelings, which were not euphoria, peace, or happiness.

Guilt may also develop when the conspiracy is utilized. The guilt may be of various types (see section on guilt diagnosis): "If only I could have told my mother that I really loved her." "If I hadn't gotten to talk to my aunt about her death, I would have felt so very guilty," or "If only we could talk at home about our daughter's death it would help me so much, but he (her husband) hits me every time I bring it up. Then I feel that I'm to blame for his pain."

The use of the conspiracy of silence is never helpful. Rather, it is always destructive and must be broken. The grief needs direct expression. A young man and his fiancee asked if I would see them. Ken told me that he was dying of leukemia and did not have much longer to live. Both he and his fiancee, Lynn, were very upset because his family believed he would be getting better, going back to college, and marrying Lynn. They continued to deny his illness and impending death, although he had all the classic symptoms of being terminally ill.

At the request of Ken and Lynn we decided to have a family session with his parents, siblings, and spouses. The conspiracy of silence had to be broken before Ken's final wish could be heard: "I want to go home to die with my family around me." It took almost 3 hours of intensive therapy before they could finally accept Ken's wishes. I was able to break the conspiracy of silence by slowly confronting the reality and needs of his impending death. Ken left the hospital that evening and went home where he died contentedly the next day.

In working with a family it is helpful to identify at least one person who would like the conspiracy to be broken. Like Ken and Lynn, that person may be so uncomfortable with the conspiracy that they initiate its demise. Others may need outside permission to break it. If the conspiracy can be broken with at least one person, the clinician is better able to assess and intervene. The following issues in the conspiracy must be assessed:

- The underlying anxieties or fantasies (of the death situation or disease) that promote the conspiracy (e.g., do they think if they talk about the cancer they will get it too?).
- How does the family "express" the conspiracy of silence (e.g., verbally? nonverbally?).
- The purpose of the conspiracy of silence for the family. (e.g., "If you don't talk about it, it will go away." "It hurts too much to talk about it.")

The conspiracy of silence leaves people feeling alone, isolated, and guilty. My clients often say that although they may want to break the conspiracy, others won't allow them to do so and respond by treating them as if they have "leprosy." Those that finally are able to break the conspiracy of silence find a great release and peace. Ken's family certainly felt this. The things that need to be done and said are now legitimate, which helps to produce "good" or "healthy" grief.

DETACHMENT

Detachment is a process whereby people "pull away" from each other because of their own bereavement pain. Detachment usually happens with people who have had a close bonding prior to the death of a third party. It may last from hours to "forever." The primary reason for detachment to occur is that people are in such pain that they cannot minister to or support others. If this process is not "lengthy," it tends to be normal, even healthy. I see this very frequently with parents who have had a child die, although it is not limited to such circumstances. Anyone in a close relationship with another, such as child-parent, parents-in-law, or adults-friend relationships, may feel detachment after the death.

For my clients, this is usually a very upsetting experience: "I've always been able to talk to him before." (Though this is often not really the case!) When families recognize that short-lived detachment is a normal reaction, it becomes tolerated through understanding.

There are several reasons for detachment:

- Protection of self or others.
- Being too pained to give support to another.
- Testing behavior.
- The initial shock precipitates withdrawal.
- People grieve in different ways and at different times.
- The marriage or relationship may have been unstable or detached before the death that triggered the response.

Initially, the detachment can result from the shock of the death. This is particularly true when the family had a short time to prepare for the loss. The period of shock is a means whereby the reality starts to become apparent. Usually people process this internally: "I can't believe this is happening to me; I'm so numb." In feeling the shock, either quietly or hysterically, they become introspective and don't relate to others, especially the more significant others (see section dealing with shock). At this initial stage, the family is protected by others and by funeral behaviors, and often the interaction with others is minimal. After this period of initial shock, however, they have to start venturing out, often with friends, to places such as the grocery store, church, restaurants, etc., where the memories are abundant. They may begin to share how painful this is or may continue to choose to process it internally.

People may choose not to talk and to detach in order to protect themselves or they may have learned that the topic is too painful for their spouse or loved one. They "think" they are protecting that loved one by the detachment. When this occurs, it is often accompanied by a quasi-conspiracy of silence. The conspiracy of silence is usually not forever, however, because the person who is detached finds someone else with whom they are able to share their pain. The conspiracy of silence only exists between the spouses or several significant others (e.g., grandparents, special friends, or other children).

Another reason for detachment is that a grieving individual's own pain may be so tremendous that they cannot support or minister to those nearest to them. Bereavement is a time when one would expect that people, especially parents, would come together. They are, however, emotionally and physically unable to do so; there is no energy left. The process is paradoxical in that they want to be close, but find it too painful. The partner reminds them of the distressing memories and that "nothing" is the same anymore.

There is a subtopic to this theme of detachment. Often following the death of a child one parent will start to feel better and begin to reattach, while the other remains detached and "down." I call this the "ping-pong" or "roller coaster" phenomenon: one is up and the other is down. It is helpful if the couple does not view this desire of one person to reattach and give support in terms of a continuum of "health and illness," but rather that one is stronger at this point and can give support. The pendulum can soon swing the other way.

A fourth reason for detachment is that there may be fantasies that loved ones may "go away." People (family members) know how painful it is to be attached to someone who dies. In their detachment, therefore, they are testing each other: "Will you go away and leave me too?" or "I don't want to get close to you, because you may go away and leave me too. This is too painful." Nevertheless, they need to be close to someone or something to lessen the pain. Usually one finds another significant person outside the home, or perhaps a child with whom they can share, or pretend to share, their pain. People may also turn to alcohol or drugs. This they believe is "safe" because it can cover the pain and will not "go away and leave them."

As they begin to share their tragic experiences, they learn which people are caring, listening, and supporting: such persons I label "helpful people." Those people who change the subject are beginning the conspiracy of silence, and are labeled "hindering people." The spouse often becomes hindering at this time, resulting in detachment.

A fifth reason for detachment is that people grieve differently. There is no one right way to grieve. Often one spouse will have expectations of the other because they do not understand the differences in people and the ways they "choose" to grieve. After 4 years, one woman still does not believe her husband "truly grieved" their son's death because he didn't cry. Crying, however, had never been a coping mechanism for the husband. In assessing family and individual themes, it is important to remember that if it wasn't helpful in the past, it probably will not serve a useful purpose during this crisis. As a result of this pressure to grieve in a similar manner, or "I'm doing it the right way," this couple had detached. Although still married, they live very separate and nonsharing lives.

Another couple had a 15-year-old daughter, Skye, who was killed in a car accident. John grieved by being extremely angry at his loss. He detached from his wife Jill and their surviving daughter, Caitlin. He turned to alcohol and became drunk most every night, which increased his anger and the emotional abuse of his family. Jill also detached, although she believed something was "wrong" with this behavior: "Why do we act like this when we need each other now more than ever?" Part of Jill's detachment had to do with the fact that she could not bear to see what John was doing to himself and the family. In her detachment, she became very depressed and multiple physical and emotional symptoms were expressed, such as sleep and eating disorders, lack of concentration, and bad nightmares. In their detachment, they were grieving very differently and neither understood what was happening to the other.

Jill made the decision that something was wrong (detachment in grief). She needed help even if he wouldn't come with her. John did come, and they, with Caitlin, have successfully "completed" grief therapy. They began to understand how each was grieving, and John learned to express his grief in healthier and more appropriate ways.

Still another reason for detachment is that the marriage or relationship may have been unstable or detached before the death occurred. Ron had had multiple affairs 12 years ago. Kay had made a decision to remain in the marriage and just "exist" until "her" children completed high school. Unexpectedly, however, a son was killed in a car–train collision. Ron and Kay were already detached. Ron began to drink excessively. Eventually the alcohol became a problem and one day he decided to commit suicide while he was drunk. Kay found him in time, but the marriage could not be saved because they were already too detached. If detachment continues over a long period of time the marriage will usually end. My research shows a high divorce rate among parents who have experienced the death of a child.

The Decision to Live Again

Sometime near the end of the first year of mourning, or into the second or third, it is critical for parents or detached people, to begin to reattach to each other. This process I term "the decision to begin living again."

In my practice and research, I found that a very important time in the mourning process is the period when a person and a couple decide, both individually and collectively, to live again. People are able to describe to me when such a decision is made and the circumstances surrounding the decision. If they cannot describe the situation, they have not made the decision. The decision making may be spontaneous or a more gradual process. Certain variables affecting this process will be discussed later.

Some experiences are very simple and gentle, in contrast to others which can be very dramatic. My father-in-law explained that about 8 months after his wife died, he had fallen to his knees one night saying he couldn't carry on like this. He felt the need to make a decision to change his outlook. Consequently, he decided he would start dating, playing tennis, and laughing again.

Usually, if grief is complicated, the decision-making process takes longer and is more dramatic. It often involves "bottoming out," much as an alcoholic does, where a life-and-death situation may occur. Such was the experience of a patient of mine. Gretchen had had two miscarriages, given birth to two normal children, and then had a child with Down's Syndrome. This child developed leukemia at the age of 3, and required much of Gretchen's time and love. She was extremely attached to Eric, and tended to neglect the rest of the family.

When Eric died at the age of 5, Gretchen was left feeling worthless, helpless, and alone. Detachment had been occurring with her family since Eric became ill. As a means of coping with these painful feelings and wanting to reattach to something that wouldn't leave her, she "attached" to alcohol rather than her family. One night after a party and in a very inebriated state, Gretchen stopped at the cemetery and made her decision—to go home and kill herself. She drove home, put the car in the garage, and left the motor running. It was at that very delicate time that she said to herself: "What am I doing this for? I have two other children, a husband, and a career to return to. I want to live." It was at that time she was willing to seek help and began to live again.

The decision-making process always seems to be a turning point in one's grief. It is at this point that the grief symptoms begin to dissipate very quickly and the person begins to reinvest in other relationships and activities.

Couples who have lost a child and experienced detachment need to reattach and make a joint decision to live again. These joint decisions often deal with categories like taking up a new sport together, building a house, planning a fantasy vacation, or having another child (see section on replacement children). The couples that are able to accomplish this seem to survive the crisis of the death of a child without terminal scars.

One must remember that thanatology is not a "hard" science and there are multiple variables that are involved in the process of grief. There is no way that I can determine the appropriate or "right" time for people to make their individual or collective decisions to begin living again. I find, however, that when people make these decisions "too soon" or "too late" there is cause for alarm, as indications of pathological grief may be developing.

Some of my families shared how they made their decision immediately. One couple, Jack and Val, who lost a child to sudden infant death syndrome (SIDS), made their mutual decision while they were in the emergency room; they went home and made love in hopes of producing a baby immediately: "We decided not to let this stop us, to ruin our lives. We couldn't let it destroy our marriage and so we just decided to not let this stop us. We got spoiled in the 2½ months we had him."

Another man said, "We made the decision the day of the funeral. I knew we'd have to cope one way or another. We'd have to pick up the pieces. The pieces have fallen apart many times, but we're picking them up one at a time. Maybe we put them back too quickly. I feel guilty about that." Guilt often accompanies the decision when it is made "too soon." Another couple, Mary and Jon, had had one twin die at 9 days of age. Mary made her decision the night Ruth died:

> What comes to mind first is that night, that Sunday night (that Ruth died), in the middle of the night and Ronnie woke up. . . . My mom and I were feeding him and we were just talking and all of a sudden I looked at the crib and I said, 'I want a new crib. I want a new crib. I'm starting over again. There is one baby now.' And that was it. . . . 'there is only one baby now and I'm going to start new.' And my mom right then said, 'Dad and I will buy you a new crib.' That is what she said. And the next day . . . they went out and we had a new crib . . . It's kind of fast isn't it? It wasn't even

24 hours that I felt that way . . . I'm sure there are people who take longer. I guess I felt I had a new baby. I can't drag this out for years because I wanted to enjoy him.

There are several important elements in this example. First, people often want to make things "alright" immediately by getting a new crib or buying something else. Again, it is ironic because you cannot make it "alright" immediately. It is like putting a bandaid on an aneurysm. The myth of "making it alright" may influence making the decision too quickly—one has to feel and work with the pain in order to make "it" alright.

Second, this woman's decision did not change her grief symptoms. She continued to convince herself that she was getting over Ruth's death. She later experienced multiple physical symptoms and depression, as well as shrining (see Chapter 3). Four years after Ruth's death she was needed to help her husband in his new office. This change triggered an increase in physical and emotional symptoms which led her back into therapy (see Chapter 5).

There are also people who never make a decision to go on living. These people tend to be ones in whom the conspiracy of silence is never broken and the emotional and physical symptoms become the inadequate coping mechanisms. One such woman was in the hospital for a bleeding ulcer operation. Her mother had died while she was in the hospital and she was referred to me for the loss. There was a picture of a young boy by her bedside. She spoke of him in the present tense and I assumed, as this woman was in her 60s, that he was her grandchild. *Never assume anything!* The boy was her child who had died at 10 years old. She had developed a conspiracy of silence, lived in the world of denial, and never made a decision to continue with her life.

When one fails to make the decision to go on living, complicated grief tends to develop. This grief may manifest itself in the form of physical or emotional problems (see Chapter 5, Complicated Grief).

There appear to be several factors that influence when and how one makes the decision to go on living. My research in this area indicates that parents with a long preparation time (long preparation group—LPG) were able to make their decisions sooner than those in the short preparation group (SPG). The LPG had 15 days or more warning that death was imminent, whereas the SPG had 14 days or less warning that their child would die.

With some warning, if allowed, people can begin anticipatory bereavement, which can shorten the survivor bereavement. For almost 2 years I treated a young woman whose husband was dying of amyotrophic lateral sclerosis (ALS). She did most of her grieving before the death and so when Philip did die she was able to make her decision to go on living, and appropriately so, quickly. She was given much pressure, however, from significant others that she was not "mourning" correctly and was "not respecting Philip's life and death" because she was moving quickly. These "significant others" were not aware of all the anticipatory work she had accomplished.

It tends to take women longer to make decisions about living, especially if a child has died. This variable tends to relate to issues of attachment to the child and often the lack of other activities and commitments in their life. "There is no reason to get up in the morning." It may not relate so much to being a woman and making decisions as it does with our role-socialization (e.g., that it is often the woman who stays home and cares for the children). When that is taken away there is a feeling of emptiness. This process can also be seen with the "empty nest syndrome" and retirement from work with no other activities to replace the previous one.

Another factor deals with the void that is left by the death. As with Gretchen, who almost committed suicide, her life space dealt almost totally with Eric. When he died she thought she had nothing left. He had required almost 24-hour care, which left little time for other members of the family or extracurricular activities. The amount of the void can influence when and how a decision is made (see Figure 2-3).

The other issue is attachment. Traditionally, the women in our culture are the caregivers to husband, children, church, society, and the like. Being primary caretaker often, although not always, means that women are more attached to the children. When the attached person is lost, it takes longer to make a decision to continue living and reorganize one's life space. When one is very attached to someone the grief is always more pronounced and prolonged. *One will not feel grief unless one is attached.*

Indeed, the past memories are very painful, but I have found that those who can confront the pain, share with one another, not detach for long periods of time from one's spouse, and who have a varied life with other commitments and activities are able to make their decision sooner to go on living. Those who are "mono-centered" (a neologism meaning having a limited sphere of activities and attachments) have a more difficult time in making a decision, and it usually takes longer because there has been little improvement in the past, for whatever reason. Therefore, it is often too frightening to begin new activities, even without the added burden of death. On the other hand, I also need to warn that work and outside activities can become too great an escape from the reality of the loss. Finding some

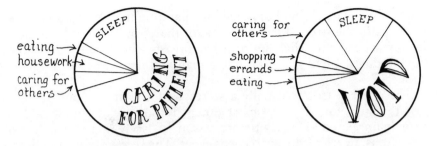

FIGURE 2-3. Twenty-four hour activity clock.
Left: before death; *right*: after death.

middle ground is most helpful in coping with one's grief: feeling pain
and gradually getting away from the pain. I am told time after time
that once a firm and healthy decision is made, there is a feeling of
peace and strength.

GUILT

Following a death, guilt is probably the most powerful factor that
holds the key to the survivor's mental and physical health. Guilt is a
feeling of culpability with offenses of commission (actions they regret) or omission (inaction they regret).

As with other themes, the patient has felt guilt in the past and used
it as a means of trying to cope with a difficult situation. Guilt is a
learned and socialized feeling.

Not everyone will necessarily experience guilt as a survivor theme.
One man said that he felt intimidated, rather than guilty, over his
son's death. Others express shame.

Guilt, if present, is a normal part of the grieving process. It is the
component whereby the client blames himself or others for the death.
In grief, guilt is a conscious feeling rather than an unconscious
neurotic feeling. It may develop, however, into neurotic or psychotic
issues or may potentiate issues that have been repressed. Guilt is
very complicated and multifaceted. In this section, I will explore the
following guilt issues: reasons for guilt in grief, types of guilt, variables in the expression of guilt, dealing with guilt, guilt instillers,
guilt movies, and counseling a person who is experiencing guilt.

Reasons for Guilt in Grief

People tend to express at least two reasons for the guilt they are
feeling. One is the legitimate reason for what happened: "My child

got hit by a car. If I had only held his hand tighter he couldn't have darted into the street. I feel so guilty for that;" or "I should not have let my wife ignore that lump in her breast—she would have been alive today if I had stood up like a man and made her see a doctor sooner."

The other reason is usually a secret, and a torturing one at that. For the survivor, it is the most potent reason for the guilt and is usually unrelated to the legitimate reason. In "secret guilt" usually no one else is aware of the antecedent event. The secret guilt often deals with past "sins" or wrongdoings, which have often been kept from others: "My child died because I had had an affair and now I am being punished." The fantasy always involves issues of guilt. The secret guilt is also used as a means of structuring an answer to an unanswerable question: "Why did my daughter die?" In our western education, we are socialized to believe the myth that there is an answer, somewhere, to any question. In reality, there are no answers to some of the questions in life: "Why do children have to die?" "Why is there injustice?" "Why isn't life fair?" "Why do 'good' things happen to 'bad' people?" "How can terrorists get by with their behaviors?"

In therapy, it is important to discover whether there are secret guilts that the patient relates to the current death. Once the person can verbalize and understand these secrets there is a great sense of relief.

Often, these secret guilts are reinforced by other people. (See Chapter 2, Guilt Instillers). One minister potentiated a mother's secret guilt by saying: "You must have done something very bad to have deserved this (daughter's death); certainly this has to deal with your unforgiveable sins." A young woman, Pat, and her husband lost a 2-month-old baby to SIDS. Pat's minister told her that Jennifer's death was because of her past drug use. This information only increased her secret guilt: although Jennifer was lying next to her in bed when she died, Pat had had a good deal to drink the night before and believed she could not hear her "yell" because she was "hung over." This secret guilt had "eaten at her" so much that she made a suicide attempt and I had to admit her to the hospital. Although it seemed evident that there must be some secret guilt, she refused to admit to it for over 2 weeks. Later she said she had difficulty admitting it because of her minister's previous remarks. She had felt so guilty and "dirty" and believed that by admitting her secret it would cause her more embarrassment and pain.

Theoretical Background of Guilt

In my practice and research, I realized that people exhibit many different types of guilt (Johnson-Soderberg, 1982; Johnson, 1984; Johnson, 1986). I have found that it is helpful if the type of guilt can be diagnosed, since the treatment varies according to the type. It may benefit the reader to have some understanding of the literature regarding guilt before the various types are explored. I shall review Hoffman's social learning perspective on guilt (1970), moral internalization research (1974), sexual differences in the expression of guilt (1975), and research on guilt as it relates to grief and mourning (1976).

Social Learning. Social learning theory defines moral development in terms of behavioral compliance of social norms. Moral development involves learned behavior patterns resulting from rewards and punishments. Identification with authority figures is accomplished through the process of role modeling and imitation. Although there are many theorists in this area, Hoffman's theory forms the basis of the guilt types I utilize in counseling.

Hoffman (1970, 1976, 1977) suggested that guilt occurs when a person learns that the prerequisites of feeling guilty are the following: (1) one has learned that another is separate from oneself, (2) one has developed parallel empathetic responses or replications of another's feelings and thus feels compassion, (3) one has learned sympathetic distress for another, and (4) one can cognitively recognize that she or he has caused another's plight. The person must not only be aware of the consequence of his or her actions, but must also have obtained role-taking abilities and recognize that he or she has the power to choose actions. The person then has the prerequisites for self-critical or self-blaming behaviors (Hoffman, 1974, 1976).

Once a person feels guilty several things happen. Hoffman believes that if a person feels guilt, he or she might transfer it into a derogatory feeling about the other. "He's just an alcoholic and that is why he's a bum." Culturally, people may feel there is nothing one can do for some people. For instance, the Hindus believe that the Untouchables in India cannot be helped because they are living out punishments for sins in past lives. Hoffman (1976) also believes guilt is a response used to cause distress to another person: "Why didn't you know she was going to die?" I suggest that one can also cause distress in oneself: "If I'd watched my diet maybe I could have avoided my heart attack."

Hoffman's theory (1970, 1976) states that there are two kinds of guilt: personal, or true guilt, and existential guilt. *Personal guilt* is defined as the result of a commission, things the person did, or omission, things the person did not do and wished he or she had done, or in other words, inaction. I believe personal guilt may be actual or fantasized. Existential guilt is described further on in the chapter.

Commission is the earliest form of guilt that develops. It occurs when the child's empathetic response and the awareness of harming another occur together; for example, where a parent points out to the child that it is not appropriate to hit another person. Omission occurs when the child gains additional cognitive abilities to "construct a mental representation of an event that might have occurred but did not," such as what a child could have done to help a drowning child. Thus, the child may be to blame for the continuation of another's distress because he or she did not act, or did not take an effective action to decrease another's distress.

In Hoffman's story completion study for moral internalization, he noted that most subjects showed guilt over both commission and omission. He believed that the child is taught to feel guilty for commissions, but he doubts if the child learns guilt for omissions. He suggests that guilt over omission is due to the child's empathic response to awareness of a central figure's performance in an altruistic act in which he or she did not partake, due to their own egoistic goals. Consequently, omission may be related to sympathetic distress, when a person is aware that he or she could have done something for another but did not. Thus, Hoffman's theory states that the child develops empathetic distress, which is then transformed into sympathetic distress or guilt. The resultant reaction depends upon the causal attributions made by the individual involved (Hoffman, 1974, 1976; Hoffman & Saltzstein, 1967).

Hoffman further refined and categorized personal, or true guilt, into conventional guilt and humanistic guilt. Both types of guilt may be a result of either a commission or omission. *Conventional guilt* is based upon learned social accommodation that occurs in response to social norms, role expectations and cultural conventions. Humanistic guilt is based on commissions or omissions that result from harm to oneself or others.

In *existential guilt* the person does not perform a commission or omission but "feels culpable because of circumstances in life beyond her control" (Hoffman, 1976). For example, a person may feel existential guilt when seeing a homeless person, although he or she has not done anything to cause this. This type of guilt usually incorporates social and ethical situations that conflict with one's values and or beliefs. This type of guilt may, however, take on qualities of true guilt.

Although not delineated by Hoffman, there seems to be a third type of guilt which requires a high level of cognition: *anticipatory guilt*. In this type of guilt, a person must not only have the ability to visualize the commission or omission, but also must be able to predict commissions and omissions in the future: "If I don't see and talk to my mother before she dies, I will feel so guilty" or "If I don't put my child in a car seat and we are in an accident, I will feel guilty."

Moral Internalization Research. Moral development, defined as the internalization of "socially sanctioned prohibitions and mandates," is the second area in this discussion of the genesis of guilt. The development of guilt in the moral development of young children and its involvement throughout the life cycle, has long been a neglected area of research. This fact is interesting since guilt plays such a predominant role in psychoanalytic theory. Guilt is also a motivating force in our culture and creates a common, identifiable feeling resulting from either commissions or omissions.

Aronfreed and his associates (Aronfreed 1964; Aronfreed, Cutick, & Fagan, 1963) hypothesized that self-criticism, which seems to stem from punishment, is learned by children as an anxiety-reducing response. In their studies and in a similar study by Grusec (1966) the experimentor administered punishments to the child and labeled the consequences when he or she made any errors in difficult tasks. These researchers found that children did learn self-blaming labels, especially when the experimenter was a highly nurturing person. These experiments, however, were performed in laboratories and it is questionable whether the experimentors had any impact on the internalization of self-criticism, guilt, and moral internalization of the subjects. Hoffman (1977) believes that these children may have learned to "parrot" the experimentors' labels. It is not clear whether parroting is identification or internalization. Therefore, in reality, the children may not have seen themselves as committing a commission or omission, but rather equated self-criticism with guilt.

There is further research indicating that a child's guilt development is centered around the results of punishment. Sears, Rau, and Alpert (1965) used a "disappearing hamster" to measure conscience development in 4-year-old children. The children were told by the experimentor to watch the hamster. While they are distracted with stimuli—such as toys, games, and records at the other end of the room—the hamster disappears. After the hamster reappears, the children's development of conscience is measured by the degree and quality of guilt as expressed by their affective arousal. The results of this research indicated that the children have a high amount of arousal, but the specific nature of this arousal is unclear. Is the arousal due to a fear of punishment from the experimenter, or is it a guilt response? The ethical issue of causing these children to have a high conscience arousal has been criticized, in this, as well as other similar experiments (Hoffman, 1977; Milgram, 1963; Regan, Williams, & Sparling, 1972).

Semiprojective story completion is a method used by Allinsmith and Greening (1955), Hoffman (1974), Hoffman and Saltzstein (1967), and Miller and Swanson (1960) to measure guilt. In this method, children listened to stories that involve a protagonist who is about the same age but not necessarily the same sex as the child. The protagonist was involved in "wrongdoing." The children then complete the story, hopefully exposing their own internal feelings. The story completions are scored according to guilt intensity, quality, and behaviors that follow a commission or omission. The children did feel guilt, with girls expressing more intense guilt.

Moral internalization research is important in understanding guilt. Moral internalization is the process whereby the child learns that there are behaviors that are "wrong" and when those behaviors are performed, guilt results. Children do feel guilt and the research indicates that the guilt develops from punishment. Yet, when research is done to analyze this concept, the guilt-producing situations tend to be artificial, and they usually occur in a laboratory. The control groups in such situations are weak, the quality and intensity of guilt are measured with questionable methods and the moral internalization indices (e.g., labels) are weak. With such a weak foundation upon which to build and gather data, one then questions whether the researchers are testing imitation rather than internalization (Aronfreed, 1964; Aronfreed, Cutick, & Fagan, 1963; Grusec, 1966; Hoffman, 1977; Johnson & Kalafat, 1969; LaVoie, 1973; Regan, Williams, & Sparling, 1972).

Sexual Differences in the Expression of Guilt.   Moral internalization research on the guilt in children shows that a majority of all children feel guilt. This result is in the contrast to Freud's theory. Freud proposed that because boys have to resolve the Oedipal complex and consequently identify with the father, they have a greater internalized moral structure and act autonomously within that structure. He believed girls do not resolve the Electra complex as fully and, therefore, do not identify with the parent as dramatically. Consequently, their superegos are always immature (Freud, 1933,

1961). Thus, Freud suggests that boys and girls may experience guilt differently.

Hoffman (1975) also studied the sex differences in moral internalization and the content of moral standards by the use of semi-projective story telling. He studied fifth and seventh graders and their parents. He stated that there are three aspects to internal moral orientation: *Behavioral:* resistance to temptation and pressure to do otherwise even without external sanctions; *affective:* guilt intensity when one trespasses; and *cognitive:* creation of internal moral judgment, about behaviors, fear of detection, anticipation of punishment, attribution of external morality, and consideration of others.

Hoffman's findings do not support Freud's theory. Hoffman (1975) found that females have significantly higher humanistic, internalized moral standards than males. On guilt intensity, it is interesting to note that girls and their mothers are higher on maximum guilt (experienced by the hero, usually early in the story) with mothers being higher on terminal guilt (what one does with guilt) than the boys and fathers. This possibly suggests a developmental aspect of affective quantities of moral internalization with guilt intensity increasing with age. This contradicts Piaget's theory which said guilt was more intense in younger children.

Both generations of males show a more consistent, but not significant, guilt response. Males more often respond to the stories with fear of detection and punishment. They also put a greater emphasis on achievement (Hoffman, 1975). The achievement aspect could also suggest a developmental aspect prominent in males, with fathers being more achievement oriented than their sons. The achievement aspect suggests that boys would be more egoistic or self-oriented than girls. Hoffman's data seems to support this expectation. Another assessment, which may account for the socialization of moral internalization in males based on achievement and fear, is the Protestant ethic or Horatio Alger theory: Males should work hard and strive to succeed.

Additional data on moral internalization are found in Hoffman's discipline research (Hoffman & Saltzstein, 1967; Hoffman, 1970). His research indicates that parents tend to discipline girls by talking, reasoning, inflicting little physical punishment, and by giving much affection and support. Parents of boys typically discipline them with physical force (power assertion). Mothers are more affectionate to daughters, use more guilt induction and less power assertion; boys are punished with more power-assertion techniques. Hoffman found that guilt induction produces internal moral standards, whereas power assertion produces external moral standards.

Hoffman found that guilt was related to early discipline experiences. This finding may support who expresses guilt regarding death. The internally motivated person may feel more guilt when deviation occurs and the externally motivated person may fear being discovered. Women may be more internally motivated, more empathic, and more humanistic. Consequently, they may experience more intense guilt in death situations. Men may be more externally motivated, less empathic, and react with conventional commissions and omissions.

Hoffman also studied moral identification and guilt in seventh grade children by looking at father absence of at least 6 months. He collected no data on mother absence, and guilt again was measured by story completion. He found that father-absent boys scored significantly lower on the guilt index than boys in the control group. There was no difference for father-absent girls. Consequently, there seems to be little relationship between guilt arousal and identification. At this age, however, the presence of the same-sex parent could have an impact on guilt arousal. Before such conclusions can be reached, further research with mother and father absence must be conducted.

Hoffman's study suggests that there are no sex differences in moral judgment. However, the females in his study tended to display more guilt and behaved more morally than males, even with the absence of external sanctions. This result is supported by other research that found females were more likely to return valuable items, whereas males would have done so only if there had been a witness (Gross, 1972). In the Milgram experiment, females resisted pressure to behave immorally to raise the level of shock to a victim. Therefore, it seems that females are more humanistic with more internalized moral standards while males are more achievement oriented with external moral standards (Milgram, 1963; Kilham & Mann, 1974).

Sex-role socialization may also give credence to why women seem to express more guilt. Johnson (1963) explored the theory that females traditionally have been socialized for the "expressive" role in our culture. The female role is focused on giving and receiving affection, being responsive to the needs and feelings of others, and keeping harmony. Males are socialized toward playing the instrumental role; they have traditionally been the family's link or liaison to the larger society.

If one accepts the theory of the traditional expressive role of women and the instrumental role of men, then it is plausible that men and women may express guilt differently. Thus, when a family confronts a crisis, such as dying or death, mothers may feel guilt more readily over expressive issues: "I feel so guilty for leaving her in the hospital all alone." This reaction is due to their identification with the expressive role in this life-threatening situation. It also seems apparent that in such a family crisis, men would identify with the instrumental role situations: "I felt a little guilty because I couldn't afford all expenses for hospitalization and doctor bills." These roles may be enhanced by the expectations of significant others of the same sex and role type; grandmothers may instill guilt in their daughters when the role of "mothering" of the grandchild is not being met; grandfathers may instill guilt in their sons if they show emotions after the death of their grandchild: "You shouldn't cry; just get on with life."

In addition to sex-role socialization, several researchers attribute the development of guilt to identification with parental behaviors, self-criticisms, and self-punishments (Sears, Maccoby, & Levin, 1957; Sears, Rau, & Alpert, 1965). They base their investigations on psychoanalytic theory. According to Sears, Maccoby, and Levin's research, the young child wants approval, love, and nurturing. These needs cause a dependence on the parents. When the parents disapprove of the child's behavior, the child will copy parental behaviors associated with discipline, including self-criticism, self-punishment, and self-control. Appropriate behaviors are rewarded and the young child learns to imitate parental behavior in order to gain, and then maintain, approval.

Hoffman's findings tend to contradict Sears' research, although a different age population is used. Hoffman (1975) researched a set of seven moral indices in lower- and middle-class seventh grade children. He did use some questions on identification, although not enough to draw conclusions (e.g., "Which person(s) do you admire or look up to the most?" and "Which person do you want to be like when you grow up?"). He found no significant difference between identification measure and the quality and intensity of guilt in these children. In this age group, however, peer rather than parental relationships are more important. Further, enough credence is not given to the possibility that children identify with both parents. If this is so, a sexual difference would not necessarily be seen.

The question of sexual differences in the development of guilt in young children is an important one. Researchers have tested situational factors that produce guilt, such as punishment (Aronfreed, 1963; Aronfreed, Cutick, & Fagen, 1963; Milgram, 1963), harming or helping others (Aronfreed, Cutick, & Fagan, 1963; LaVoie, 1973; Milgram, 1963; Regan, 1971; Staub, 1971), breaking or taking objects (Gross, 1972; Regan, William, & Sparling, 1972), sex-role socialization (Hoffman, 1975; Johnson, 1963), behavior following guilt (Freedman, Wallington, & Bless, 1967; Green & Quanty, 1977; Regan, 1971). Research thus far indicates that guilt is based upon parental punishment, with sex-role socialization also playing an important function.

At present, the research does not clarify whether the identification process of the child with the same-sex parent significantly contributes to guilt development or not. Areas such as affective atmosphere of the home, role-modeling of the parents, cultural and religious beliefs, age, experiences, and the method of transmission of parental values and beliefs may contribute to the quality and intensity of guilt. Yet too many variables in the research exist for concrete conclusions to be drawn from this factor alone. For the clinician, however, sexual differences do seem to have a role in the treatment and understanding of guilt.

Research on Guilt as Related to Grief and Mourning

Guilt as part of death and the mourning process is a topic that has not been extensively or thoroughly researched. There is one well-researched theory that analyzes guilt as it relates to the crisis of death. Robert Jay Lifton's 1967 classic, *Death in Life; The Survivors of Hiroshima,* explores the thought that the Hibakushas, the survivors, felt guilty because of the "closing-off" or denial process they experienced. Lifton's guilt theory will be presented because it addresses death guilt rather than moral development in children.

An initial reaction of the survivors of Hiroshima was to close-off what was happening around them. This major defense helped them to function as "normally" as possible while undertaking the unbearable tasks of caring for the injured and burying the dead: "I feel nothing, then death is not taking place all around me." Lifton writes: "it [closing-off] was a way of creating emotional distance between survivors and the intolerable world immediately around them." Guilt would not be felt if the closing-off process was successful.

However, the psychic closing-off could not totally protect from the "threatening stimuli from without or within." Within, it took the form of self-condemnation through guilt and shame for being alive. There was a strong need to justify one's own survival while others died. The guilt then interfered with and yet stimulated the closing-off process. If the closing-off process was reinstituted, delayed guilt occurred until the guilt could break through once again.

The delayed guilt was evidenced by survivors recalling the voices of those who died, while they were rescued at the expense of others. The survivors then saw themselves as bad people because they did not help the others. "In every corpse I saw myself. What if the survivors didn't help me?" Lifton found that people remembered the guilt feelings rather than the external event . . . the "living hell" that forced them to make the decision to help or not to help someone at the time. The guilt that the Hibakushas felt was due not only to the deaths themselves, but also to the influence the deaths had on the survivors' symbolization of life and on what survivors felt they could or should have done.

The survivors' guilt, especially that of the children, was often interpreted as a form of punishment for misbehavior: "We did nothing bad—and still our parents died."

Guilt provided a way to formulate a structure of an illness or other event within a framework of cause and effect. The guilt could give reason or meaning to a crisis. It is a means of coping with something one does not understand. However, the guilt needed to be understood and resolved. Lifton pointed out that if the guilt was not resolved, the survivors were closed-off at an unconscious level; guilt then reappeared for the Hibakushas in other forms such as illness (e.g., conversion hysteria, anxiety reactions, or thoughts of attempted suicide).

Parents whose children were killed expressed a "special kind of guilt associated with failure to carry out the fundamental psychological task in caring for the young—giving life to them and maintaining it in them." Often they would reconstruct the death event in their fantasy in order to make them more culpable.

There often were ambivalences and resentments, which became magnified after the death because their own needs or discomforts prevented them from caring for the injured or saying their final good-byes.

The guilt issues became very complicated and intertwined: ignorance, closing-off, ambivalence, conflicts in responsibility and priorities; guilt–anger–abandonment alternating with relief–gratitude–restored nurturance, and even joy.

The Hibakushas then felt more guilty because of these positive feelings, and the vicious circle was created. They condemned themselves for being alive and also for feeling relieved that someone else was dead instead of themselves. The prospects of their continued health, life, and pleasure added to this guilt. Lifton's analysis describes guilt as a complicated and multifaceted feeling in the life and death experiences such as a nuclear explosion.

In a study of the grief of bereaved psychiatric patients, Parkes (1965a, 1965b) found what appeared to be a strong connection between mental illness, guilt, and self-blame over a death. Parkes interviewed 21 widowed patients whose psychiatric symptoms occurred during the terminal illness or within 6 months of the death of a parent, spouse, sibling, or child. He then matched for age and sex in a subsample (N = 14) with widows from a study by Morris (1958) who analyzed normal grief patterns. He found a striking difference: the bereaved psychiatric group expressed more guilt and self-blame than the normal grief group (p = <0.001). This important study suggests the possibility that guilt over a death may be a contributing factor to a decrease in emotional health.

The "Harvard study," conducted by Glick, Weiss, and Parkes (1974), reports that 9 of 22 men were not as successful in managing guilt as they were in controlling anger immediately after the death of a spouse. Guilt was the result of a feeling that they had contributed to their wives' deaths (e.g., blaming themselves for making the wife pregnant when the wife died in childbirth). This descriptive study found that men tried to control recall more than women. Although this study indicated that men had difficulty in handling guilt immediately after the death of their spouses, it did not indicate why, nor did it explain the differences between men's and women's expressions of guilt.

A study by Benfield, Leib, and Vollman (1978) found that mothers express "more" grief than fathers in a newborn infant postmortem interview. Grief was based on seven reactions: anger, guilt, irritability, loss of appetite, preoccupation, difficulty sleeping, and sadness. The only significant index was guilt. Mothers reported feeling more guilty than fathers. The parents' grief did not relate to the child's duration of life. This study did not specifically explore guilt but reported that guilt may be an important reaction to grief and possibly more prevalent in mothers.

In addition to experiencing guilt in bereavement, guilt has also been researched with terminally ill people. A 1953 study by Abrams and Finesinger described the guilt experienced by 60 adult patients with various types of cancer. Verbatim interviews were used to determine patient attitudes. The study reports that 93% of these people had feelings of guilt, although only a "few" actually stated they felt guilt. The patients equated their guilt with feelings that their illnesses were either their own fault or the fault of others. Consequently, the researchers may not have been measuring guilt, but rather were uncovering "secret" causes for the patients' illnesses. Guilt, however, may still have been involved in their blaming process.

Abrams and Finesinger (1953) also found that these same patients were preoccupied with ideas that indicate guilt. The patients, however, were vague and did not specifically analyze these feelings. They also noted that relatives often expressed the same attitude of guilt as the patient; however, the exact number of relatives demonstrating this attitude was not determined. Although they did not substantiate their findings with data, the researchers believed that these feelings of guilt caused adult patients to deny their symptoms and consequently delay seeking treatment. These guilt feelings inhibited their ability to communicate and fostered "attitudes of inferiority, inadequacy, dependency, and feelings of rejection" in the patients.

Using case studies, others have attempted to describe the presence of guilt in dying people. Friedman (1973) found that guilt was often accompanied by a sense of failure. When guilt increases, a strong need for expiation developed. Friedman believed that the expiation often resulted in self-punishment. He dealt with various losses, not only death. These assumptions need further research, but do indicate that guilt, if present and not resolved, can hinder a healthy resolution of the loss.

Gardner (1969) studied 23 parents of severely ill children. He tested the psychological processes they used to help explain "inappropriate" guilt reactions. He found that some parents' guilt supports the psychoanalytic theory that guilt is based upon an unconscious hostility toward the child. He developed the Affective-Hositility Score by asking the parents questions. These questions, however, were directly related to traditional sex-role typing, with the result that if a girl did not like to play with dolls as a child, she would get a low or "hostile" score. Such questions may have biased the outcome. Gardner also found that parents used guilt as a causal relationship. Because guilt became the reason why the tragedy occurred, guilt became a tool to relieve anxiety rather than a defense to protect from anxiety for these parents.

Gardner studied couples' guilt rather than the individual parent's guilt. He assigned couples to three experimental groups: blamed self, blamed others, and no need to blame others. The last group was the control group. He interviewed the parents to place them in the proper group. The group labels may indicate that he was studying blame causality rather than guilt. His research attempted to identify specific reasons for guilt and to show that guilt can be a normal reaction to grief.

Guilt Types

Guilt is a very complicated process and feeling. Since it is such a persistent factor in grief, I have developed a decision tree to help the clinician diagnose the various types of guilt. This process also tends to assist in treating the patient. First, one must determine the guilt statement(s). Second, one should determine whether the cause is based upon a present, past, or future act, or whether the person just "feels" guilty with no apparent commission or omission. One should then be able to identify the type of guilt that the person or family is experiencing (see Figure 2-4).

Personal Guilt.   Personal guilt is a result of a commission or omission and will be retrospective. First it must be determined if the guilt is unimagined (U). This would mean it was the result of an actual commission (things done) or omission (things not done). Imagined (I) guilt is the result of a fantasized commission or omission. For example, one woman felt guilty because she did not acknowledge the lump in her breast for a very long time and then needed a radical mastectomy. Her guilt was based upon the fact that she did not seek early treatment. Therefore, her omission (not having a checkup) is unimagined personal guilt (U).

Personal imagined guilt begins with phrases like "I should have," "If only I had," or "I wished I had." It may be imagined if the event did not occur. In addition, the guilt may be based on realistic assumptions, but the thought remains a fantasy. Such were the feelings of a father whose daughter was in an intensive care unit as a result of a horrible car accident. He said to me, "If only I had insisted that she put on her seatbelt, maybe she would have been okay."

The guilt is further subgrouped into internal [(to oneself = self-grounded (S)] versus external [(distress to others = other-grounded (O)]. An example of self-grounded guilt is the woman who did not go for early treatment for the lump. An example of other-grounded guilt is the woman who let go of her 3-year-old child's hand, giving him the opportunity to dart into the street where he was run over by a truck. She felt her behavior affected another, causing "distress," and therefore, she felt guilt as a result of an omission toward another person (Personal, Unimagined, Other-grounded guilt = PUO.)

There are two further subtypes: humanistic (H), which results from commissions or omissions that affect, or harm other humans or oneself. For example, a diabetic woman, who was a nurse, gave birth to a 13 lb 9 oz baby. She believed that if she had monitored her diabetes more carefully and had eaten less during her pregnancy, the baby would not have been so large. The baby died of anoxia in a critical care unit 9 days after birth. Conventional guilt (C), on the other hand, results from a deviation from a social norm, role expectation, or cultural convention. A little girl had fallen out of a tree and was unconscious in the intensive care unit. Her mother centered her guilt around the conventional issues of being a working parent: "If I had been home this never would have happened."

Anticipatory Guilt. Anticipatory guilt involves predicting that one will feel guilty in the future if certain circumstances occur. Anticipatory guilt is grounded in fantasy and based upon future commissions or omissions. Therefore, the guilt is not felt in the present. This type of guilt starts with phrases like "if" or "I should." Since the situation has not occurred as yet, anticipatory guilt can only be imagined; "If I start smoking, the chances are greater I'll get cancer and that would make me feel guilty."

Anticipatory guilt may not be significant in the present in determining the quantity or intensity of guilt, unless it eventually becomes a type of unimagined guilt or involves psychopathology. It is used for future decision making or prevention of guilt in the present. I see this type of guilt more frequently with long-term illnesses or with illness in an older person: "If I don't visit Grandma before she dies, I will feel very guilty" (Anticipatory, Imagined, Other-grounded, Conventional guilt, AIOC). In addition, it may involve a crisis time: "If the nurse doesn't let me into the critical care unit before she dies, I will feel so guilty" (AIOC).

As a clinician, it is helpful to intervene with this type of guilt as soon as it is verbalized, so that it does not become a personal-unimagined guilt. It is far easier to prevent guilt than to undo it in the future. Often, only a very simple act is needed, such as saying goodbye, seeing, touching, or saying something where there has been an issue of unfinished business. If the patient is in a crisis situation, I always ask if there is any anticipatory guilt, or if there are things that need to be done that, if left undone, would make them feel guilty.

Existential Guilt. The third type of guilt is existential. With this type there has not been an actual commission or omission, but the person feels culpable because of circumstances beyond his or her control. The issues usually deal with social and ethical values or beliefs. There are three conditions necessary to feel existential guilt: the ability to identify with another's plight, to cognitively feel at an advantage, and to then feel helpless (Hoffman, 1976).

Existential guilt incorporates the involvement of social and ethical situations that conflict with one's values or beliefs. It occurs with more global issues where one may not be personally involved. It often is a resolution guilt for the other types of guilt. For example, the parents of an 8-year-old child who died from a terminal cardiac

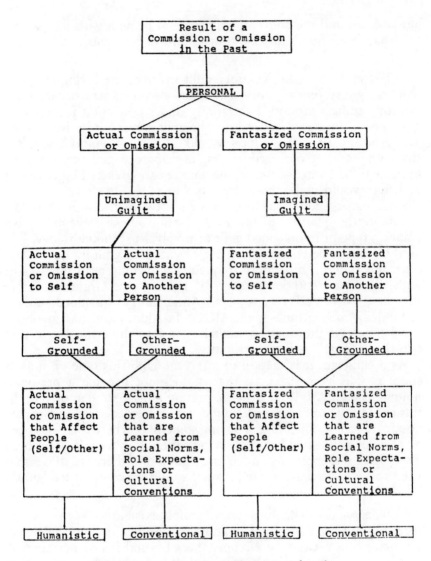

FIGURE 2-4. Decision tree: types of guilt.

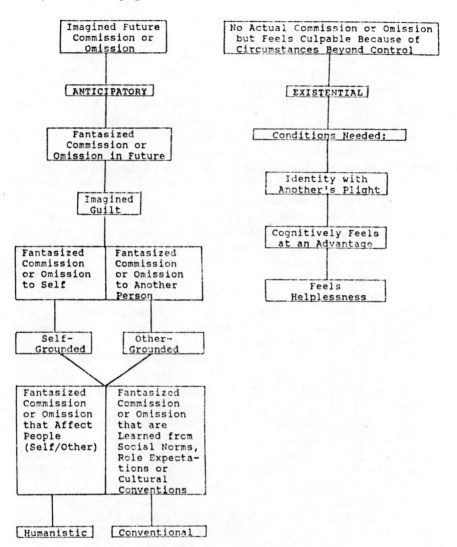

FIGURE 2-4. *(Continued)*

condition were feeling RIOH, PUOH, and PIOC guilts. As we worked with the guilts in therapy, they eventually realized that they had done nothing wrong, they just "felt guilty." Their guilts changed from RIOH, PUOH and PIOC with intervention, to existential guilt, "She died and we are still alive."

War veterans often feel existential guilt when they have survived their friends in combat. In addition, people often experience this type of guilt when, for example, they watch the news of the starving people in Africa and then sit down to a large meal. Existential guilt often leads people toward action, such as sending money to Africa.

The following examples show how the guilt diagnoses are determined using the decision tree (see Figure 2-4): Please recall the example of the nurse who was diabetic and pregnant with her second child. She felt that she had gained too much weight and kept saying that the baby was going to be too big. The physician told her that she was "overreacting and not to worry . . . what did she know, she was *only* a nurse." The baby was too big to be delivered vaginally (13 lbs 9 oz) and died of anoxia 9 days after delivery. Trudy expressed her feelings: "I have a lot of guilt over how I got so big . . . I was concerned a lot about my pregnancy because I knew I was a diabetic and diabetics have big babies and I thought that he was bigger." Using the decision tree one can identify this mother's guilt as personal, unimagined, other-grounded and humanistic (PUOH): Personal: weight gain as a result of commission, Unimagined: actually happened (Trudy gained too much weight because of her eating habits and being diabetic), Other-grounded: affected fetus, Humanistic: commission affected child.

Another family's 3-year-old son was hit by a car. The parents, Jane and Mark, had been working on Mark's parent's lawn. Jane drove home to get some tools. Sven, their 3-year-old son, asked Mark where his mother was. Mark said that she had to run home for a minute but would be right back. Without Mark knowing it, Sven went down the street on his tricycle, heading toward their house, which was a couple of blocks away. He had to cross a very busy street and was run over by a passing car. Jane came upon the accident when she was returning to her in-laws' house. She expressed many "if only" statements like, "If only I had told Sven to be sure to stay there and don't come." This is an example of personal, imagined, other-grounded, conventional guilt (PIOC). It is personal and imagined: a fantasized omission which should have occurred in the past, Other-grounded: dealt with another person, Conventional: role expectations of the protecting parent.

In my research I found that mothers expressed significantly more retrospective imagined guilt than fathers (Johnson-Soderberg, 1982).

Perhaps mothers in our society are expected to be the ones to protect children from all harm and then if they are harmed, take the guilt. These are difficult expectations with which to deal.

Expressions of Guilt

In my research, I interviewed 14 couples who had had a child die and were in their first year of bereavement. Eight couples had a short preparation time for death (SPG), with 2 weeks or less warning that death was imminent.* Six couples had a longer preparation time for death (LPG): about 15 days or more warning that death was imminent. The parents ages ranged from 24 to 54 and all were white middle-income families. Mainly Christian religions were represented, but one couple professed athesim. Nine of the children who died were boys, and five were girls. The primary focus in the research was parental guilt.

The results showed that the SPG expressed more guilt statements than the LPG over two interviews (one with both parents, one separately, and a third which was debriefing).

Through the interviews, a total of 451 guilt statements evolved from all of the parents. Every parent in the SPG expressed guilt feelings, as did all but one man in the LPG. (This man had several guilt statements but did not label them as such.) The SPG had more guilt statements than the LPG and women had more than the men (Table 2-1).

The results of a student's *t*-test, correlating preparation time and guilt, showed that the SPG had significantly more guilt statements than the LPG ($p<0.01$) (Johnson-Soderberg, 1982). This may be due to the fact that the SPG had less time to prepare for the death of their child and, therefore, could not "prevent" or "undo" their guilt.

These findings also showed that mothers expressed more guilt than

TABLE 2-1. Distribution of Guilt Statements

Death preparation group	Total number of subjects	Guilt Statements		
		Women	Men	Total
Short (SPG)	16	207	120	327
Long (LPG)	12	83	41	124

*Although 15 days is not very long, there are clinical indications that even "some" preparation time has an effect on survivor bereavement.

the fathers ($p<0.02$) and the SPG mothers ($p<0.06$) and fathers ($p<0.02$) expressed more guilt than the LPG mothers and fathers. The implications of these findings are that the SPG had more guilt. If guilt is a factor affecting the physical or mental health of a parent or a couple, then the SPG parents may be at higher risk than the LPG parents. Another interpretation is that these SPG parents could better express and verbalize their guilt, a positive sign that they are dealing with the problem.

It is also apparent that as the number of guilt statements increase for one spouse, they also increase for the other. A Person's r analysis was performed on the relationship between mother's and father's guilt statements. This analysis accounted for 52% of the variance, with a significance level of <0.004 between the mothers' number of guilt statements and the fathers', which represents a relationship of moderate strength between the two. It was found that as the mother's number of guilt statements increased, so did the father's; the opposite was also true. Therefore, it could be that there is a contagious effect with guilt among couples as one parent's guilt increases so does the other's and vice versa (see Figure 2-5).

Coping with Guilt

The parents coped with their guilt in a variety of ways. Some kept it a secret and felt tormented and sick inside. Some would work harder, others became very religious, some drank more, and others developed the conspiracy of silence so that they did not have to deal with "it." Those that talked and cried about their guilt and eventually moved toward altruistic responses as a means of undoing their guilt seemed to "heal better." Usually these altruistic responses came with their "decision to start living once again" (see section on the decision to live again). Those who did not deal or cope with their guilt in a healthy manner became emotionally or physically sick.

Guilt Instillers

In addition to the guilt already felt, there were also people who would instill guilt in the survivor either in fantasy or reality. For the most part, this reinforced guilt feelings. People often comment to me that one reason to not have contact with people was to avoid the guilt-instilling people, who only made them feel worse.

My research shows that there were more direct guilt-instilling statements from "so called" close family members or significant others (Johnson-Soderberg, 1982). For example, a mother said to her

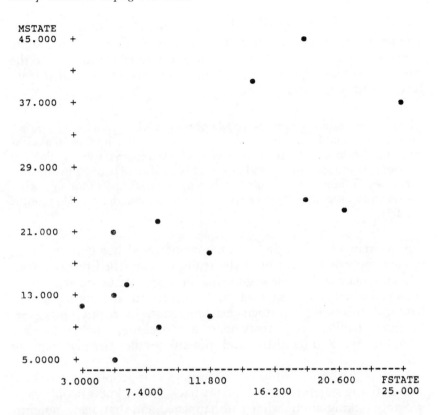

FIGURE 2-5. Scatter plot of mothers' and fathers' total guilt statements.

daughter, after the death of her granddaughter, "Why didn't you know something was wrong with Ruth? You should have been a better mother and insisted that she be taken to the doctor." Another mother told her daughter, after the death of a grandson, "You shouldn't have gotten pregnant with your diabetes. You knew you had a chance of your child dying. Couldn't you have been satisfied with one child?" Such comments tended to accuse the parent directly for an omission or commission. These statements continued to reinforce the existing guilt feelings with such themes as parenting, God, and pregnancy.

Distant friends or family tended to be more passive or indirect in their guilt instilling statements. In these statements they did not directly use the parents name or situation of the death. The statement only "implied" that they had done something wrong. For example, one guilt-instilling woman said, "If my children ever go astray, become disobedient, or go far from what I desire for them, I would pray to God to 'take' them." The grieving mother told me that that statement was not a bit comforting. A friend said, "Well, some people are just not meant to be parents," not referring directly to the woman, but making the comment after her friend's child died from Reye's syndrome. Another woman said,

> I had a few stupid comments. I had one person who was a friend, she is a good friend and I was telling her about Kathy's baby who was 16 months . . . no, I told her about the one who was 21 months. I was telling her about this and she said, 'Oh, that would be really bad because by the time they are 21 months old, you're really attached to them.' I thought, 'what makes you think that I wasn't attached to mine, since he was 2½ months old?'

This woman said that the interaction increased her guilt feelings, because she was wondering if she really was attached to her baby.

Clients believe that these guilt instillers are not necessarily malicious and often believe that the guilt instillers are attempting to help them rid themselves of their existing guilt. In reality, however, the guilt instillers comments tend to "backfire," either directly or indirectly, and confirm and potentiate the already nagging guilt.

Women also expressed paranoid feelings that people were making guilt-instilling statements "behind my back." They knew people were probably talking about what had happened and that again potentiated their own guilt feelings.

In my research, all but one of the guilt-instilling people were women (Johnson-Soderberg, 1982). One begins to wonder if sex-role socialization teaches some women, but not men, to feel or instill guilt. It may also be a threat to the traditional role expectations. If a woman believed that it was a "mother's role" to protect her child and then the child died, this role had been threatened. The guilt instiller could be projecting his or her own fears into another's situation. If women are using the "traditional role" as a measuring stick for success, then they can feel better about themselves in putting someone else down for their omission or commission. It is a very sad and tragic example of how women can hinder, rather than help, their own sex.

Rarely do I find that men instill guilt in other men or women. Women, on the other hand, instill guilt in both. One man said, "my wife is always trying to make me feel guilty—she says I'm not grieving correctly, I don't cry enough, and I don't really miss Ben."

Guilt Movies

In my research, the phenomenon of a "guilt movie" emerged. A guilt movie is a repetitive, compulsive, and often secret "movie" or flashback of the person's most intense guilt feeling. The movies, for the most part, are in color and occur sometimes hundreds or thousands of times a day. One father said:

> I always thought it (guilt movie) was kind of a repetitive nightmare or something, only not when you're asleep—just during waking hours when you are obsessed by one thought or feeling—like some drama being played out in your head over and over and over again. There's no escaping from it.

Once this finding emerged, I began asking all parents if they had movies. They would be amazed and say "yes." None of them had previously expressed their haunting fantasies. Sharing them brought a great sense of relief that others had had the same experience and that they were not going "crazy." They had been certain that they were hallucinating. It frightened parents. They felt that if they described the experience, even to their spouse, that they would be committed to a psychiatric unit.

Often the movies were sacrificial in nature. One mother handed her baby over to the nurse for surgery. The baby died during the surgery. Another father saw himself lifting his 10-year-old daughter onto the surgery cart. She later died in surgery.

Other movies dealt with guilt surrounding the scene of death or just prior to the death. Families who had children struck by a car saw the accident occurring or the scene of the accident. One father said, "The accident scene is emblazed in my mind. Then as I'm seeing this awful scene, I hear myself saying, 'If only I had told him not to follow me' " (ROC).

The parents who had more than one feeling of guilt were able to rank them from the most intense to the least intense. The woman who had diabetes said that she could "definitely say the birth weight was the most intense guilt feeling, having a boy rather than a girl, and lastly, not going to the cemetery." Trudy's husband mentioned three types of emotions:

> Yes, probably the most intense (guilt) was the first one that I was responsible for what Tommy was going through. It was probably most intense because it was a very brief period and like I said, when the

doctor told us it was all over, there was nothing else he could do. That was probably the worst day of my life. I don't know what I would have done. I don't know how I would have solved it . . . that was really the most intense one. I have never experienced any guilt that strong. Next would be the helplessness. You always feel that something can be done even if you cannot control it, at least you can do something. But in this situation, I felt like I couldn't do anything that would be able to solve it. The other one was kind of like after the fact: it's just the feeling that I could have supported her (Trudy) a little better and that is the least intense of the three.

Mary, the mother whose twin died, said, "Turning my back on her was the most intense" (the twins were born by cesarean section, and it was too painful for Mary to lie on her left side, so even though there was some indication that Ruth was ill, Mary had to turn her back to the baby and lie on her right side). "And then, second, of course, I thought she was pale and I didn't do anything soon enough. But definitely turning over in bed." For the father whose little boy was run over by the truck, the primary guilt feeling was that he had had multiple affairs, and the secondary one was his drinking problem.

Nancy was a flight attendant. Her child died of a cardiac problem. Her most intense guilt was that she had worked too hard during her pregnancy. "It was almost like I was trying to make something happen and that makes me feel very guilty. I don't know if I will ever get rid of the guilt." Nancy has since developed bulimia.

The most intense guilt feeling was always associated with a guilt movie. This was a very consistent finding both in my research and in practice (Johnson-Soderberg, 1982). It is important, therefore, to assess the guilt feeling, and to rank those feelings and the associated guilt movies. People typically experience one movie repeatedly, and that movie can be very intense and frightening; it would "just come out of nowhere. I would not even be thinking of her."

MASOCHISM

Masochism is a process whereby the person learns, through various external stimuli, that suffering, submission, and self-punishment are ways to respond to, internalize, act, and interact with others. This develops through a long process of socialization, involving many factors including fairy tales, religious teachings, media, and role teaching by parents and significant others. This is passed from generation to generation because of the sex-role identification.

Many theorists, Freud in particular, believed that the masochistic person enjoys the suffering that is so much a part of his or her life. In reality, no other way of life is known. The masochist's way of coping with crisis is to suffer, which becomes a defensive and compliant style with no alternatives. They use the same coping patterns over and over, even in dying and death situations.

In her recent book, *Sweet Suffering: Woman as Victim*, N. Shainess (1984) provides comprehensive background symptoms and alternatives for the masochistic personality. Although masochistic themes are found in men, I agree with Dr. Shainess that they are more prevalent in women.

> . . . women in our society bear such liabilities as inferior social and economic status, lesser biological strength, and reproductive handicaps that masochism is a special problem for them. In nearly four decades of practice as a psychiatrist and psychoanalyst, I have all too frequently encountered masochism in women and only occasionally in men. Both women and men have early experiences that dispose them to masochistic behavior, but the cultural elements that continually reinforce masochistic behavior in women are largely absent for men. Women, in this sense, experience a really double whammy. Many emerge from their childhoods with a damaged sense of self. Then the culture in which they live ratifies that distorted image rather than helping them to repair the damage. And the odds are longer for women in the struggle to overcome masochism. To eradicate something as stubborn, compulsive, and destructive as masochism, people need all the help they can get. Our society, in its attitudes and judgements, gives women precious little of that. (p. 3)

Shainess (1984) views masochism as having two facets: one deals with feelings (fearful of others, self-doubt, unable to resist, refuse, offend, or insist on limits, very guilty, offering constant apologies, self-punishment and self-denial) and the other is the process by which those feelings are communicated to others, or masochistic style (non-assertiveness, dependency, never questioning, taking things at face value, accepting of someone else's premise, quick to apologize, or use of self-damaging words, or "kick-me" statements) (pp. 5–11).

The masochistic feelings and communications can be learned from the very earliest stage of social development. Children's literature often carries many masochistic messages. From Snow White who cooked and cleaned for seven men before being "rescued" by a prince, through rhymes such as "Peter, Peter pumpkin eater, had a wife and could not keep her," and the like.

The apple theme from Snow White is a continuation of the historical and biblical archetype beginning with Eve's acceptance of the apple in the Garden of Eden, causing her to be banished from the

Garden and to be long-suffering, and resulting in God's promises of men's mastery over women and of painful childbirth (Gen. 3:16). An example of this continued belief can be found in the distress of a 90-year-old woman with whom I came in contact. The woman was very concerned because of the easy delivery of her granddaughter, who had studied the Lamaze techniques. The grandmother felt that it was not biblical not to suffer!

Many aspects of submission are learned early because the child is taught to fear authority figures, especially men, such as God, fathers, physicians, and ministers. Children, especially girls, also learn submission through biblical teachings. For example, several of the most misinterpreted, misunderstood, and manipulated texts in the Bible are:

Likewise you wives, be submissive to your husbands.

(1 Pet. 3:1)

Wives, be subject to your husbands, as to the Lord, for the husband is the head of the wife as Christ is the head of the church, his body, and is himself the Savior. As the church is subject to Christ, so let wives also be subject in everything to their husbands.

(Eph. 5:22–24)

Women should keep silence in the churches. For they are not permitted to speak but should be subordinate, as even the law says.

(1 Cor. 14:34–35)

The culture, the original language, and the mores of the time need to be considered in the interpretation. It becomes very dangerous to take these words literally without full knowledge of the past.

Besides biblical texts, one sees these issues being acted out in contemporary life. Women keep the house without benefits. If they work, they are paid less than what a man makes. They are often called "girls," by themselves and by men, which implies their low status in life. It has only been recently that women have begun to assume power positions in government, in private industry, and in the professions.

Women through the centuries have learned these behaviors through the church, society, culture, and interpersonal relationships. The masochist's reason for being is to suffer. They perpetuate the "pattern of suffering in life, primarily by processes of communication that alert other people to her submissiveness and her fear of their power over her" (Shainess, 1984, p. 2).

Shainess (1984) developed a questionnaire that deals with the symptoms of masochism: desire for approval, fear of offending, self-doubt, fear of authority, fear of abandonment, feelings of humiliation and guilt, self-punishment, nightmares of helplessness and flight, and sense of being the center of critical attention (pp. 13–15). This often is a primary theme with clients, especially women. As with other themes, it is usually a coping mechanism, although unhealthy, from the past and is again called into play during the dying and death process.

I was treating a 46-year-old woman, who was initially referred because her husband had left her and wanted a divorce. They had been married for 24 years and had four adopted children, the oldest of whom had been killed in a car crash a year before her husband's departure. The conspiracy of silence had been in operation, not only in their marriage, but in Greg's death. They had never talked about "it," were not involved in funeral arrangements—a friend took care of everything, nor did they grieve together. Within their marriage, they never expressed themselves or understood each other's behavior, never shared their problems ("intelligent people don't have problems, and if they do you push them under the rug"; "sex was always painful for me") or their own joys ("I never had my own joys"; "Greg's successes were mine"). Darrell, the husband, had begun to realize that "something" was wrong about 14 years earlier. In his search for intimacy, he began to have secret affairs. Darrell was a well-respected professional person who had been leading a double life, believing that was his only alternative. In those behaviors, he was also exhibiting masochism.

Jane, on the other hand, lived a fairy tale all of her life: "If you are good nothing will happen." "You go to college so you can meet a 'professional man', get married; he will always protect you; you will have children and live happily ever after." It is ironic that the masochistic person believes that if she gives and gives all of her life that someday she will be rewarded. In order to achieve this, however, she must sacrifice her personal needs, desires, and goals along the way. If she wants something, she learns to manipulate to achieve it (there are even books that teach women how to accomplish this). Jane keeps her part of the bargain: "to care for my husband, be dependent upon him, let him call the shots, nurture him and the children (playing the role of servant), and maintain the home." His part of the contract is financially to support her and remain faithful to her. When she was betrayed, she could not function and life lost its meaning.

Jane, as with other masochistic people, lost power over the years both to her husband and her children. Family members constantly criticized her and blamed her for all problems ("Mom you should know where my gym shoes are," "you really are a lousy cook"). She progressively felt more powerless. She didn't discipline the children and phrases like "wait until your father gets home" became a way of showing that she deferred the power to her husband. Jane deprived herself more and more of power, and as the children learned to respect only their father, who they viewed as having power in the home and at work, she felt isolated and abandoned. When her fairy tale was finally destroyed, she became very depressed, which is one way to withdraw. Her other means of withdrawal was her frequent suicide plans and attempts: "Life is not worth living without him. He's the only one for me."

In the two major losses, Greg's death and Darrell's departure, she continued to cope in a masochistic fashion. She attempted to transfer her dependency to me, to her friends, and to her hospitalization. She punished herself by weight loss, headaches, colds, insomnia, depression, by not expressing anger ("ladies don't get angry"), by her suicidal plans and attempts, and by her refusal to make good long-term decisions for her life, believing that she had no future without Darrell. How can society, culture, the church, and interrelationships say it is healthy to be submissive? When the love object is taken away the person is often defenseless, powerless, and physically and emotionally unhealthy. Jane's story is not unusual; this happens to many women in this country, and yet we continue to support fairy tales and masochistic issues in women.

One often sees this refusal to make a decision to go on and this extreme suffering in women who have had a child die. They grieve and refuse to give up their grieving. The grief will be as potent today as it was 10 years ago. Masochistic behavior is their way of coping and they know of no alternative but to continue to suffer.

Masochistic behaviors can be life-threatening in other ways: The man who covered his grief with a conspiracy of silence manifested that grief in ulcers; the woman who developed ulcerative colitis after her mother's death; or the woman who developed arthritis after the suicide of her father. The goals in death situations continue to be that of self-punishment, suffering, and submission.

Jane gave me a very revealing pencil drawing that Greg had done before he died. She had not known he had drawn it until much later. He had had multiple learning problems over the years and one of his major strengths was his drawing. This picture reflects, probably for Greg as well as Jane, fairy tale issues. There is an "earthquake" and the unicorn is looking back on the crumbling castle from the middle of the river. There is a tear in her eye. The picture is done in black and white, which adds to the feelings of depression and sadness (see Figure 2-6).

In the death and dying situation, the masochist has the opportunity to use masochism to the ultimate degree by continuing to suffer,

FIGURE 2-6. Greg's drawing.

being submissive, or inflicting self-punishment. These people are often the ones who will exhibit physical, emotional, and relationship deterioration. They may experience potent grief and never make the decision to get on with their lives. Others, however, because of their pain, might be able to seize the opportunity for change and health of a type not previously experienced by them.

SUMMARY

This chapter has dealt with grief themes of scapegoating, conspiracy of silence, detachment, guilt, and masochism. These family themes that come to play in coping with death provide a broader framework for assessing families who have had a death within the family. The themes also give a historical perspective on family dynamics. Each theme has components of healthy and unhealthy ways to cope with the death of a loved one. I encourage my patients to keep talking with safe people; to share their feelings and stories; to surround themselves with helpful people; and to express their grief actively in picture drawing, writing a journal, running, singing, dreaming, or working on changing something attributed to the death (e.g., start a MADD chapter, candlelighters, etc.).

REFERENCES

Abrams, R., & Finesinger, J. E. (1953). Guilt reactions in patient with cancer. *Cancer, 6*, 474–482.

Allinsmith, W., & Greening, T. C. (1955). Guilt over anger as predicted from parental discipline: A study of superego development. *American Psychologist, 10*, 320.

Aronfreed, J. (1963). The effect of experimental socialization paradigms upon two moral responses to transgression. *Journal of Abnormal and Social Psychology, 66*, 437–448.

Aronfreed, J. (1964). The origins of self-criticism. *Psychological Review, 71*, 193–218.

Aronfreed, J., Cutick, R. A., & Fagen, S. A. (1963). Cognitive structure, punishment, and nurturance in the experimental induction of self-criticism. *Child Development, 34*, 281–294.

Benfield, D. G., Leib, S., & Vollman, J. (1978, August). Grief response of parents to neonatal death and parent participation in deciding care. *Pediatrics, 62*, 171–177.

Bermann, E. (1973a). Death terror: Observations of interaction patterns in an American family. *Omega, 4*, 275–291.

Bermann, E. (1973b). *Scapegoat: The impact of death-fear on an American family.* Ann Arbor: The University of Michigan Press.

Bowlby, J. (1980). *Attachment and loss: Loss, sadness, and depression* (Vol. III). New York: Basic Books.

Freedman, J. L., Wallington, S. A., & Bless, E. (1967). Compliance without pressure: The effect of guilt. *Journal of Personality and Social Psychology, 7*, 117–124.

Freud, S. (Ed.). (1961). *Letters of Sigmund Freud.* New York: Basic Books.

Freud, S. (1933). *New introductory lectures on psychoanalysis.* New York: Norton.

Friedman, J. J. (1973). Depression, failure, and guilt. *New York State Journal of Medicine. June,* 1700–1704.

Gardner, R. (1969). The guilt reaction of parents of children with severe physical disease. *Amer. J. Psychiat. 126*, 636–644.

Glick, I., Weiss, R. S., & Parkes, C. M. (1974). *The first year of bereavement.* New York: John Wiley & Sons.

Grusec, J. (1966). Some antecedents of self-criticism. *Journal of Personality and Social Psychology, 4*, 244–252.

Gorer, G. (1965). *Death, grief, and mourning in contemporary Britain.* London: Cresset.

Green, R. G., & Quanty, M. B. (1977). The catharsis of aggression: An evaluation of a hypothesis. In L. Berkowitz (Ed.), *Advances in experimental social psychology* (Vol. 10, pp. 1–37). New York: Academic Press.

Gross, A. E. (1972, September). *Sex and helping: Intrinsic glow and extrinsic show.* Paper presented at meeting of the American Psychological Association. Honolulu.

Hoffman, M. L. (1970). Moral development. In P. H. Mussen (Ed.), *Carmichael's manual of child development,* (Vol. 2, pp. 261–317). New York: Wiley.

Hoffman, M. L. (1974). Developmental synthesis of affect and cognition and its implications for altruistic motivation. *Developmental Psychology, 11,* 607–622.

Hoffman, M. L. (1975). Sex differences in moral internalization and values. *Journal of Personality and Social Psychology, 32,* 720–729.

Hoffman, M. L. (1976). Empathy, role taking, guilt, and development of altruistic motives. In T. Lickona (Ed.), *Moral development and behavior: Theory, research, and social issues* (pp. 124–143). New York: Holt, Rinehart and Winston.

Hoffman, M. L. (1977). Moral internalization: Current theory and research. In L. Berkowitz (Ed.), *Advances in experimental social psychology* (Vol. 10). New York: Academic Press.

Hoffman, M. L., & Saltzstein, H. D. (1967). Parent discipline and the child's moral development. *Journal of Personality and Social Psychology, 5,* 45–57.

The Holy Bible, revised standard version. (1952). New York: Harper & Brothers.

Johnson, M. (1963). Sex role learning in the nuclear family. *Child Development, 34,* 319–333.

Johnson, R. C., & Kalafat, J. D. (1969). Projective and sociometric measures of conscious development. *Child Development, 40,* 651–655.

Johnson, S. (1983, January/February). Guiding adults through bereavement. *Nursing Life,* 34–39.

Johnson, S. (1984). Counseling families experiencing guilt.

Johnson, S. (1986). The client experiencing grief. In J. Durham & S. Hardin (Eds.), *The Nurse Psychotherapist in Private Practice.* New York: Springer.

Johnson-Soderberg, S. (1981, July). Ibsen's little Eyolf: A study of grief themes. *Advances in Nursing Science, 3,* 15–26.

Johnson-Soderberg, S. (1982). The ethos of parental bereavement and guilt. (Doctoral dissertation, University of Michigan, 1982). *Dissertation Abstracts International,* (University Microfilms).

Kilham, W., & Mann, L. (1974). Level of destructive obedience as a function of transmitter and executant roles in the Milgram obedience paradigm. *Journal of Personality and Social Psychology, 29,* 696–702.

Kübler-Ross, E. (1969). *On death and dying.* New York: MacMillan.

LaVoie, J. C. (1973, January). Individual differences in resistance-to-temptation behavior in adolescents: An Eysenck analysis. *Journal of Clinical Psychology, 29,* 20–22.

Lifton, R. J. (1967). *Death in life: Survivors of hiroshima.* New York: Vintage Books Edition.

Lindemann, E. (1944, September). Symptomatology and management of acute grief. *American Journal of Psychiatry, 101,* 141–148.

Milgram, S. (1963). Behavioral study of obedience. *Journal of Abnormal and Social Psychology, 67,* 371–378.

Miller, D. R., & Swanson, G. E. (Eds.). (1960). *Inner conflict and defense.* New York: Holt.

Morris, P. (1958). *Widows and their families.* London: Routledge and Kegan Paul.

Parkes, C. (1965a). Bereavement and mental illness: Part I. A clinical study of the grief of bereaved psychiatric patients. *British Journal of Medical Psychology, 38,* 1–12.

Parkes, C. M. (1965b). Bereavement and mental illness: Part II. A classification of bereavement reaction. *British Journal of Medical Psychology, 38,* 13–25.

Parkes, C. M. (1970). The first year of bereavement: A longitudinal study of the reaction of London widows to the death of their husbands. *Psychiatry, 33,* 444–467.

Parkes, C. M. (1974). *Bereavement: Studies of grief in adult life.* New York: International Universities Press.

Regan, D. T., Williams, M., & Sparling, S. (1972). Voluntary expiation of guilt: A field experiment. *Journal of Personality and Social Psychology, 24,* 42–45.

Regan, J. W. (1971). Guilt, perceived injustice, and altruistic behavior. *Journal of Personality and Social Psychology, 18,* 124–132.

Schoenberg, B., Carr, A., Kutscher, A., Peretz, D., & Goldberg, I. (Eds.). (1974). *Anticipatory grief.* New York: Columbia University Press.

Sears, R. S., Maccoby, E. E., & Levin, H. (1957). *Patterns of child rearing.* Evanston, IL: Row, Peterson.

Sears, R. S., Rau, L., & Alpert, R. (1965). *Identification and child rearing.* Stanford, CA: Stanford University Press.

Shainess, N. (1984). *Sweet suffering: Woman as victim.* New York: Bobb-Merrill.

Staub, E. (1971). Helping a person in distress: The influence of implicit and explicit 'rules' of conduct on children and adults. *Journal of Personality and Social Psychology, 17,* 137–144.

Westberg, E. E. (1961). *Good grief—A constructive approach to the problem of loss.* Philadelphia: Fortress Press.

Worden, J. W. (1982). *Grief counseling and grief therapy: A handbook for the mental health practitioner.* New York: Springer.

CHAPTER **III**

Grief Symptoms

The exhibition of certain types of behaviors, reactions, and feelings is a necessary component of healthy grief, and is a means of coping and giving expression, physically and emotionally, to the pain of grief. Symptom formation not only is an expression of grief, but also allows for the gradual distancing and detachment from the dead person. I generally refer to these reactions as "grief symptoms." These differ from the long-standing family themes that come to play in dealing with grief as discussed in the last chapter in that they are responses that emerge specifically as a result of the death and may not have been a previous mechanism of coping. In fact, since many of these symptoms have not been experienced before they become frightening and secret: "Am I going crazy? I've never felt this before."

VARIABLES AFFECTING GRIEF SYMPTOMS

The process of symptom formation is complicated. The factors and variables are multiple and not easily separated. The pain of grief, however, needs to be expressed or it may be translated into pathological physical or emotional symptoms. Parkes (1972) said, "if it is necessary for the bereaved person to go through the pain of grief in order to get the grief work done, then anything that continually allows the person to avoid or suppress this pain can be expected to prolong the course of mourning" (p. 173).

No one experiences grief in the same manner, nor can one feel the intensity of the pain of another. One can sympathize but not empathize, even if you have been in a similar situation. This is a time in one's life that is only yours, as in one's birth and death.

As stated above, there are many variables that affect grief symptoms: the sex of the person; individual differences; family, cultural, social, economic, and spiritual influences; preparation time for death; the "hole" that was left by the dead person; attachment at the time of death; preventability of the death; and additional life changes. These variables will be further discussed.

Sexual Differences

Through my research (Johnson, 1983; Johnson-Soderberg, 1982), and that of others (Clayton, 1974, 1975a, 1975b; Crisp, 1972; Reese, 1975; Wiener, Gerbee, Battin, & Arkin, 1975), it is seen that women tend to verbalize more symptoms than men. That does not mean that men don't feel or express grief symptoms, but many are socialized not to show their feelings, and certainly not in front of other people, even those closest to them. We need to conduct more research in how men grieve, because there are men who have healthy grief without using generally accepted expression modes. In addition, one needs to consider the individual differences, since not all women cry and not all men are stoic.

Individual Differences

One hypothesis that I have developed regarding the personal differences is based on the work of Myers-Briggs. Their premise is that people are different from each other. Our differences are not good or bad. We must correct the myth that everyone must think, feel, create, behave, and respond in the identical way. "Pygmalion" and "My Fair Lady" are examples of how people (Pickering and Higgins) attempt to change others ("Eliza" Doolittle) to their own concept of what a person should be (a "lady").

Although we have the capacity to change, we basically remain our own person. Therefore, for years we may have been conducting therapy backwards: instead of guiding people to learn conformity to certain behaviors, feelings, and reactions, (like Eliza) perhaps we need to know who the person is *first* and then work with their strengths in changing destructive patterns of response, decision making, and function.

Myers-Briggs says that there are 16 personality types, with a possibility of 32 mixed types (Keirsey & Bates, 1978). There are four pairs of preferences that make up these 32 mixed types: extraversion (E) or introversion (I), sensation (S) or intuition (N), thinking (T) or feeling (F), and perceiving (P) or judging (J) (eg. ESTP, INFJ, etc.). It is not my intent to summarize the entire work of Myers-Briggs.

However, if one uses their concept in the grief situation, it makes it understandable that some people may find comfort in being social (E) while others experience comfort in their own territory and need less socialization at this time (I); some approach grief from a practical standpoint (S), while others are innovative (N); some people "feel" through their grief (F), while others "think" (T); and some just want to "wrap it up" (J) while others process it longer (P). It is the combination of these categories that makes each person's approach to grief unique.

For example, I had been working with a woman whose son had been run over by a school bus. She had multiple grief symptoms and was able to express her feelings. Her husband refused to "get into" therapy during the first year of bereavement. After the first anniversary, he decided to join the sessions because of their marital problems. She was constantly pressuring him about his grief and feelings regarding Tom's death. He could not respond. One of the initial assessments dealt with his lack of expressed feelings about the death. When I changed the question from, "What are you feeling?" to "What are you thinking?" the difference was pronounced. He could understand that question: That was how he was socialized, how he functioned in the business world, and what made him comfortable. I was able to assess his grief using an approach different from "feelings" and he understood himself and his "pain."

In grief therapy, it is helpful to become familiar with the Myers-Briggs test. This has been a very helpful tool in helping couples understand their spouse's, as well as their own grief reactions. It is a good tool especially with those who are not responding in a similar fashion as their spouse, or even the therapist. Table 3-1 is a summary of four pairs of personality preferences.

Contagious Family Effects

As reported in my research, in the guilt section of chapter 2, as one spouse's guilt increased so did the other's. This also appears true for other symptoms of grief. Although I have no hard research data to support the contagious effect within families, I do have clinical data. Families often experience a depression together, although the expression of it may vary. If one is feeling powerless, helpless, or hopeless,

TABLE 3-1. Myers-Briggs Personality Preferences

E (75% of population) versus I (25% of population)	
Sociability	Territoriality
Interaction	Concentration
External	Internal
Breadth	Depth
Extensive	Intensive
Multiplicity of relationships	Limited relationships
Expenditure of energies	Conservation of energies
Interest in external events	Interest in internal reaction

S (75% of population) versus N (25% of population)	
Experience	Hunches
Past	Future
Realistic	Speculative
Perspiration	Inspiration
Actual	Possible
Down-to-earth	Head-in-clouds
Utility	Fantasy
Fact	Fiction
Practicality	Ingenuity
Sensible	Imaginative

T (50% of population) versus F (50% of population)	
Objective	Subjective
Principles	Values
Policy	Social values
Laws	Extenuating circumstances
Criterion	Intimacy
Firmness	Persuasion
Impersonal	Personal
Justice	Humane
Categories	Harmony
Standards	Good or bad
Critique	Appreciate
Analysis	Sympathy
Allocation	Devotion

J (50% of population) versus P (50% of population)	
Settled	Pending
Decided	Gather more data
Fixed	Flexible
Plan ahead	Adapt as you go
Run one's life	Let life happen
Closure	Open options
Decision making	Treasure hunting

TABLE 3-1. *(Continued)*

Planned	Open-ended
Completed	Emergent
Decisive	Tentative
Wrap-it-up	Something will turn up
Urgency	There's plenty of time
Deadline!	What deadline?
Get show on the road	Let's wait and see

Source: From *"Please Understand Me,"* by D. Keirsey and M. Bates, Del Mar, CA, Promethius Nemesis Books. Reprinted with permission.

others in the family often have similar feelings. Every grief symptom is different in expression, but there are many that pervade the family.

Preparation Time

As previously expressed, the preparation time before death can effect symptom formation. People with a short preparation express many more and prolonged grief symptoms. People who have a longer time to anticipate the death and who use that time to prepare for the tasks ahead tend to have a resurgence of and increase in symptoms at the time of death and in the first month. Longitudinally, however, these people tend to make their decision to start living again "sooner."

Cultural, Social, Economic, and Spiritual Influences

There is interplay, often subtle, between these *interrelated* factors. Quiet, but powerful, messages are given by our society and culture that grief should not last "too long." When I ask people who have not grieved or allowed themselves to grieve, how long grief should last, the average suggestion is usually between 48 hours and 2 weeks. I would agree that this is the consensus not only of the lay community, but also of professionals. The family is protected at the time of death and during the funeral time. Others will take care of them, bring in food, stay with them, run errands, and even make decisions for them. These behaviors by significant family members and friends usually continue for about 2 weeks after the death. Then, however, begins the myth that they are "done with", "over the worst" of the grieving and should be "getting on with life." Yet, grieving has only just begun.

Many of the families with whom I have worked say that they are "forgotten" 2 weeks to a month after the death. People avoid them and treat them (and the death) as though they had leprosy. They feel contaminated, alone, and uncared for by family members, friends, and the church. As Geoffrey Gorer (1965) says, "Giving way to grief is stigmatized as morbid, unhealthy, demoralizing. The proper action of a friend and well-wisher is felt to be the distraction of a mourner from his or her grief" (p. 130).

People are expected to return to work within a couple of weeks, if not before. How many people work for a company that will allow significant amounts or frequent grieving time? I spoke to a group of insurance executives several years ago on this very matter. A president of a company called me several weeks later to let me know he had made a policy change: "now 3 days may be taken for the funeral of a family member instead of the previous 1 day." This was a 200% improvement!

Our society has also a myth in its work ethic: that work will make people feel better. Granted, work can be a wonderful and an often-needed escape from grief. One needs time, however, to grieve and that time must be taken. Taking time may be difficult when one is "forced" into the routines of life without that time or space. Financially, people are usually forced back into the workplace. If this is true, I try to help my clients schedule time to do their grieving. They must feel the pain in order to recover.

Many grieving people tend to cut off their pain because of outside pressures. There are a number of ways one can accomplish this: deny any painful feelings, avoid thinking of painful events, idealize the dead person, immediately put away all reminders of the person (e.g., pictures, clothes), move to a new house or city, through alcohol and drug abuse, go on a vacation or cruise, or remarry or have a baby quickly. Then one does not have to deal with their own pain of loss, or even denying that the death occurred. Queen Victoria was a classic example in her denial of her husband Prince Albert's death. She had his shaving water brought to his room every morning and there was always a place set for him at the table.

The Void that is Left

The void that is left by the person's death is an important factor when evaluating symptom formation. The number and duration of symptoms will be different for those whose grandmother died and who only saw her on holidays and birthdays than for those who were the primary caretaker of a child who needed 24-hour care. When that child dies it will leave a huge void in that person's life space.

It is usually those people who are left with a large void who come into treatment. I often have them draw a pie-picture of their daily activities before and after the death. They, as well as myself, can then better understand the impact of the death. A rule of thumb that I use is: the larger the void, the longer and more pronounced the grief symptoms (refer to Figure 2-3, p. 31).

Attachment

In addition to the void remaining in one's life, one must also assess the degree of attachment to the dead person. A large void does not necessarily mean the person was closely attached. For example, I had been treating a woman whose alcoholic husband had died suddenly of a heart attack. She had "hated him" for the years of abuse that she and their daughters had received. She began to realize that she had been detached from him for many years.

It is difficult to measure attachment or detachment in any reliable form. However, people are usually able to express how much they were attached by phrases like: "Oh, I loved her so " or "I am finding it difficult to live without her." The attachments can take forms other than love or admiration. I treated one husband who was extremely attached to his wife, who was dying of cancer. The attachment, however, dealt with "maid" issues: "Well, who is going to cook me dinner, sew on my buttons, clean the house—how could she go and leave me like this?"

If the attachment is strong in terms of bonding or love, the grief will be more pronounced and extended. If not, replacement people or things are usually found (marrying quickly, getting a maid, or moving).

There is also much pain with people who are "forced" into detachment prior to the illness or death and then have much retrospective guilt: "If only my father could have understood why I left home at such a young age. Now that he is dead, he'll never understand." "I wish my parents could have shown me they loved me—now they are both dead and I'm all alone." Through the process of life experience over the years, these people often understand themselves and the previous conflict better. However, the retrospective guilt cannot always be undone and results in deep wounds. It is often helpful in therapy to discuss issues of forgiveness of self and others, have the survivor write a letter to the deceased, or utilize a Gestalt technique of the "empty chair" conversation with the deceased (see Interventions).

Preventability of the Death

The issue of preventability is an extremely powerful one for those who experience it. The retrospective guilt is extremely potent. They constantly say things like: "If only I had gone and checked on the children, then I would have known they were playing with matches. But I thought they were old enough to know better." "If only I had told Janelle she couldn't use the ladder to get that damn tennis ball off the roof." or "If only we had insisted that Grandpa have that angiogram, then maybe he wouldn't have had that stroke so soon after the last one." Retrospective guilt is probably the most common theme connected with preventability, and it also tends to increase other symptoms.

For example, a family that I was treating had a daughter who had fallen off an extension ladder. She and her brother had continually lobbed a tennis ball onto the roof. They thought it was great fun going up on the roof after it. Steve was smaller and younger than Janelle. After the third trip to the roof, the ladder, with Janelle on it started to fall and Steve could not hold it. Her heart was punctured by the extension hooks. The mother felt very potent retrospective unimagined guilt (RUOH), as mentioned above. Steve, however, was feeling retrospective imagined guilt (RIOH). He believed that he should and could have held the ladder.

In our play sessions, Steve continually worked out that scene of Janelle on the roof, the ladder falling, and Janelle lying on the pavement bleeding while he ran for help. The goal of this play was for him to realize that he had done all that he could do to help Janelle. Although we were making progress in our play, it was not until I had his father take the extension ladder out and put it against the garage wall that Steve understood that not even his father could have stopped that ladder. It would have defied the principles of physics. It was very painful for Steve's parents to take that extension ladder out, but the relief that Steve felt in reducing RIOH was tremendous.

The situation was different for Barbara and Roger: "I should have watched them more closely. Even though we insisted that they not take the ladder out—why didn't we go out and check to see if they were obeying." The accident "may have" been prevented; one will never know. However, the torture that families feel in preventable deaths like accidents, suicides, or homicides are very different from other types of death, such as terminal illness, "old age," congenital problems, or other natural causes. Such families must live and hopefully come to peace with the "what ifs."

Multiple Life Changes

In addition to the death, one must also assess what else has happened in this family's life over the last year or so. One needs to assess both the positive and the negative issues because positive issues can often create as much change in life-style as negative ones (e.g., winning the lottery for a million dollars will change life-style, becoming successful may take you away from home more often, a new baby CERTAINLY changes how days are filled . . . and nights!!!!!).

I treated a woman for a very long time who was an excellent example of the problems that multiple life changes can bring. Her history showed that she was married to a physically abusive husband and that she had made two previous suicide attempts. Several years before "the worst year of her life," she divorced the abusive husband and married a supportive man. They wanted to have a child, but she had difficulty becoming pregnant. After many fertility tests, which are stressful in themselves, she became pregnant and was due to give birth in October. Her mother was dying of cancer in a distant state and died in September. The distance and pregnancy created much stress. Sue and Wes were also building a house, virtually by themselves. In October, Sally was born and in late November they moved into their house. Ten days later she received a phone call saying Wes had fallen off a utility pole and was killed.

The multiple life changes, both positive and negative, affected the potency and length of Sue's grieving. In addition to verbal assessment of life changes, I use Holmes and Rahe's Social Readjustment Rating Scale (Holmes & Rahe, 1967; Holmes & Holmes, 1970). This scale shows the relative difficulty of adjusting to 43 different life changes such as death of a spouse, divorce, change in financial status, change in responsibilities at work, and the like. Each of the 43 changes is assigned a point value, which reflects its position on the scale.

Holmes and Rahe found that they could predict the likelihood that a person would become ill based on the number of changes he or she experienced in a 12-month period. For example, if a person has a combination of changes totaling over 300 points in a 12-month period, he or she would have an 80% chance of becoming ill during the next year. A person who has less than 150 points would have a 30% chance of becoming ill.

My research (Johnson-Soderberg, 1982) contradicted Holmes and Rahe's opinion that the death of a spouse was the most stressful life change one could experience. They assigned 100 points to this change, 63 points to the death of another family member, and 37 points to the death of a close friend. The death of a child is never mentioned. In my study, all but one parent freely stated that the death of a spouse would not have been as traumatic as the death of their child had been. A child's death is especially devastating because a child is a physical and emotional extension of the parents—their original creation. The attachments are different.

Although the scale is helpful, it does have some drawbacks. It is written primarily for men, it leaves out many life changes, and it does not specifically take into account the death of a child. I find the scale to be very helpful, however, in assisting the client/family to recognize all that has happened to them during the 12 months following the death of a loved one. The families are then able to put their grief in perspective. Further, other aspects of life-change often emerge from review of the scale because the family is confronted with questions that may not have been approached in verbal therapy.

Many times, for example in a crisis situation, it is not appropriate to utilize a scale. It is important to estimate the changes, positive and negative, that the patient is confronting. For example, I was called to an emergency room because the physician and nurse did not know how to handle a hysterical woman whose son had been missing for 2 days and was later found drowned in the river. It would have been inappropriate to hand this woman a questionnaire. In any case, she was in shock and would have been unable to read it. I was able to discover while talking with her that there were many other negative situations in her recent life. This information assisted in the crisis therapy. All of these factors are important for the therapist and patient/family to consider in order to understand the potency and length of the grief. This information also will help plan treatment goals and interventions.

DESCRIPTION OF GRIEF SYMPTOMS: FEELINGS, PHYSICAL RESPONSES, AND BEHAVIORAL REACTIONS

There is an endless list of grief symptoms. All of these symptoms are "normal," although some occur with more frequency than others. However, if these symptoms continue over "long" periods of time (two or three years) without much significant change, there is reason to believe that the grief may become pathological (see chapter 5).

One of the earliest research attempts to identify grief symptoms was done by Eric Lindemann (1944) after the 1942 Coconut Grove Fire in Boston. This is a classic piece of work. Lindemann discovered a pattern in bereaved people and described characteristics of acute grief. These are as follows:

1. Somatic or bodily distress of some type
2. Preoccupation with the image of the deceased
3. Guilt relating to the deceased or circumstances of the death

4. Hostile reactions
5. The inability to function as one had before the loss
6. The development of traits of the deceased in their own behavior

Others have added to the list of symptoms (Johnson, 1983, 1986; Lindemann, 1944; Westberg, 1961; Worden, 1982).

Worden (1982) uses the terms "clinical" and "statistical" when referring to normal grief. Clinical is defined by the clinician as normal behavior and statistical refers to the frequency of the behavior in the bereaved population. I would agree with Worden's theory that the more frequent the statistical behavior, the more normal it is. I do not believe, however, that all the symptoms have been uncovered as yet, such as guilt movies, and therefore may be clinical but as yet not statistical. I consider any symptom clinical and normal, unless it lasts for several years.

I consider acute grief symptoms to be *normal,* while many clinicians view these as pathological. It is interesting to note that many of these symptoms indicate "craziness" and persons presenting such symptoms could probably be admitted to the psychiatric unit. Extreme symptoms frighten the person, especially when they are bizarre and prolonged. The grieving person often then tries to hide the symptoms because the reactions of others toward their grief confirms that society expects overt symptoms to dissipate within a couple of weeks. We have more tolerance for people who have had an appendectomy or depression.

Because the symptoms are so complicated and numerous, it is helpful for the therapist to categorize them when assessing symptoms. The following categories will be utilized to explore the symptoms of grief: feelings, physical responses, and behavioral reactions. It is essential in treatment to assess and diagnose the symptoms and evaluate how they change over time (see Table 3-2).

Feelings

Shock: Shock seems to be a truly universal feeling with everyone who has suffered a loss through death. There always seems to be a feeling of "I can't believe this is happening." The shock may only last minutes or hours, or may still be in effect many months after the death. In extreme cases, shock may last, to some extent, for over a year. Factors such as short preparation time and preventability of the death seem to lengthen the period of shock. It seems that in many of the families I have treated, the purpose of shock is initially to protect

TABLE 3-2. Common Grief Symptoms

Feelings	Physical responses	Reactions and behaviors
Shock	Vacant or hollow feel-	Depersonalization
Hysterical	ing inside	Time confusion
Tranquil	Backaches	Difficulty concentrating
Anger	Aching arms	Suicidal ideation and/or
Guilt	Anorexia or weight	plans
Sadness	gain	Increased accidents
Powerlessness	Xerostomia	Social withdrawal
Helplessness	Dyspnea	Preoccupation with
Hopelessness	Hyperventilation	dead person
Relief	Sighing	Storytelling
Emancipation	Lump in one's throat	Secret behaviors and/or
Pining	Migraine headaches	thoughts
Anxiety and fear	Sleep disturbances	Hallucinations
Fatigue	Nightmares	Phobias
Loneliness	Crying or total inability	Obsessions
Depression	to cry	Compulsions
Self-hatred	General malaise	Flight behaviors
	Nasal congestion	Alcohol abuse
	Scratchy eyes	Drug abuse
	Food does not taste	Affairs
	right, if at all	Running away
	Uncontrollable shaking	
	Overactivity	
	Oversensitivity to stim-	
	uli	
	Muscle weakness	
	Weight pulling from	
	back of neck, down	
	arms and shoulders	
	Lack of strength	
	Multiple somatic symp-	
	toms	

Source: Adapted from "Guiding adults through bereavement" by S. Johnson, 1983, *Nursing Life,* January/February, 34–39. Adapted with permission.

the survivor so that they may "slowly" process the reality that the person will never be here again.

I was treating a mother, father, and son for acute grief. Their daughter had just graduated from nursing school and they were of course, very proud of her. In the middle of the night there was an explosion and the entire house caught fire. The smoke was so thick, no one could see. Jan, the mother, went ahead through the kitchen at the request of her husband, John. She was to unlock the three bolts and run for help. John came behind with their children, Kristen, 20, and Ryan, 14. The smoke became so blinding they lost each other. John and Ryan got out. They thought Kristen was behind them, since they had kept in voice contact. Kristen must have turned around and gone back to her room for something; the firefighters found her under her bedspread. The shock of losing their daughter, their house, and all their possessions was tremendous. The shock lasted several months for Jan.

The shock was so prolonged that, in my clinical judgment, it needed to begin breaking down so she could continue grieving. This was accomplished by taking her on a tour of the ruined house. She expressed much existential guilt, although she said she was not "feeling" the guilt as yet. The shock can numb the person so that they may be able to verbalize a feeling, but not actually feel it. The reality began to sink in—that it was a wonder that any of them got out of the house alive.

Once the shock state is broken, the person can proceed with grieving. I never break the shock, however, unless it is very prolonged. Shock is a needed defense in processing the loss; some need it longer than others. The length of shock usually depends upon the preparation time before the death and the sex of the survivor (women tend to remain in shock longer than men; men are often "forced" into decision-making roles such as identification of the body, making arrangements for the funeral, insurance calls, etc.) We often protect women from those "ugly" things, and yet, are we really helping their grief? (see Chapter 6, Use of Pictures). Additional factors include the preventability of the death and age of the dead person (a child's death causes longer periods of shock; this also applies to loss of adult children).

Based upon my research and practice there tend to be two forms of shock: tranquil or hysterical (see Figure 3-1). *Tranquil shock* is a process where the person is aware of what is happening around him, but he is not a part of it. He describes himself as detached, both from his body and the environment. He often is not able to speak, experiencing a "calming" or "numbing" effect internally and have a slowing of body functions (e.g., bowel, bladder, appetite, etc). This was the response of a young man who was accused of murdering his family. He did not urinate for 1 day or have a bowel movement for 3 days. He described himself as living in a "fog." Interestingly enough, he was arrested because he was not exhibiting an "appropriate grief

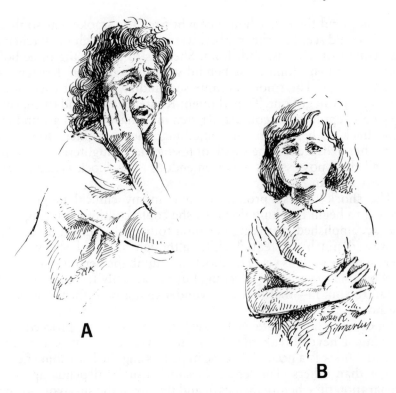

FIGURE 3-1. Shock.   **A:** Hysterical shock. **B:** Tranquil shock.

response." Yet, his response was very similar to his response to other crises in his life.

Hysterical shock is more in line with that anticipated with a tragic loss: people may wail, cry, yell, scream, feel nauseated, or pound their fists. Although anticipated, we are very uncomfortable with this behavior. If such behavior is exhibited in the emergency room the staff, and often family members, are usually so uncomfortable that they use minor or even major tranquilizers to "calm them down."

People who are in shock, especially hysterical shock, need to be observed for their own protection. They may try to hurt themselves or even make a suicide attempt. I was called in on an emergency case where a couple's only child had died of SIDS. The mother who was in hysterical shock, went into the bathroom and slit her wrists.

Anger: Survivors show anger, like guilt, in many forms. People often just get angry, for no apparent reason. The anger may not be directed toward anyone in particular, "just whoever is around at the moment." They may get angry over an insignificant incident, like dropping a stack of papers. This tends to be displacement of anger. The underlying issue of the displacement is that one is angry that someone died.

Some, who are usually angry in life anyway, direct their anger toward a scapegoat. A father, Tim, whose daughter died in a car accident involving a drunk driver, went to the state attorney's office yelling and screaming because he felt that justice was not done in the trial of the driver of the car. He wanted to shoot the attorney. With scapegoating, violent acts can occur because the person loses control of his or her anger.

Others often turn the anger toward themselves. This usually causes depression and carries potential risk of pathological bereavement symptoms and may also cause active or passive suicide attempts: "life is not worth living without my love."

Anger is normal and healthy. It must, however, be expressed appropriately. Appropriate anger is recognizing that one is feeling angry and expressing it without harm to self or others. Anger can be talked out, and it can also be released through physical activities like running, swimming, walking, or hitting a punching bag. One does not need to be afraid of anger; it is important to find the best way to express and deal with the anger. One also needs to assess whether the anger is truly anger or whether it is a covering feeling for something else. Tim, as previously mentioned, was extremely and inappropriately angry. Granted, he was angry about his daughter's death, but he was using his anger to cover his feelings of helplessness, powerlessness, and sadness. Those feelings had never been acceptable to him, and he did not know how to express them. In therapy, we worked on several issues: to understand and identify all of his feelings, to avoid using anger to cover other feelings, to understand all of his feelings, and to express his anger in an appropriate manner. When he felt violent he was to exercise or hit a punching bag. Eventually Tim could talk out his anger without hurting himself or others.

People often express guilt to me for feeling angry with their spouse, children, and especially, God. I tell them it is okay to be angry, but that they must recognize the reason for their feelings. If anyone can take it, God can! I explore with them texts in the Bible that mention God and Jesus' anger, such as Mark 11:15–19 and 3:5; Luke 19:45–48; Eph. 4:26–27; and Psa. 6:1 and 30:5. Anger is a God-given feeling, just like love. One problem in our culture is that we are frightened by anger because we see the destructive results, such as crime, war, rape, and the like. We need to educate people in ways to express their anger so that it will not be damaging.

It is also important to determine if the client has a tendency to inflict pain or harm on himself (cutting a finger, burning hands in the fireplace, falling down). Continually breaking or loosing articles are also symptoms. People need to become aware of the reasons for their anger when these incidences occur. It is helpful to ask why they are afraid to express anger or dispel it appropriately. The more a person is aware and understands what is happening inside himself, the more choice he has in eliminating the anger.

Guilt: What else can be said?

Sadness: Sadness is expressed in many ways. People often cry, but again only if crying has been a coping mechanism in the past. People can appear sad without crying: the affect is flat, eyelids usually lowered, lips together, shoulders rounded, little eye contact with others, and when sitting, the legs are usually crossed.

The sadness is also expressed internally. My patients will explain that the sadness at first covers the entire body: "my whole body aches." After several weeks, or months, it usually centers somewhere in the abdomen or upper chest, often around the heart or mid-line: "I have an aching in my stomach." "My gut just hurts." "It's like a knife in the back" (see Figure 3-2).

The drawing in Figure 3-2 was done by a woman whose husband died of Hodgkin's disease. Her grief pain was like she had been "stabbed in the back." She is a minister and faith issues were abundant. "How could God take my young and talented husband?" The drawing from the left hand shows more pain, depression and depth than the right hand. The right-hand drawing shows the knife as being external (Omar's death); the left hand shows the knife as internal— or the torturing pain of grief. The left hand also exhibits more depression by the darkness.

I have found that the lower the pain is in the body, the more difficult it is to work out (see Figure 3-3). I have had people tell me their grief pain was very deep, (e.g., "in my toes"). Usually when the person does "good" grief work this pain will move upwards toward the throat, change in intensity, and eventually leave. It is fascinating to watch this release. It is often a gradual process, but may come spontaneously when some unfinished work is done.

Mary, the woman who had the twin die at 9 days old, had placed much of her sadness in her throat: "It's always there. I feel like I have a knife stuck in my throat. I'm always swallowing, trying to get it down." (Symbolically, she wants to keep the grief-sadness by push-

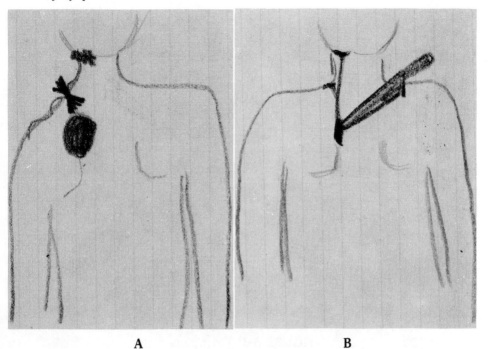

A   B

FIGURE 3-2. Drawing of grief pain.   A: Left-hand representation.
B: Right-hand representation. (Used with permission.)

ing it back down into her stomach, rather than "vomiting" it out.)
She returned to therapy three years after the death.

In assessing the grief she really could not let go of the sadness, as
was externally exhibited by her shrine-producing behavior. She had a
trunk, which she had moved to the end of her bed. It contained all of
Ruth's clothes, toys, and blankets. She would secretly go through
them every night and say goodnight to her picture. If anyone came
upon her she would get extremely angry and force them out of the
room. I had her bring some of the most potent clothing to the office,
which was extremely difficult for her. She was never able to say
good-bye to Ruth, and this was the critical point of the unfinished
business. I suggested she dress one of the infant dolls that I have in
the office and say good-bye, but she could not do this. However, the
clothing was potent enough for her to use it to say good-bye (See
Chapter 6 section on good-byes). Her shrining was coming out of
secretness; when the vicarious good-byes were said, the knife in her
throat "came up."

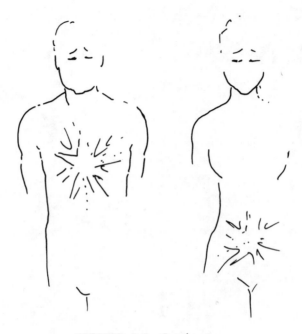

FIGURE 3-3. Grief pain.

I treated a 58-year old man who had multiple losses as a child. He was an Adult Child of an Alcoholic (ACOA) which had a tremendous impact on him. In addition, he and his wife had three children who died and were left childless for 28 years. Two years ago while driving to Cape Cod to pick peaches, Norm and his wife were in a car accident near the Cape Cod canal. The accident was not their fault. His wife was seriously injured but he came through without injury. He became very depressed with much existential guilt: "I didn't do anything, but I feel so guilty for all her injuries. She was unconscious and I needed to sit and watch her until they could get her out of the car. I felt so helpless! Now, she's left with all these terrible effects of the accident."

We dealt with his multiple losses, which he had always pushed "inside" prior to this. In dealing with his sadness, I asked him if he could draw it. From his right hand he drew a black container image (Figure 3-4A), which had streaks of "sadness." From his left hand the image was larger and less controlled (Figure 3-4B). He cried as he looked at his sadness drawing: "there is reality to my sadness." To me there was something symbolic about the pictures. As I turned it sideways I realized it was a picture of the Commonwealth of Massa-

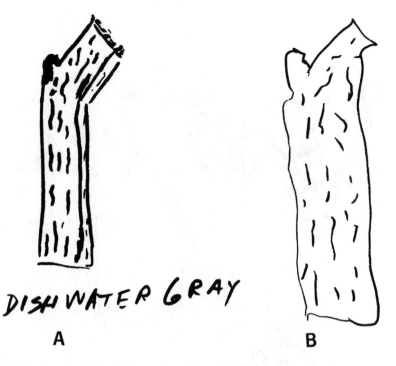

DISH WATER GRAY

A   B

FIGURE 3-4. Pictorial of Norm's grief. **A:** Right-hand representation. **B:** Left-hand representation. (Used with permission.)

chusetts without the Cape! The picture became more of a reality of what he was attempting to avoid: his sadness and depression regarding the accident at the Cape.

He got the "flu" that night and vomited. "I felt such relief—like vomiting up that sadness. It's gone." Allowing his sadness to become a reality and "getting it out" was a turning point in his grief work.

Children are fascinating to watch as they work out their sadness. It usually comes out of some orifice: the nose, mouth, ears, or some may even defecate it (see Figure 3-5). Figure 3-4 reflects children's drawings illustrating this concept. People who are doing difficult and painful grief regarding their sadness may even vomit.

I often use coroner pictures when the patient was unable or "forbidden" to see the body (see Chapter 6, Use of Pictures). Often the pictures are *awful* and difficult to look at. While confronting the reality and sadness people will often feel nauseated or actually "vomit" the sadness. However, relief is usually felt and the knot

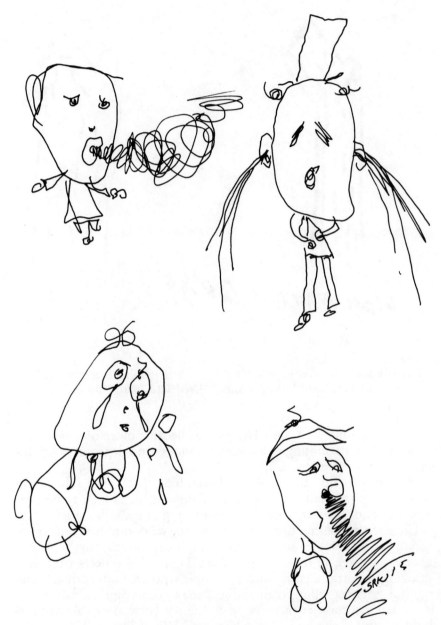

FIGURE 3-5. Child's drawings showing exit of grief pain.

of sadness has either moved to a level closer to an orifice or is gone.

Powerlessness and Helplessness. These are vulnerable feelings for the survivors. It makes them feel that there is nothing else that can be done. People describe powerlessness or helplessness as a sinking feeling. Often people will delay decisions or actions that will only increase their feelings of powerlessness. (e.g., "It took us almost a year to order the gravestone. We felt once that was done there would be nothing else to do and that made us feel more powerless.")

Another type of powerlessness or helplessness comes when the survivors feel they cannot cope or "go on" without their spouse or loved one: "My husband always did the banking. I have never even deposited a check; I don't know how to do it. I feel so helpless." This type of helplessness and powerlessness deals with everyday living situations, and also indicates a dependency on the person who died. "I couldn't stay by myself after my husband was killed. My parents had to stay with me for almost 3 months."

Through therapy people can learn that it is acceptable for people *to gain power* wherever possible. The couple whose 15-year-old was killed by a drunk driver collected money for a scholarship fund in memory of the child. They also planned and had made for their church a tapestry which said, "Love one another." This gave them a feeling of having some power and direction in their lives. Although tasks like this are not a "cure-all," they do bring about some positive and productive feelings.

Hopelessness. When there is no hope left in life, or death, it is a very lonely time. There is nothing left. One needs hope: "I hope I get better." "I hope the pain isn't too bad." "I hope my family is okay after I am dead." Even though the hopes may change, there is still hope for something. When there is no more hope one usually finds an extremely depressed person. Barbara, the woman whose daughter fell off the extension ladder, had no hope; there was no reason for her to live. After several months she started to experience some hope when she found that she did not shake as long and as hard every morning when she awakened. Her hope, although minimal, became, "maybe I am healing."

Although the hope may be minimal, it is important to have something for which to hope. As hopes grow in the bereavement process, I find the person gets closer to the time when they start to think and talk about a decision to go on living. The hopes start small because they need to relearn that it is all right to trust the future and themselves. This is an extremely difficult process because one often has no reason to trust the present or the future.

A woman I was treating had lost her husband, two daughters and her parents all in a 5-year period. She had very little hope or trust: "If I get attached to people, they will probably just go away and leave me, like the rest of them did." With all of her experience she had learned not to find hope or she would be disappointed. It was very traumatic for her, and for myself, when I had to move. That was one more loss that reinforced the hopelessness.

Relief. Families often feel relief at the time of death, especially after a long terminal illness. The relief is often followed by guilt: "I shouldn't feel relief that my husband died. Now I feel guilty for feeling that." For several years, I was treating a woman who was taking care of her invalid husband. One Sunday afternoon she had taken him for a ride in the country. He had a cardiac arrest and she was certain that he was dead. She ran from the car for help. As she was running she could feel her arms stretching out into the air and she felt a strong sense of release and freedom. She immediately put her arms down, stopped running, and felt guilty for feeling relief.

Emancipation. Along with relief often comes emancipation. This is especially true when the survivor has lived under some sort of harmful or restrictive environment. A young woman who has multiple sclerosis had much difficulty accepting this diagnosis. She had not had strong mental health since childhood. Her father was an alcoholic and had been violent in the past. When her father died suddenly of a heart attack she felt sad, but also relief that she was finally free from his wrath. Like relief, emancipation often produces guilt. Finally she could accept that these were normal feelings and admit that life had been difficult with her father. People who feel emancipated, however, often tend to idealize the dead person to compensate for "feeling so happy he is dead."

Pining. Pining is one of those onomatopoeic words that so beautifully describes the feeling that it represents. It is the yearning to be with the dead person once again. In pining one will search for the lost person, will hear his voice or his presence, or will unconsciously set a place for him at the table. Barbara said, "I go to Steve's school to get him and I search the hallways for Jannelle. When will she come?

How I yearn to see her coming down the hall. She should be there . . . but never comes. That makes my yearning all the more."

The pining behavior should diminish if the grief work is being done, but one often finds that at certain anniversaries, rights of passage, or on special occasions the pining returns. Even when grief is complete this feeling still occasionally recurs.

Anxiety and Fear.   Experiencing a feeling of anxiety is almost universal. It is a defensive reaction to a threatening situation. The symptoms of anxiety are also symptoms of fear: "fight–flight" reactions, worry, panicky feelings, and fright. C. S. Lewis (1961) experienced this anxiety after his wife died. He wrote, "No one ever told me that grief felt so like fear. I am not afraid, but the sensation is like being afraid. The same fluttering in the stomach, the same restlessness, the yawning. I keep on swallowing." (The swallowing may have been his attempt to push grief "down.")

Survivors also experience symptoms of anxiety like restlessness, difficulty in concentrating, disorganized thoughts, and difficulty sleeping. Physically they may experience diarrhea, vomiting, tachycardia, frequent urination, and sweaty palms and feet. During the death or in survivor bereavement, vague symptoms of anxiety may be experienced or may progress from hypochrondrical complaints (e.g., ulcers, colitis, hypertension, asthma, panic attacks, and obesity), to a full-blown phobia or obsessive-compulsive neurosis.

Anxiety is a normal feeling when confronting a death situation, but the patient must be helped to decrease and control the anxiety so it will not become debilitating. I recommend the following to the families I treat:

- Keep life as consistent as possible; do not make any changes—don't even go home a new way. Do not add extra anxieties and stresses when you are feeling so much already.
- Do not think about too many things at once.
- Do not force yourself to do something, like read, when you cannot concentrate; it will only frustrate you more.
- Do not overplan your days. Allow yourself resting time.
- Recognize when you are feeling signs of anxiety and take steps to alleviate them (relaxation techniques, listening to comforting music, taking a walk, etc.).
- Learn how you are really feeling: is it anxiety or is it anger, sadness, guilt, etc., taking the form of anxiety.

Fatigue. My patients often remark how tired they are all the time: "I can never get enough sleep." Grief takes a great deal of energy and people need to give themselves quiet and resting times. If they are not able to sleep, that increases the fatigue. Unless a patient is totally sleep-deprived, however, I do not recommend hypnotics, sedatives, or minor tranquilizers, which tend to repress grief symptoms, especially dreams. In my treatment of people I utilize their dreams and evaluate how they change over time as the grief work is being accomplished (see Chapter 6). It is normal to have sleep interrupted. During the first several months of bereavement I strongly recommend that resting times are scheduled especially if the patient has poor sleep patterns at night.

Loneliness. When someone dies there are strong feelings of loneliness. In addition to feeling the loneliness, the survivors feel alone; something/someone is missing. It is very difficult to be alone and not lonely. It also takes a very long time to arrive at the position of wanting to reinvest in another relationship. People feel they are in a catch-22 position: they are so lonely without the deceased person but if they attach to someone else they, too, may go away and leave them. If grief work is accomplished, they usually decide that reinvestment is worth the chance. Often loneliness becomes an important driving force for healing.

Depression. Depression is a very complicated process in grief because it could be a normal reaction or could become (or is) pathological. It is often difficult to diagnose. All these types of depression can manifest similar symptoms: sleep disturbance, weight gain or loss, sadness, withdrawal, guilt, loss of self-esteem, nightmares, feelings of inadequacy, lack of concentration, pessimistic attitude, suicidal thoughts and plans, lack of energy, anxiety, hypochondriacal complaints, and psychomotor retardation.

Although grief-related depression may be classified as a dysthymic disorder it may be accompanied by psychotic symptoms, like hallucinations and delusions. It also may resemble schizophrenia because affect may be superficial, inappropriate, and/or unconvincing. There may be "twilight states" with religious ecstasies, violent anger, or stupors. In addition, the grief depression may appear to be situational, where the person feels better when he is away from a stress-producing environment. For example, many people feel much better when they go to work, but as soon as they return home they feel depressed.

There is a fine line between a "clinical depression" and a grief depression. Grief depression may represent qualities of a variety of depressions. Although differentiation may be difficult early on, it is important to assess any changes in symptoms after the first several months. If the symptoms have increased significantly, a clinical depression is probably present. This is especially true for symptoms involving sleeping and eating patterns, guilt, self-esteem, and social withdrawal. Even though the grieved person may still be experiencing these symptoms, they should be decreasing or fluctuating. The changes may be ever so slight so that the person is not aware of the change, but a perceptive clinician should be able to note them.

The *Diagnostic and Statistical Manual, Third Edition* (1983) *(DSM-III)*, published by the American Psychiatric Association, suggests assessment of the following behaviors to determine a clinical depression:

> . . . A full depressive syndrome frequently is a normal reaction to such a loss, with feelings of depression and such associated symptoms as poor appetite, weight loss, and insomnia. However, morbid preoccupation with worthlessness, prolonged and marked functional impairment, and marked psychomotor retardation are uncommon and suggest that the bereavement is complicated by the development of a Major Depression.
>
> In Uncomplicated Bereavement, guilt, if present, is chiefly about things done or not done at the time of the death by the survivor; thoughts of death are usually limited to the individual's thinking that he or she would have died with the person who died. The individual with Uncomplicated Bereavement generally regards the feeling of depressed mood as "normal," although he or she may seek professional help for relief of such associated symptoms as insomnia and anorexia (p. 333).

The diagnosis of clinical verses grief depression is much more complicated than implied in the *DSM-III*. At the time of death and bereavement, often previously repressed or unfinished business arises, which is another variable to consider when diagnosing a major depression. This was noted when working with the heart transplant patients at a large university. The men exhibited a major depression and could not confront their heart transplant or possible impending death. As we went back into their history we discovered that all of them had fathers who had died of heart attacks. Much unresolved grief was involved. It was not until each man came to some peace about his father's death that they could confront their own crisis. This has become a rule of thumb for me: *always explore a patient's history for major losses and its effect on the present situation.*

Past losses can affect the diagnosis of a grief depression versus a major depression. If possible, it is helpful to deal with the past loss early in therapy. The patient may appear to have a major depression relating to the present crisis, when in reality it is based upon the past loss. For example, a 32-year-old woman, Agatha, had been admitted to the psychiatric hospital with a major depression after her husband told her that he wanted a divorce. He felt she was "overreacting." It was not until I could uncover the secrets that tortured her (i.e., her father had sexually abused her from age 8 to 15; she had seen him beat her mother; finally, she was the one to find him after he had shot himself) that she could deal with all that unfinished business and pain. A major depression is often the smoke screen concealing previous crises.

Self-hatred.   Self-hatred also may appear either because the survivor is feeling depressed, has unresolved issues, or feels inadequate because of losing old roles and having to develop new roles. It is normal to feel this way. However, it is important that the self-hatred not be internalized, which can lead to depression or suicidal intentions. It is also helpful for the patient to be able to verbalize the self-hatred so it may be processed through reality testing, appropriate expressions, and developing appropriate role-changes.

Physical Responses to Grief

There are multiple biological and physical manifestations of grief:

Feeling Vacant or Hollow Inside.   This is often experienced in the stomach or abdomen areas.

Backaches.

Aching Arms.   This is especially true for parents who have had a child die. They will describe that their arms actually ache to hold their child one more time.

Anorexia or Weight Gain.   People traditionally respond as they have in previous crises: "I always lose weight when I'm under stress" or "I eat a lot when I'm anxious." Over the last 7 years, however, I have seen more weight gain than loss, even with those who have lost weight in the past. People often find that food is the only comfort or pleasure remaining to them and symbolically they may try to "fill up that empty space inside."

Xerostomia. Sugarless gum or candy is helpful to have in one's mouth. There is also a wonderful product called Moi-stir®, which is a mouth spray or synthetic saliva that is very effective for xerostomia from grief, strokes, or medications like major tranquilizers.

Dyspnea, Sighing or Hyperventilation. Often the person has a difficult time breathing, which may be very frightening. Many say they find that they seem to "forget to breathe." Symbolically it may be a means of questioning their own living.

Lump in the Throat. Many complain of a "lump in the throat." This lump often comes when tears are being held back. In addition, the lump may be continuous and become a place to put their sadness, which is perceived by the person as "something is there" (in the throat). Symbolically, these people often try to "swallow" and "keep" their grief pain, rather than "letting it out." If this behavior is occurring, it may take longer for whatever reason(s) to work through the grief.

Migraine Headaches. People complain about headaches when, often, headaches have not been a problem in the past. They seem to be caused from sinus pressure from crying and the stress of readjustment to living without the dead person. Teaching relaxation techniques is very helpful to my clients.

Sleep Disturbances. Total insomnia or early morning awakening is typical. I encourage my clients to get up and do something such as washing the floors, watering the garden, walking, or talking. They report feeling better by getting physical exercise rather than lying there thinking.

Nightmares. Often these are very frightening and the patient may then choose not to go to sleep because he is more frightened about the nightmares than staying awake. Again he is caught in a catch-22 position. I use the dreams in therapy and encourage patients to keep a pad of paper and a pencil by the bed so they can write down the dream immediately. Dreams are really our friends and give symbolic expression to the reality of grief. If the person becomes extremely sleep-deprived, however, sedatives may be needed (see Chapter 6).

Crying or No Tears. This depends on what tears have meant to the person in the past. People who have used crying in the past as an expression of sadness will usually continue to do so after a death. Many people, especially men, have been taught not to cry: "It's a sign of weakness." Therefore, tears may not occur even when permission is given. When tears do not occur there can be a problem in a relationship because people who cry often believe the noncryer is not grieving, which is not necessarily the case. It is important, however, that the sadness be expressed somehow if not through tears.

General Malaise. "I just don't feel good. There isn't anything specific, but I just feel lousy." A sense of well-being is often lost.

Nasal Congestion. I often hear complaints of nasal congestion, which is usually due to an increase in crying.

Scratchy Eyes. This symptom also seems to occur as a result of crying. Often wet or cold packs placed on the eyelids are comforting.

Food Doesn't Taste as Good as it Used to, if at All. With a grief depression, the person may also display signs of vegetative symptoms of weight and sleep loss or gain. People complain frequently that food does not taste right, if at all. Food may develop negative responses resulting in increased weight loss.

Uncontrollable Shaking. This symptom is often seen at very difficult times of the day, like early morning or dinnertime. The clients describe it as almost like a seizure and they cannot stop. It is usually accompanied by feeling very cold. It may last minutes or even several hours.

Overactivity. People often explain that they feel so "jumpy" and restless that they cannot sit still. They may find themselves walking or running for extended periods or driving aimlessly for hours. This seems to be related to high anxiety levels.

Oversensitivity or Undersensitivity to Stimuli. Senses may be deadened or stimulated because of grief. These symptoms seem related to the type of shock the person is experiencing: I see oversensitivity more with hysterical shock and undersensitivity with tranquil shock. Responses to lights or noise may be exaggerated or depressed. This is often very annoying to the person.

Muscle Weakness and Lack of Strength. This may be located in a previously weak area (e.g., back, knees) or throughout the body.

Weight that Pulls from the Back of the Neck, Down the Arms, and Shoulders. People express that this is very painful and heavy. It is unlike any headache or other sensation that they have ever felt. It is a feeling similar to being in traction, although most people have never experienced traction.

Lack of Strength. Many people complain of a physical weakness that may or may not be localized to a part of the body. Norm had had multiple losses from childhood, and had 3 children die in adulthood. A serious car accident that involved himself and his wife brought him into treatment. Norm was a strong and muscular man, but in his grief he lost "all my strength" in his chest and arms. His chest was also the place where he had put his sadness. As he began to heal it became evident to him that he regained physical strength and power in his chest and arms. I often see the loss of strength associated with powerlessness, resignation, and lack of hope.

Multiple Somatic Symptoms. Numerous, and often unrelated physical symptoms may be expressed, for example, "stomachaches," skin rashes, or twitches, in addition to the physical grief symptoms I have explained. These multiple symptoms often occur when the grief is not being expressed appropriately. Grief needs expression, and if not allowed direct expression it will find other indirect ways to be expressed. Granted there are many physical and emotional symptoms that the survivor is feeling and should be experiencing as they detach from their loved one. However, usually people do not enjoy pain and want to alleviate it as soon as possible. It is at this point when an appointment is made with their physician and medication is usually prescribed. However, it is the pain and symptoms that have to be felt and then let go of in order to work through one's grief. Medication will usually cover the symptoms and eventually the symptom will be expressed in another form.

For example, an elderly woman, Betty, was seen frequently by her physician after the death of her husband for a number of symptoms: First, it was her stomach, which was hurting; then palpitations; and finally, a rash on her chest. During each encounter the physician prescribed medication, without diagnosing the "real problem": her grief pain was being expressed and in the same area. Finally, he suggested that she see me. Appropriate healing could then be initiated.

For years I have been trying to explain grief to physicians and nurses. Often these professionals will treat the symptom and not the cause. Their treatment of "choice" too often is drugs, but this only deepens the symptoms, and the patient will return shortly with other hypochondriacal complaints. The patient is asking for help but often does not know how to ask for it other than by physical expression of symptoms.

One wonderful pediatrician finally heard what I was saying about treating the cause instead of the symptoms. An 8-year-old boy and his mother had come to her with his multiple physical complaints. The mother desperately wanted some medication for him, but the pediatrician said, "You need to start at the beginning," meaning with the trauma resulting from his father's suicide 4 years earlier.

The somatic symptoms are normal, and even healthy, as long as the person can recognize that they are part of the grief. When the symptoms are used to "cover" for the pain, it is a reason for concern. The somatic symptoms are then converted into physical and emotional symptoms as a symbolic expression of the grief pain (e.g., holding feelings inside, vomiting symbolizing revulsion and disgust, arthritis—becoming immobile and helpless, or anesthesia—so as not to feel pain).

Behavioral Reactions to Grief

Depersonalization/Time Confusion.   Nothing seems real to the survivors. They feel as though they are in a fog. Many people say that it is like being "jet lagged." Although the body is here, it feels as though it has been left behind somewhere.

Difficulty Concentrating.   People find it very difficult to concentrate for any length of time. Most are unable to read, remember what has just happened, put events in sequence, or even know where they have been. This is due to an increase in anxiety level, which impedes concentration. In addition, patients often lose their ability to function in their usual family environment. Many of my clients tell me that they don't remember where they've been driving, which frightens them a great deal. It is similar to an alcoholic black out, without the alcohol.

Suicidal Ideation.   Often people feel extremely suicidal after a traumatic death. It may only be a verbalization: "I don't want to live anymore," or an active attempt. This is a normal reaction to a loss, that life may not be worth living at that time. One should always consider any suicidal thought or plan as serious and explore and watch for suicidal symptoms: a specific plan, withdrawal, loss of interest, sleep and eating pattern change, and less interaction with people (see Chapter 6). It is difficult to assess how suicidal a person is because the symptoms of normal grief are so similar. However, the one difference is the existence of a plan. This may be verbalized or kept a secret so they will not be stopped.

Many, especially with strict religious backgrounds, think that suicide is a "sin." Because of their beliefs, they may not actively develop a plan, but may attempt suicide in passive ways: getting into an accident, falling down the stairs, "forgetting" their hypertensive drugs, or in diabetics, for example, may increase their insulin and induce an insulin reaction.

Although suicidal thoughts are normal, it becomes dangerous if they are instituted. It takes qualified assessments to determine whether the patient needs to be hospitalized for his or her own protection. The woman who had multiple losses and changes in 3 months felt very suicidal after her husband was killed. She verbalized it and without much assessment, a nurse sent the sheriff to her house to bring her to the psychiatric unit on Christmas Eve. She was forced to leave her 6-week-old baby and was admitted to the hospital. She could not convince anyone that she was not going to kill herself, but only "felt like dying." Having to leave her baby was indeed another loss for her, which complicated her grief. In cases where the death and losses are complicated and multiple, it is often more advisable to first try some alternatives: have someone with the person at all times, even when going to the bathroom; allow the person to express his/her feelings to others; or "make" the person get into therapy. This gives the therapist time to assess the problems. One may not have the luxury of time and may need to make the best clinical decision with the information at hand. Hospitalization should be the last resort since it can be more traumatic and represent yet another loss for the person. It also can delay grief, because the person is out of his surroundings, which makes the death more unreal.

In making a decision not to admit, one must also evaluate the family support: will the family watch the suicidal person or might there be sabotaging in behaviors that may unconsciously encourage the suicidal person to act out his or her thought or plan? For example, "forgetting" to put away razor blades, guns, or medication. I had a young woman patient who I felt was suicidal after her infant son died of SIDS. The family appeared to be supportive and caring; her mother and husband were willing to watch her and said they would remove all harmful instruments. Her husband fell asleep, however, and she was able to get to the bathroom where she slit her wrists.

If the suicidal thoughts or plans continue "long" after the death, there is reason to be concerned about the impact of complicated grief. Many times an actual suicide attempt can be a turning point in grief and be responsible for the initiation of some good decisions to get on with life (e.g., the woman who came home drunk after a party and decided to kill herself, then asked herself what she was doing, and made a decision to initiate treatment).

If a suicide attempt is not a turning point, one is probably dealing with a very depressed, passive-aggressive personality, "You can't make me want to live." This was the case of Jane. She didn't want to live without her unfaithful husband and couldn't live without her son, Greg, who had died the year before. She always had a suicide plan. Her behavior was so extremely passive-aggressive that she could not recognize her husband's collusive behavior of not taking all dangerous medication out of the house. Because of her resistance her support network deserted her: "There is nothing we can do anymore, if she doesn't want to try." This made her feel lonely and increased the depression and passive-aggressive behavior.

Increased Accidents. Although this may indicate passive suicide elements it also can be a way in which people punish themselves for surviving (survivor guilt): "Why am I alive and my daughter is dead?" They feel they have no right to be alive and often, unconsciously, search for ways to hurt themselves. In addition, accidents can occur because a person is not concentrating well and, therefore, not paying attention to environmental hazards.

The clinician needs to assess the seriousness of these behaviors. I would handle the information very differently if the person just "happened" to cut their finger with a knife because they were not paying attention to what they were doing versus someone who had repeatedly voiced the wish to die, but could not actively commit suicide. One woman told me that she would never think of suicide, because if she did she believed she would never go to heaven and see her family. Nevertheless, she was continually placing herself in situations that caused pain to herself; walking out in the middle of the street and being hit by a car, falling down stairs, bumping herself, and "accidentally" cutting her fingers as she prepared food.

Social Withdrawal. This is a "chicken or the egg" reaction: do people tend to become introverted and homebound because of the "hindering" or nonsupportive people in the world or is it just more comfortable for them to be alone in grief? It is probably a combination of both.

I encourage my patients not to place themselves in situations where they feel unsafe; do not enjoy the company of certain people, being in large crowds, or where they do not know many people. Such situations are too anxiety producing. Anxiety should be decreased, not increased.

It is all too easy, however, to be a hermit: "There is no reason to go out." I try to help my patients to recognize the fine line between having successful interactions and gaining confidence in life and having to protect themselves against hindering people.

I really understood this process only when my father-in-law died. My husband and I were very sad, and there had been a whirlwind of decisions and traveling to take the body to a distant state for burial. We sang in a classical choir at that time, which had always been a safe, comforting, and fun place for us. We had just returned from the burial and wanted to sing for our own benefit. It would have been safer to have stayed home, as not one person acknowledged our presence, Papa's death, or our grief.

Preoccupation with the Dead Person. Survivors spend a great deal of time thinking about the person who died. The thoughts often become compulsive in nature. The thoughts tend to idealize the person: "He was really the best husband in the world." "If anyone was perfect, she was." In addition, many thoughts deal with recapturing the dead person: "Maybe if I become more religious, God will let me see him one more time." "I think I'll go to a séance." "I carried around his watch and ring so I could be closer to him."

As the months go on, it is appropriate and healthy to move from the preoccupation and acknowledge the "bad points." Often these acknowledgements, secret or verbal, make people feel guilty, but it is important to realize that none of us are perfect; we all have our good points and our bad.

Story Telling. Along with preoccupation often comes the verbalization of a story of the history of the events leading to the death. (See Chapter 6, on Interventions, Storytelling.) Storytelling is a very interesting phenomenon. It tends to be a repetition of what happened from the time they found out that something was seriously wrong through the funeral behaviors. In my research and practice I find that the stories are most often told by women, and the shorter the preparation time for death, the longer the story tends to be (Johnson-Soderberg, 1982). The function of the story tends to be twofold: it is a way of structuring events and trying to make sense out of what happened, and the verbalization of the story, which is told over and over to whomever will listen, is a means of sharing and releasing the grief and pain. However, because many are uncomfortable with death and need a conspiracy of silence, people often stop the story or choose not to listen to it. The more the person can share his story about loss, the more realistic it becomes to them.

Over the years, I have come to appreciate this aspect of grief as a very potent issue. In developing the story it tells me that the patients are willing to confront the reality of the loss; they aren't denying what happened but rather are meeting it head-on. When one knows all that happened, why, and when, they are able to come to peace with their grief. It is those that refuse to share their story or have missing details that tend to develop complicated grief. In addition, it may be very bothersome not to have information, but there may not be sufficient energy to gather the missing components.

One of the first tasks in therapy is to determine if the patients have a story, how it is developed, and what pieces of information need to be gathered. The themes that are typically missing include the exact way of death or a refusal to believe in the death, which is caused by not being allowed to see the body and saying goodbye.

I find it very helpful to contact the coroner when trying to reconstruct the whole story. The coroner's office usually keeps records that include pictures of the incident. These pictures, although often very painful, are a useful tool in reconstructing the story (see Chapter 6, Use of Pictures).

Secrets.   Secrets can range from guilt movies to behaviors that the survivor plays out without anyone knowing. Women tend to admit more secret behaviors than men (e.g., smelling the clothing of the dead person, which is one way to attempt to regain the dead person); often people will fondle, or take to bed with them, a toy, blanket, or picture of the dead person, especially if it is a child. They may have developed shrines within the house, and although rituals may be carried out in secret, other members of the family know there is a special area that must not be "tampered" with. One woman kept a used, but clean, diaper in the wastepaper basket in her daughter's room until the next child was born. Her husband knew it was there, but the significance of it was never told to him.

Some secretly go through photo albums or home movies. Others may carry a favorite picture, a lock of hair, or wear an article of clothing or jewelry. They also may have the need to travel, often great distances, to see the "homestead" or family graves. These secrets are a means to remember the dead person and an attempt to recapture them. People do not share their secret behaviors in fear that others may think they are crazy. The behaviors, however, are comforting to them.

Others have torturing secrets that usually relate to guilt feelings. They secretly believe they are the cause of the death. One woman whose child died of SIDS believed she really had killed the child because she had been drinking the night before and was "so out of it" that she did not hear the baby cry. It took a very long time for her to be able to express this, but once she did, reality testing and education regarding SIDS could take place.

Hallucinations. These are any sensory process where the survivor hears, smells, tastes, feels, or sees the deceased. Often they are very desirable occurrences, because it is a means of recapturing the dead person. On the other hand, they are often kept as a secret because "people will really think I am crazy if I tell them what happened." Hallucinating may be frightening.

My patients have reported many of these secret experiences. One woman said her lights would go on in the house and her dog would bark. This occurred at the same time every night, which was her husband's typical time to come home from work. She walked out to the kitchen and saw his form standing by the counter. This happened numerous times during the first 2 weeks of bereavement. Another woman said her dead husband would come to her in bed and they would make passionate love. Others may not see the person, but will smell a cologne that she always wore, hear the sounds she always made, such as a special whistle, or feel a familiar touch on the arm or face.

Korry, a young boy whose father committed suicide, kept this torturing hallucination, dream, or experience a secret. This later affected his functioning in school and at home. The night his father committed suicide his mother and father had been fighting. The father had been physically abusive in the past and Korry and his mom fled from the house for safety. They went to a friend's house and Korry went to sleep. He awoke in the middle of the night to see his father standing over his bed, saying good-bye to him, and telling him to keep safe and well. Korry was very young at the time and was extremely frightened by this. It was not until the next morning that they found out his father had committed suicide. In his therapy he finally spoke of this experience, drew a picture, and shared it with his mother. He felt great relief through sharing this and discovering that many people experience hallucinations. Hallucinations usually occur during the first several weeks after the death, although many of my clients report them at holidays, anniversaries, or other significant times in their lives. The occurrence usually is not as frequent after the first several months. I find it very difficult to diagnose or label these as hallucinations; possibly there is a "spiritual" realm.

Even as I write this, I wonder if my readers will think I am crazy if I say that I have had similar experiences? For example, the night after Ken's death (the young man with leukemia who wanted to go home to die), I awoke with a start to see Ken standing over my bed. He put his hand on my arm and said, "thank you." Was I hallucinating, dreaming, or did it happen?

Survivors need to be aware that this may happen and that they are not "going crazy." If the behavior continues and interferes with everyday functioning, however, then it may have the elements of pathology.

Phobias.   After a death, survivors, both children and adults, often develop phobias that may or may not be accompanied by obsessions. Phobias may range from an anxiety disorder with a persistent fear about an activity, situation, or object to a phobia disorder, such as agoraphobia.

Phobias are usually irrational fears. In grief, however, they are not always viewed as irrational; "this has happened to me before (a death), it could happen again." As with any phobia, issues of separation anxiety and being alone are usually prevalent. One woman experienced her entire family dying within a period of 5 years (both parents, husband and two daughters). It was very frightening for her to reorganize her life because the threat of loss was always there for her.

Many of my patients, especially women, will experience panic attacks at a shopping center or grocery store. This is not uncommon. Such attacks are usually associated with avoidance behaviors of the issues. Steps are taken to deal not only with the avoided topics, but also issues of the separation anxiety, loneliness, and powerlessness (see Chapter 6).

Children often develop phobias after the death of a loved one. It may be slight, like becoming afraid of the dark again and needing to have the light on at night or it may progress to a full-fledged crippling phobia. A 7-year-old was brought to me because of a school phobia after the death of her grandmother. This was a very intelligent child who had not been allowed to participate in the funeral or grieve openly. Secretly, she thought she had killed her grandmother by not drawing her enough pictures.

Her phobia became crippling: she could not go to school, and if she did go out, her frequent urination forced her to retreat; she was also unable to get to sleep at night. The sad thing was that her teacher was not understanding of the problem. Luckily, however, her principal and parents were. It is very difficult for a child, or an adult, to make behavioral changes when they do not feel safe. This only increases the anxiety and the phobic behaviors.

I utilized a behavior modification approach to reintroduce the child to the classroom gradually. We used a favorite puppet, "Peedie," to protect her at night, and he would come to the office so we could conduct play therapy. He became her "protector," much as did Dumbo's magic feather, which he thought allowed him to fly. Peedie was able to accomplish the same thing. She knew there was "game-playing" in these activities but until she could understand her behaviors, decrease her anxiety, and mourn her grandmother she needed the "crutch."

It was also necessary to place her on Tofranil®. This medication helped decrease the anxiety so that I could work more with the phobia. Rarely is medication needed, unless the person is crippled by the symptoms and prior interventions are not successful. It must be understood by the patient that the medication is not going to cure the problem, but only help decrease the anxiety so that the *real* issues can be addressed.

In therapy, she made a list of things that frightened her and over the months we evaluated how they changed:

- Scared of teacher
- Scared that "I'm going to die and go back to the hospital"
- Nervous about school a lot
- Scared from grandma's death
- Scared that my mom, dad, grandma, and grandpa will leave me
- Really scared that my mom and dad are going to take a knife and cut me open
- Worried about my health
- Think that my grandma died because of me and my art work
- Sometimes don't pay attention to people and work that they give me and don't know how you do it and they get mad at me for not listening to the directions
- I just don't know why but at night I say I'll go to school but then in the morning I won't even touch the door
- Think a lot about my grandma's death and cry a lot

Obsessions/Compulsions. Obsessions and/or compulsions may also develop. This may be attached to phobic responses or may be isolated incidences. For example, a widow may find that she is compulsively checking the door locks or that she is obsessive about her deceased husband. These are normal responses and often involve learning new roles, "My husband always locked the doors at night; that was his job."

Often these behaviors have a secret and undoing element: "If I wash my hands 10 times a day, then I'll be 'clean' again." Others may believe these behaviors or thoughts give them power in a powerless situation.

Flight Behavior.   People often attempt to cover the pain of grief by the use of flight behavior, such as drugs, alcohol, affairs, or running away. This behavior often gives the person a false sense of security, yet when they "awake" the pain and grief are still there. It is very difficult for family or friends to encourage people who are utilizing flight behaviors to receive treatment. A woman, Donna, age 36, had had a child (Katie) die 8 months prior to her entry into treatment. It was difficult for her to deal with the death, but her husband, Curt's, coping behavior involved running away for months at a time and the abuse of alcohol and drugs. Besides the grief for Katie, she also had to deal with her anger, pain, and grief about Curt.

SUMMARY

This chapter explored the variables that affect the development and expression of symptoms of grief. In addition, multiple and complicated grief feelings, physical responses, reactions, and behaviors were discussed.

REFERENCES

American Psychiatric Association. (1980). *Diagnostic and statistical manual of mental disorders.* (3rd ed.). Washington, DC: Author.

Clayton, P. J. (1974). Mortality and morbidity in the first year of widowhood. *Archives of General Psychiatry, 30,* 747–750.

Clayton, P. J. (1975a). *Weight loss and sleep disturbance.* In B. Schoenberg, I. Gerber, A. Weiner, A. Kutscher, D. Peretz, & A. Carr (Eds.), *Bereavement: Its psychosocial aspects* (pp. 72–77). New York: Columbia University Press.

Clayton, P. J. (1975b). "The effect of living alone on bereavement symptoms." *American Journal of Psychiatry, 132,* 133–137.

Crisp, A. H., & Priest, R. G. (1972). Psychoneurotic status during the year following bereavement. *Journal of Psychosomatic Research, 16,* 351–355.

Holmes, T. S., & Holmes T. H. (1970). Short-term intrusions into the life style routine. *Journal of Psychosomatic Research, 14,* 121–132.

Holmes, T. H., & Rahe, R. H. (1967). The social readjustment rating scale. *Journal of Psychosomatic Research, 11,* 213–218.

The Holy Bible, revised standard version. (1952). New York: Harper & Brothers.

Johnson, S. (1983, January/February). Guiding adults through bereavement. *Nursing Life,* 34–39.

Johnson, S. (1986). The client experiencing grief. In J. Durham & S. Hardin (Eds.), *Private practice in psychiatric mental health nursing.* New York: Springer.

Johnson-Soderberg, S. (1982). *The ethos of parental bereavement and guilt.* (Doctoral Dissertation, University of Michigan, 1982). *Dissertation Abstracts International,* 1–222, 502.

Keirsey, D., & Bates, M. (1978). *Please understand me* (pp. 25–26). Del Mar, CA: Prometheus Nemesis Books.

Lewis, C. S. (1961). *A grief observed.* London: Faber & Faber.

Lindemann, E. (1944). Symptomatology and management of acute grief. *American Journal of Psychiatry, 101,* 141–149.

Parkes, C. M. (1970). The first year of bereavement: A longitudinal study of the reactions of London widows to the death of their husbands. *Psychiatry, 4,* 444–469.

Parkes, C. M. (1972). *Bereavement: Studies of guilt in adult life.* New York: International Universities Press.

Rees, W. D. (1975). The bereaved and their hallucinations. In B. Schoenberg, I. Gerber, A. Wiener, A. Kutscher, D. Peretz, & A. Carr (Eds.), *Bereavement: Its psychosocial aspects* (pp. 66–71). New York: Columbia University Press.

Westberg, E. E. (1961). *Good grief—A constructive approach to the problem of loss.* Philadelphia: Fortress Press.

Wiener, A., Gerber, I., Battin, D., & Arkin, A. M. (1974). The process and phenomenology of bereavement. In B. Schoenberg, I. Gerber, A. Wiener, A. Kutscher, D. Peretz, & A. Carr (Eds.), *Bereavement: Its psychosocial aspects* (pp. 53–65). New York: Columbia University Press.

Worden, W. J. (1982). *Grief counseling and grief therapy.* New York: Springer.

CHAPTER IV

The First Year of Bereavement

words only have meaning when listened to—
words of joy . . .
love . . .
pain . . .
sorrow . . .
give sorrow words

elizabeth*
(used with permission)

In the next two chapters, the first several years of bereavement will be discussed. This chapter will be subdivided into sections that discuss the first 2 weeks after the death, 2 weeks to 2 months, 2 months to 6 months, and 6 months to a year. These time frames are certainly not meant to be exact but rather only arbitrary parameters that give form to understanding of the first year of bereavement. It is just as ludicrous to be rigidly bound by these suggested time frames as it would be to worry about the number and order of Kübler-Ross' now famous stages of death (1969). Tasks of the first year will be explored.

In Chapter 5, the second and third year of bereavement will be discussed, along with the slow and quiet progress toward recovery or the painful process of pathology.

---

*Elizabeth is a client of mine who had a very painful loss. One of her ways of expressing her grief was through her poetry. I will be sharing some of her poetry in the next two chapters.

This first year is a very difficult and painful time for survivors. If the death was a significant one, the symptoms may be pronounced and multiple. The reality then becomes a constant bombardment of pain, and the memories are not yet sweet and peaceful. The survivors find little comfort or release from their torture. Grief becomes all encompassing, engulfing, and consuming, in time, energy, and thought.

It is the process of moving the pain toward recovery that will be explored in the next several chapters. I hope that the caretaker can have a greater appreciation for the survivors' needs and can take appropriate steps to prevent or undo problems. It is important to assist the survivor, in understanding that he or she is not alone, that his or her feelings are normal, and that there is help available if needed.

There are many tasks of mourning that need to be accomplished during the first year of bereavement. The discussion of the four tasks of mourning in Worden's (1982) book are quite helpful. These tasks are: to accept the reality of the loss, to experience the pain of grief, to adjust to an environment in which the dead person is missing, and to withdraw emotional energy and reinvest it in another relationship. These are important tasks and essential if the survivor is to achieve healthy grieving. It is these tasks that I term "grief work"—and it is hard work. The grief work and resolution of themes and symptoms become the goals in therapy. I will also explore other tasks that are more specific. Some tasks will relate to certain populations (e.g., parents who have had a child die or widows/widowers), but they may have relevance for others.

FIRST TWO WEEKS AFTER THE DEATH

Time of Death

There is much helplessness and pain in watching someone die. It may be one of the loneliest feelings in a person's life to know that now the person whom he loved and cared for is alive and soon will be dead. The survivor will never again be able to see, laugh, cry, hug, or celebrate life as it is known on Earth with this person. When the person dies, they are gone. Things will never be the same. Death in itself is a mystery and difficult to comprehend. It happens to us all.

Death, like birth, is something we must do alone. We can have helpers: one's mother *helps* deliver us; the father may support the mother; the physician, nurse, or midwife may also help in the process. The helpers are available, but it is the small infant that must make his or her way through the cervix and down the vagina. And, so it is with death. There can and should be helpers. The greatest fears about death are of pain and dying alone. But one must "do" one's own dying. In acknowledging that process, the survivors can often put the dying in perspective: the survivors can help the process and for that they can feel some comfort and power in a powerless situation. We can never actually do the dying for another, even though we wish we could take away or experience the pain and suffering for a loved one.

Once the person has died, people describe an overwhelming feeling of emptiness. There may be crying and great emotion, or there may be nothing. It is during this time that people often feel fear and anxiety. They have witnessed life being extinguished from another person, which is frightening. Many want to run away to decrease their anxiety. Those moments immediately after a death can be very important in initiating healthy survivor bereavement.

We have been "wrong" for many years in wisking the infant away from his or her parents immediately after birth, unless there is an emergency. This is a time when initial bonding, examination, and joy can be experienced. It is an important time for both child and parent. So it is immediately after a death. This important time can be used to "unbind" from the person who has died. Good-byes can be said and survivor grief can begin to be expressed.

The caretaker, be it nurse, physician, or clergy, often needs to give permission to stay and perform these important tasks. It always amazes me that at the time of death the family often expresses the feeling that they do not "own" that person anymore. A couple may have been married for 50 years, but now the widow feels as though she cannot and should not touch her husband. I always give my families permission to stay as long as they need and do what they need: if you want to crawl into bed and hug that person one last time—*do it!* If you need to rock your baby—*do it!* If you would like to participate in the "postmortem" care—*do it!* These are means to begin the survivor grief. One must do what one needs to do because one will never have the opportunity again as it is presented immediately after the death. When these initial good-byes have been accomplished, the distancing and separation can begin.

Over the years, I have seen more and more health care providers better understand this need, resulting in their giving families the time they need to be with their loved one. To you, these enlightened providers, I am thankful. Granted, allowing the family to have time may interfere with your schedule, but whom are we treating? We must always keep in mind that our patients and families are the center of our treatment plans. It is important to give this permission both verbally and nonverbally. Even as you give this message verbally, nonverbally you may be exhibiting a hurried and intolerant message. Therefore, it is helpful to be aware of all levels of communication.

Often the families are uncomfortable remaining in the room after a death. Asking them if it would be helpful for you to stay with them gives them permission to do what they need, but also tells them that you care for them as a family. Because of the shock of the death, you may need to anticipate their needs: there may be people you could call for them, or if their clergy has not yet arrived they may want you to contact him or her. It is also helpful to give them permission to talk about the good and bad memories, what their life was like, and express their pain. Above all, do not hurry them. Some families may only need a few minutes, while others may take hours. I have never had a family who "stayed too long," but I have had those who left "too early."

Sometimes the body has been mutilated. In these circumstances clinical decisions must be made as to whether the family should be allowed to view the body at this time, or later at the funeral home. I find it helpful to assess the body to see if there are parts that could be viewed by the family, such as an arm or leg. "Seeing is believing" and usually I find, at least in the long run, the reality is easier to confront than the fantasies. With one's senses they are confirming the reality that this is their loved one who is dead. By not seeing, usually doubts, nonclosure, regrets, and guilts develop. I explain and describe what they will see in order to prepare them.

I never force anyone to see a body, but through the years a common issue for people who come into treatment is that they never were able to see their loved one or say good-bye to them. Consequently, there is no closure and often there are doubts that the person is dead. One man whose wife and daughter died in a house fire was advised by the funeral director not to see their bodies, although they were not burned. Five years after their deaths he still could not believe, on an emotional level, that they were dead. In addition, by never saying good-bye and bringing closure to the past, it is impossible for him to form intimate relationships with women in the present. Of course, this is only one part of the reason for not committing to a relationship, but it is a large one.

I was asked by an emergency room physican and nurse to see a woman whose son had apparently drowned in the river. It had been several days and they had not yet recovered the body. Besides dealing with her initial shock and grief, she could not believe that he could have made such a terrible mistake as to fall into the swift river. This gave an opening to discuss viewing his body when it was found. She was not ready to hear it, because she could not believe he had actually fallen into the river. I had several days to prepare her and when they eventually found him, she realized the need to see and say good-bye to him, although she did not see his entire body because of the distortions from the drowning.

This inital "unbonding" time is important and necessary. It should not be rushed and often much permission-giving needs to be expressed to the family. The family should never be forced to do something that is not comfortable for them; one must always question whose needs are being met. Often the family is too grieved or passive to ask for what they need, if indeed, they know what they need. That is when encouragement, suggestions, or permission-giving from the caretaker can be extremely helpful.

Informing Family and Friends

Soon after the death it is the task of the family to inform others of the death. This is a very difficult task, especially if the death was unexpected. Yet it is also helpful and necessary, because it is a chance to tell and retell the story. The more the story is told, the more "comfortable" the survivors become with it and it assists in promoting the reality of the loss. It is helpful to encourage the family to tell and retell their story as they inform family and friends. This telling serves as a means to begin to confront the reality of the loss and to obtain missing data to the story, which is often easier to gather at the time of death rather than in the future.

Funeral Arrangements

Coming home from the hospital after a death, or after having the body removed from the home, is an extremely lonely time. The family is usually in shock, no matter how long ahead of time they were aware the death would occur. At the same time there are pressures to meet and tasks to accomplish. Although many people prefer to be involved in arrangements, it is also the time to allow others to help. I encourage my families to find a helpful person or persons, usually of their own sex, who can be what I call their "alter ego."

An alter ego should be someone that has some understanding of that person, who knows how to care for the survivor, and has some understanding of how to anticipate and meet their needs. Often these people are the ones who feel comfortable enough to appear without being asked. These people can be particularly helpful since the shock and sadness can, initially, be overwhelming. One man described his shock and the need to have another person who would be able to direct him:

> The lack of direction, the lack of ability to determine what to do next. You don't know. It is not so much what society expects out of me but golly, I don't know what to do. Where do we go from here: You don't really realize the full impact of it (death) even though he hadn't died at that time (their 3-year-old son). I really felt I needed somebody to direct me, to take me to this place and that place. I think that sensation was evident really the first 2 days. Well, especially the first day, that was the most.

One must realize that not everyone will feel they need or want a person like an alter ego. If this type of person has not been helpful in the past, he or she will probably not be helpful now. To make this decision, it is useful if one understands and knows what is needed ahead of a crisis. If the person is able to be open and helpful, survivors will probably find this comforting and supportive. If not, it will not be appropriate. No matter what is comfortable for the person, it is important that somehow he finds some comfort. Believe me, you need all the comfort you can possibly get.

In addition, people can be "too helpful." These tend to be the people who need to rescue others, who overprotect, and who cannot see the necessity for the survivors to participate. The role of the alter ego is to be helpful, but not to "do it all." The survivors need to make as many of the decisions regarding funeral behaviors, obituaries, and services as they are able. This allows for grief to be expressed, but it is also a means to do what they wish and need, for the last time, for their loved one. There is often a feeling of power and peace in those decisions, in an otherwise powerless situation.

I treated a family whose son was killed in an automobile accident. The shock was tremendous. Both of the parents had passive personalities, so it was very easy for a rescuing friend to come in and make all the decisions regarding the funeral, insurance, services, etc. He decided for them that they should not see their son, the car, or talk to the police. He was trying to be helpful by being "protective." And yet in the long run both parents had regrets and delayed grief because of their lack of participation in the decision making.

It is a fine line that the alter ego must walk: they must be helpful enough to anticipate needs and yet perceptive enough to know what decisions and to what degree the survivors need to participate. They can encourage the survivors to discuss memories, both good and bad; to think of special music or verses for the service; and to assist in any of the tasks to make the funeral as meaningful as possible. If this can be accomplished there are few, if any, regrets or guilt. Most of all, the survivors are well on their way to healthy bereavement.

Rituals

Obituaries.   Another task that the survivor needs to accomplish is the writing of the obituary. How does one put all the needed information about a life into several paragraphs? It seems almost "sacriligious" to attempt to make sense out of a life in a short space and then expose it to the world. And yet, the obituary is a very important document that shares with the world the who, what, where, when, and how of this person's life and death. It contains historical information, and therefore, specific dates and events that are helpful to survivors and history.

As our culture becomes more comfortable in dealing with death, maybe we can approach our own, and our loved ones', death with more comfortable responses as well. People do not really die of "a long illness" or "a short illness." They die of such ailments as cancer or heart disease or an accident. That is nothing to be ashamed about; it is the reality and history of that death.

In addition, I encourage my families to make the obituary as personalized as possible. What will the survivors miss about this person? Is there a message that this person would leave to the world? For what will they be remembered? A young woman whom I was treating while her father was dying of cancer insisted that the obituary included this phrase: "In memory of our dad, go hug a person today." Although her family was "afraid what people would think," they consented. The positive reactions, from significant and nonsignificant people, were overwhelming. The following is another example of an obituary where a personal response was written. The family eulogized the grandfather by saying, "He will be remembered for his work in the hospice, Men's Garden Club and church; making people happy; his congeniality; and his good looks." The family knew he would have enjoyed that and it gave them a smile and peaceful feeling to be able to say those words.

Flowers.   Another decision that the caretaker can assist the family with in their decision making is whether the family wants to have a memorial instead of flowers. This is a personal decision and again, the family should do what is helpful to them. If seeing and smelling flowers is helpful, then that is what is needed. If a memorial is chosen it is important to state that strongly in the obituary. Usually the funeral director can be extremely helpful is phrasing the statement, but something like, "In lieu of flowers, memorials may be sent to . . ." or "Please omit flowers," can be added.

As a caretaker, it is often helpful to confront one's own ideas, beliefs, and values about death. A helpful process might be to write one's own obituary. What would you want in your obituary? It may be helpful to share it with a friend or spouse.

Visitation and Funeral Services.   Most funeral directors can be extremely helpful to the survivors. I find many who are able to guide the family in their own needs. As with any purchased service, it is helpful to encourage families if at all possible to investigate and make their decision regarding a funeral director before a death occurs. Although there are incompetent people in any field, funeral directors are not necessarily "out to get you." They are extremely important and usually care about the families they serve. I find most allow the family to plan and decide what is helpful and useful.

I encourage my families to be as involved in the decision-making and rituals as they would like. I give them a strong message: *dare to grieve.* Do what is helpful for themselves and their family. The ritual should have meaning, otherwise there is no purpose in performing it.

We had a 3-year-old in our hospice organization who died at home after a long battle with leukemia. The parents decided that it would be helpful and meaningful for them to bathe, dress, and say their good-byes at home. When they had finished their rituals and good-byes they called the funeral director and carried her to the hearse. Other families have gone to the funeral home and dressed their loved one. Everyone does not need or want to be so involved, but for those who need it-*do it.*

If it would feel good to put "things" like pictures, blankets, toys, or a letter in the casket, I encourage families to *do it!* It is not going to help the dead person travel better over the "River Styx," but it does help the survivors feel as though a part of them is with that body. This is based upon the old story about "who pays the Ferryman, Charon?" (The Ferryman would only take souls who had received burial rites across "the flood." The rest would have to roam until it was their turn. Their loved ones would put a gold coin under the tongue of the dead loved one in order to pay the Ferryman to take him across the River Styx (Bullfinch's Mythology, 1964).)

A grandfather loved to have his little glass of Scotch every afternoon. A family member bought a miniature bottle of J & B Scotch and put it in his pocket in the casket. Grandfather didn't *need* his Scotch anymore, but this was something special that the person needed and wanted to do. No one needs to know about it if it makes the survivors uncomfortable. Not everyone has the same needs, but giving the survivors permission to do whatever is meaningful is helpful and prevents regrets.

The survivors are celebrating this person's life, especially the good parts. In order to do that, the service and the funeral need to contain aspects of that person. An elderly man died who loved to fish; beside his casket stood his fishing pole. A young man played in a band; the drum stood silenced next to the casket. Another young man played football; pictures of Steve in uniform were seen around the room. Linnea had a favorite teddy bear; next to her in the casket was the bear. Papa's casket was filled with cards that our daughter's school friends had made; he would have loved being surrounded symbolically by these children so special to him.

The following poem was written by a client of mine who has MS and whose father died suddenly of a heart attack. This was read during the service and was a help to many. It reflects her struggle with attachment and separation.

> There's a song in my heart though you're gone. I can
> say I know you're far better off—the love of roses are
> yours, I loved you so. I can't miss you anymore than
> now. I'll only cry a little longer, don't worry, I'll
> be alright. I'll share with you in that peace
> someday. The Lord, Our Father, bless you for the
> Lovin'. For giving the change of seasons; for taking
> him now out of pain.
> I must grow now that I'm lost.
> There's silence.
> The tree's leaves have fallen and along
> With them, too, I'm bare.
> My Joy is last gone and my comfort is but a blanket to
> keep warm as I'm cold.
> If we could only talk together I'd say
> Thank-you.
> There's a song in my heart though you're gone.
> I know you're far better off.
> You're smiling so.
> I know you're in His arms.
> Know that I'll always love you.

SUE MARSTON
(used with permission)

One goal of a funeral is to celebrate the person's life, which is often related to religious and life experiences. The survivors are usually able to receive comfort and support from people, "the church," cards, flowers, and food. In this initial grieving time, it also is another phase where separation can occur. Separation is another goal of the visitation and funeral. In observing visitations and funerals, I usually find that the family will initially stand very close to the casket, often touching or "fidgeting" with the body. Once I observed a mother holding her dead infant; she was not yet able to separate herself from him. As the visitation proceeds, unknown to the survivors, I usually see a bodily distancing from the casket. They begin to move further away from the casket and physically detach. They will often walk around the room, returning at intervals to check "things out." Although people are unaware of their behavior, this is a healthy process and displays the need and usefulness of visitations.

This is a very difficult and stressful time for the family. Many are in shock (see Chapter 3, Feelings), and remember very little about the funeral. But usually there is a general feeling or behavior which is remembered. With stress high, often there are arguments, displaced anger, and hindering behaviors. The caretaker can prepare the survivors and help them recognize the probability that these negative things will happen. It is then possible to assist the survivors in protecting themselves from hindering people. It is important for them to assume that not everything will be "perfect," but rather the best will be done. Often a caretaker or alter ego can be helpful in mediating problems.

For example, I had two sisters referred to me by a funeral home because their brother had died in a very bizarre fashion. They were confronted with issues about their brother that they had never known; he had a secret life. For them it was very upsetting to think of being at the visitation where people might ask "too many questions." The three of us were able to develop strategies to handle these potentially hindering situations. They felt more confident in having a plan and the visitation went smoothly.

Grave Visiting.   Grave visiting is a very personal matter. It is helpful to some and hindering to others. Grave-visiting behaviors need to be assessed for avoidance and denial, as well as a helpful ritual. Some people secretly believe if they do not go to the grave the person may not be dead. I have had many patients who do not know where the grave is because they refuse to believe the loved one is dead.

On the other hand, many will compulsively visit the grave. This is normal in the first year. It is a means to feel closer to the loved one and, although a painful experience, they often feel better for going. This seems to be due to the fact that they allow themselves to grieve at the grave. If the compulsive grave visiting is continued over the years, it has the potential for pathology. This is because the person is not willing, on some level, to concede to the death and reorganize his or her life.

In addition, the grave visiting may develop into secret shrining behavior. The secret develops because the person is often fearful that others will think they are crazy, and therefore, do not want others to know what they do and say. If the behaviors continue to be potent, they can develop into a pathological response (see Chapter 5).

Grave-visiting behaviors are initially an attempt to regain the lost person. It is healthy because it helps confront the reality that the person is dead and is "no longer here." Most of my clients remark that the visiting is most helpful in the first 6 months, after which they find their visiting decreases. Once the first task of mourning is realized, I often see a decrease in grave visiting, which often is around the sixth month. At birthdays, anniversaries, and holidays, however, the behaviors may again increase.

There is often a need for special behaviors on those occasions. It gives a feeling of power, when there actually is none. What good does a grave blanket do at Christmas time? What good does a special bouquet of flowers do on the anniversary of the death? It does not do one thing for the dead person: a grave blanket is not going to keep them warmer; the flowers won't make them happier. The survivors are really doing it for themselves. It allows them to grieve, and to do something actively. The rituals then can and should have meaning for the survivors—otherwise *do not do it!* These special rituals may not help the dead person, but it certainly does not hurt the living, especially in the early phases of mourning.

John and Jill, the couple whose 15-year-old daughter, Skye, died in a car accident, wanted to do something special for her first birthday after her death. After much consideration, they decided to bring a bouquet of balloons to her grave. They felt very uncomfortable as they tied down the balloons because people in the cemetery seemed to be giving them very strange looks. Nevertheless, they felt good about their decision, because Skye loved balloons. Indirectly, they were doing something for her. They had a wonderful laugh, which is always good for the grieving person, when they visited her grave a few days later. Not only did Skye have her balloons, but there were balloons on many other graves! They said it was a beautiful sight in a very sad place. Not only did their "daring to be different" help themselves, but probably helped many other people, as well. I always tell my families to *dare to grieve* as creatively as they can. Although Skye's birthday was difficult and painful, the balloons became a ritual that had meaning and added some positive aspects to a dark day.

Many people prefer to go by themselves to the grave, especially women. They believe that they are then not restricted in what they say or do. For them, many of the grave visiting behaviors are aimed at "straightening" or "tidying-up" the plot. In many ways these seemingly compulsive behaviors are a means to gain control in a powerless situation and allows the women to continue to use their expressive role, which many believe they have lost through the death of a child (Johnson, 1963).

In addition, women tend to have a grave-visiting pattern: "I go every Sunday, and every 24th" (the day of the month the daughter died). Others "go when the spirit leads me." Usually people who go routinely have the need to have rituals, repetition, and routines in other aspects of their lives. Keirsey & Bates (1978) call these people "J" people. The compulsive like behaviors allow them to gain control, they think, in a powerless situation. There is nothing wrong with either method; it is knowing what helps each individual person.

It is all right to be ritualistic, as long as one does not feel guilty when the behavior is not accomplished or when it develops into a compulsive neurosis. It is all right to go to the grave "whenever" or very infrequently. I always give my clients permission to do what is helpful for them, especially during the first and second year of bereavement. They must also be aware, as with grief symptoms, that people grieve differently: What is helpful to one person, may not be to the other, the spouse, or other family members.

Consequently, for those in early phases of mourning, it is important to give permission to develop helpful grave-visiting rituals for themselves and possibly their family (e.g., deciding as a family on some ritual, like each bringing a special flower). Grave visiting need not be pathological, although like other grief symptoms, people keep their behaviors secret: "If my husband knew what I did and said at the cemetery, he'd lock me away for sure!"

Women tend to be the ones who express guilt over the grave visiting. One woman went once a week and said, "Only because I thought I had to. . . . A good mother should do this if she has a child die." Often they will express guilt if they haven't been: "I haven't been now for 2 months, and every time I think of it I feel so guilty. I should go."

Often there is guilt and pining that develops when their loved one is buried in a distant city. The distance prevents them from developing rituals and grieving at the grave. Substitute rituals can be developed, however, such as going to a peaceful spot and meditating or having quiet time in a church or chapel. If this is a large issue for the family, moving the body may be helpful. If not, it is always helpful for them to plan a trip sometime in the first year of bereavement to check the grave. This often promotes a feeling of peace that "all is well."

In summary, I have seen trends in grave visiting: women visit more often and prefer to go alone; men do not need or like to go to the cemetery as often as women; those men and women who have a short preparation time for death, visit more frequently in the first 6 months, which seems to be related to the shock of the loss; women tend to identify guilt with grave visiting; and grave visiting tends to decrease over time if complicated grief does not develop.

If I am fortunate enough to be with the family prior to the death, or when I get a chance to talk to funeral directors, I encourage people to think carefully about the marker. In the last 100 years, we, in the United States, have stopped providing what I believe is important and historical information on the marker. For historical purposes, it is helpful to have the full names and full dates of birth and death on the gravestone. It is also making a statement to the world that this person lived between such-and-such dates.

Another ritual which is "out of vogue" is an epitaph. I enjoy reading and finding epitaphs. These sayings certainly are a summary of the personality of that individual. Some of my favorites that I have spotted are:

Here lies the atheist
All dressed up
And no where to go

Here lies dear old Anna
Done to death by a banana
It wasn't the fruit of the thing
that made her go
It was the skin of the thing
that laid her low

If you seek my epitaph
Look around you

Remember friend, as you pass by
As you are now, so once was I
As I am now, thus you must be,
So be prepared to follow me
(this response is written below)
To follow you, I'm not content
Until I find which way you went

I told you I was sick!

If you feel inclined, roam through a cemetery and see what you can discover about the history of people; for example, in the early 1800s many women were not only anonymous in life, but also in death. Often the stones will be engraved with something like, "Wife of John Breakenridge," or "First wife of William Smith"—"Second wife of William Smith," etc., with no name or dates. The gravestone is an important reminder of who this person was and the history of the time. That information needs to be preserved. What would you put on your gravestone?

Pet Responses. In assessing family composition, it is always important to determine if there are pets who have been involved with the person who died. Pets appear to mourn and if they are aware of family activity and respond to feelings and reactions, somehow they need to be included. We have no real way to research what thoughts and/or feelings go through our pets' minds, but from clinical experience I have observed grieving pets.

Recently, there has been much publicity regarding Koko, the gorilla who speaks with sign language. She has been grieving the death of her pet kitten, All-Ball (Time, 1985). Many of my families have shared how after the death of a family member the dog will carry around the dead person's shoe for a week, hide under a bed, refuse to eat, appear depressed, howl, or protect a favorite chair of the person who died.

Animals appear to grieve both people and other animals. Buffy, a cocker spaniel, enjoyed watching the caged gerbils. She would lie on the floor for hours, tail wagging, just watching their quick, purposeful actions. The two gerbils died within hours of each other. Noticing the cage was not in its usual place, she laid down staring into the empty space with her tail between her legs.

Cats also seem to have grief reactions. One of our neighbor's cats, Clover, died and I suggested they show her to their other cat. Daisy sniffed, cried and searched for her sister. For several weeks she spent much time encircling and guarding Clover's grave. Daisy and Elizabeth, their 7-year-old, would spend hours sitting by the grave, looking, and "comforting" each other. Seeing Clover's body probably helped Daisy realize the death.

Another example is a family dog who was very intelligent. When the grandfather who lived with the family died, Tookie seemed to know. When she was told about the death she immediately put her tail between her legs and wanted to be held. She moped around the house, looking very depressed and refused to eat. It was decided that it was important for her to see Grandpa. Thank goodness the funeral

director was supportive! As soon as Tookie was brought into the
visitation room she started sniffing frantically and wanted to get to
the casket. She proceeded to sniff Grandpa up and down for about
10 minutes, never taking her eyes or nose off of him. She then looked
up and turned her head. Did she say goodby or instinctively know
that Grandpa was dead? Whatever the case, after that experience her
behavior returned to "normal."

I advocate that pets be involved, talked to, and comforted. It may
seem "weird," but it can't hurt. Even if they are not as "sophisti-
cated" as we are in our thoughts and feelings, they still have their
instincts. With their instincts, responses develop.

TWO WEEKS TO TWO MONTHS:
"The First" Time for Everything

Coming Home Without Their Loved One

> i cannot see you
> i cannot hear you
> i cannot touch you
> ever . . .
>
> elizabeth
> (used with permission)

After the funeral is over and friends and relatives leave, the reality
and emptiness of grieving begins. The first time survivors have to
walk into the house without their loved one is devastating. It is
painful and lonely. The survivors can't believe that they will ever get
through this, and there is often very little hope at this time.

It is very difficult to go home for the first time. Many of my clients
find it too traumatic and painful and refuse to "go home," often for
long periods of time. One woman lived with her parents for 6 weeks
after her husband died. Her parents decided when she should return,
although she was not ready. When she finally went home, all she
could do was sit in the rocking chair and stare into space. She was
not ready.

Another woman whose child died of SIDS also refused to go home
for over a month. She insisted that she and her husband live with her
mother, which was not an easy or supportive situation in itself.
However, she felt it was better than facing the home and empty crib.
Gradually, I increased her time and activities at the house until she

felt strong enough to return home. The activities included washing the baby's dirty clothes, which had been there since he died; putting away clothing and toys; and reorganizing the baby's room.

As they begin to confront this painful time and the memories, my patients often begin to experience what they term "crazy behavior": "I'm sure I heard Duane walk in the house and yell, 'hi mom,' last night." "I know I heard the shower go on this morning at the same time Ralph usually takes it " or "I know I didn't leave the kitchen light on; it's like Fred came back and turned it on for me so I wouldn't come into a dark house."

Daily Activities

This is the time when every activity is "The First": the first time to go to church without their loved one, to the store, to a family gathering on a holiday, to a birthday party, seeing the first snowfall, etc. Every activity is without their loved one, and the memories and pain are abundant. I have had patients tell me that they could be standing in the middle of the grocery store with their carriage filled and become so overwhelmed with grief that they had to leave. Other things that may trigger the "flight" behavior include: seeing a child about the age of the one that died or a box of cereal that they liked; it may be crowded Christmas stores, or just a memory going through their head. It is very much like a panic or agoraphobic attack, but it is a normal reaction. One is so overwhelmed with grief and pain, that defenses are weakened and one is vulnerable to attack.

People often get frightened, overwhelmed, or think they are going "crazy" because of these foreign behaviors and feelings that they often want to hibernate. By knowing that these feelings may happen one can protect oneself: the survivor may ask a helpful friend to go with them to the store; they shouldn't stay in any one place for long periods of time; often teaching them to do protective imagery before entering an anxiety-producing situation may be helpful; or if there is an invitation for dinner, it is helpful if the host or hostess knows they may need to leave early. The issue is that the survivors are attempting to reorganize their life, but they know when they have had enough and must retreat and take care of themselves. I tell my patients *to praise themselves for what they are able to do and not to kick themselves for leaving early or not being able to accomplish an activity.* These techniques are helpful in getting through the "firsts" of everything. However, these activities must be done many, many times before comfort and power are restored.

Grief Symptoms and Escapes

The grief symptoms often become very intense (see Chapter 3). Depending upon the impact of the loss, the first several months are usually very tortured. The symptoms are continuous and intense; time is not important. Survivors experience feeling "jet lagged," and they are extremely tired. Thoughts, energies, and feelings are focused upon the loss.

Because the pain is so intense, escape mechanisms are often sought. Some may find that alcohol, drugs, or affairs will momentarily stop the pain. Others will turn to their religion. Work also becomes a great escape. Some people will express feeling so much better at the office, and then, as soon as they come home, feel depressed.

This is a situational depression. The person experiences an increase in energy and power when outside of the depressing environment, but when they return to the painful environment, depression is once again felt. Most people (except for masochists) attempt to find places, people, or activities that add to their comfort and well-being. Therefore, it is very common to find that people seek out activities that provide them with a greater sense of well-being. One spouse may work longer hours, in turn increasing pressures and arguments with the spouse that is home more often.

For example, a couple I was treating not only had their child, Julie, die, but were going through extremely difficult financial problems because of Julie's medical bills. Ken enjoyed working and had always found work to be a wonderful escape for him. Kathy, on the other hand, chose to stay at home with their three children. She had always been secretly jealous of Ken's job and would consciously sabotage him by forgetting the boss was coming to dinner or by planning a family activity when she knew he'd be out of town, etc. When Julie died, Ken continually worked hard because it made him feel better about himself and his pain. Kathy was not receiving support from Ken and needed comfort. She had an affair: it was a way of gaining the support and comfort she wanted and needed, but also a means of again sabotaging their relationship.

It is very difficult to convince people, lay, as well as professional, how difficult and complicated grief is. Therefore, it is often not until it is too late that they realize they have made some harmful decisions or found themselves in deep trouble. This is why I encourage people to get into grief therapy early after a devastating loss or death. Destructive behaviors can often be prevented. The first several months are an extremely difficult time for all concerned. There is little energy to minister and help others in the family, and adding more trauma, like alcoholism, drugs, or affairs, will only increase the recovery time. These inadequate coping mechanisms are like putting a Band Aid on a deep laceration. Such treatment will only cause more problems. It is a difficult enough time, without creating more issues and problems.

TWO MONTHS TO SIX MONTHS

Myth that Grief Is Ended

> so great a sorrow
> so few to mourn with . . .
>
> elizabeth
> (used with permission)

There is also a great deal of pressure from society, because people do not want to be with the grieving. It is too painful to deal with for those who are uninvolved, or even for involved family and friends. Survivors learn very quickly with whom they can share their pain and who avoids the topic. In addition, it is often too painful for the survivors to confront others, even if the "friends" intend to be helpful. For example, it may be very difficult to have to see the babies that were born from the LaMaze group, while their baby died or to have to see the children in their daughter's class after she died in a car accident.

Our culture continues to support the myth that grief should be completed in a couple of weeks (see Chapter 5, When Is Mourning Finished?). Therefore, often survivors feel the pressure to "put on a happy face" to protect others; "they don't want to hear," and many feel they have a catch-22 situation since the nonsurvivors may feel that they have been cut off by the grieving people because "it is too difficult for them to share with just anyone." The reasons for not sharing may be many, but that does not mean grief is ended.

Helpful and Hindering People

> i've learned to weep without
> to weep alone . . .
>
> elizabeth
> (used with permission)

As they start to reorganize their life, survivors begin to venture into the world. It is difficult to realize that one's "friends" or family are truly not befriending in this process. Widows and widowers will tell me how they are not included in their old "pot-luck" group because of the death of their spouse. One patient, Lee, told me that she was excluded because the women in the dinner group were frightened that she may "steal" one of their husbands now that she was a widow! Besides dealing with the death of her husband, she also had to confront the loss of friends and peer groups. For the first time in her life she felt discriminated against because of her change in status. This is not unusual.

Nongrieving people will often make decisions for the survivors, without even consulting them: "We just thought it would be too hard for you to come to the Fourth of July picnic, so we just had it without you." This is not helpful to the survivor. It should be her decision whether she wants to go to an activity; it is impossible to answer for another.

Role Changes

In addition to all the previous changes mentioned in dealing with one's grief, there are also changes in roles. The survivor must gradually adapt to being a "single parent," a parent with two children instead of three, or being orphaned either as a young child or an adult. These changes are difficult to learn to adjust to, because most likely the survivor did not want this change. Often people have to learn how to do "things" that they never had previously attempted. This is especially true if there has been strict role-socialization within the family: "My husband never cooked; he won't be able to live without me." "My husband always did the banking. I have never even written a check. I don't know what to do."

In addition to the role changes, survivors often receive pressures from the external world that potentiate the role changes. I am often asked by parents who have had a child die, "What do I say when someone asks me at a party how many children I have?" Their hearts sink, because they want to say four instead of three or two instead of one. In addition, the survivors do not want to make the questioner uncomfortable.

I recommend that they include the dead child in the counting. That child was and is their child and is part of the family even though he is no longer physically with them; there is no reason to discount him. Often people will drop the question after asking, without pursuing where the children are and what they are doing. If it is pursued it is often helpful to say something like, "Don't feel uncomfortable, you did not know, but we have one child who is no longer with us. She died several months ago. This has been extremely painful for us." The survivors learn from reactions of people if it is safe to say more or drop the conversation. Often the survivors will not have the opportunity to drop the conversation, because the asker has disappeared in a hurry.

SIX MONTHS TO FIRST YEAR

Reorganization

By 6 months there is usually some reorganization of the individual's and family's life. The degree of reorganization depends upon the impact of the loss. Some may feel as though they have recovered; for others, the pain is just as great, if not worse. Often it is worse because they are beginning to come out of the shock, "fog," or "jet-lag" period, and the reality that the loved one is not coming back is setting in.

Symptom Formation

At around the 6-month anniversary time, there tends to be an increase in symptom formation. This is even true for those who "think" they have completed their mourning. This date becomes an anticipated and dreaded time. Often symptoms will start increasing 2 to 4 weeks prior to the anniversary. This is not unusual and is, in fact, healthy. The pain of grief must be felt for recovery to occur.

The same process will also occur at the 1 year anniversary, and may be more pronounced. The potency of this time depends upon grief work that has been accomplished, the impact and circumstances of the death, attachment to the dead person, one's own personality, and other changes in one's life. Even though grief work may have been accomplished, often there is regression during this time. Then it is necessary to rework areas once again. For example, often there is a strong need to retell their story, new and frightening dreams may occur, or the person may start deteriorating physically.

I had been treating a young woman because her best friend and another person, along with her dog, were killed in a car accident caused by a reckless driver. She had an extreme survivor guilt response for being alive while the others were dead. She continually found ways to punish herself for being alive (e.g., accidents, alcohol, and drug abuse, and by quitting her activities). The symptoms increased tremendously at the 6-month and 1-year anniversaries. At the 1-year date she could not stand the pain any longer and ran away from home, thinking a "change of scenery" would calm the pain. Of course, it did not. It is often helpful for the survivor to know that these are going to be painful times, and that there is help, although no "cure-alls."

Anniversaries

The first year is filled with anniversaries, birthdays, holidays, and special days from the past. These days are usually dreaded and approached with much trepidation and sadness. First, it is sad to realize that the person is not here to celebrate. Second, there is a stark realization that things will never be "the same" again. Third, the memories of years past are very painful at this time.

The goal during this first year of bereavement is to make it through these days. There probably will be little joy or energy, and much sadness and tears. I encourage my families to try to plan these potent days, but to also plan some grieving and quiet time. Again, the survivors must do what is helpful for them. If it is important to have helpful people around—*do it!* If there is something that they need to do at the grave, like bring a plant or balloons—*do it!* It is often helpful to search and attempt to plan something prior to the day. Explore what will be helpful and hindering.

Often there are plans made for these painful days, but when the day arrives the survivors cannot carry them out as planned. I tell my patients not to kick themselves for the change. They need to give themselves credit for planning something, with the knowledge that it may not work. When the day arrives, it is often far worse than they ever imagined. But next year it may be better.

Time does not heal; people do the healing. Therefore, the plans for this year may not work, but, perhaps, because of their grief work, the plans will work next year. I also have my patients evaluate what they learned from that day—both helpful and hindering. These experiences can assist the survivors as they plan for future anniversary days.

These days, although painful, provide an opportunity to grieve creatively. One of my families, whose son died of SIDS, baked a cake for Kevin's first birthday. They took one piece to the grave, leaving it for the birds and squirrels to enjoy. Others have planned special days with supportive family or friends. One father whose daughter, Nancy, was killed gave an anonymous check to a local dance company for Christmas. His daughter had lived in a distant city but loved to dance. These altruistic behaviors often result in some positive feelings. Although the positive feelings may not last long, the survivors are able to feel something good on a painful day.

In therapy, we start planning and discussing the anniversaries well in advance. Many will start discussing Christmas in July. Usually the client, initially, brings up the topic and often comments that he is thankful he can discuss it, since he finds many forget "the" date or choose not to talk about it. We gradually attempt to plan together what will be helpful to them, both individually and as a family. I also discuss issues of increased symptom formation such as nightmares, crying, anger, guilt, and eating disorders. My clients become well educated about grief, and most of them say this education is helpful in understanding the process.

My clients are usually thankful when someone else remembers their painful days. A hug, flower, card, or phone call can be very helpful. That behavior is saying two things: "I too remember your loved one." and "You are an important person to me and I would like to help your pain." These acts are appreciated. The survivors feel so alone during these times and it is helpful to know that others do care.

Cleaning Out Clothing and Personal Effects

This is another painful task that usually takes place, to some extent, during the first year of bereavement. Some people choose to clean things out right away. Often there are regrets if this is done under the pressure of shock or others' needs and desires. Many of my families have come home from the hospital after their infant had died, or had had a stillbirth, only to find some good intending person had cleaned and rearranged everything—"like nothing ever happened." "It" did happen; there was a life, no matter how short! These acts are done with the goal of "I was only trying to help!" Initially, it may seem helpful, but often regrets and guilt, which are difficult to undo, may arise. There is also an issue of "protection," but people should not be protected from the pain of grief. These "helpful" people are always excellent examples of how people do not understand grief, yet think they are helping. Whose needs are they meeting?

Cleaning out a room or house is exhausting and should never be done all at once, especially if it is a potent death. It is usually more helpful to the survivors if they can gradually make these changes at home. It is the survivors who should make the decision as to when cleaning or changes should begin and where the clothes and articles should go; this takes time. I give my clients permission to take their time and move slowly in this area. There usually is no reason to rush this process, and, if it is rushed, regrets often result. It is unlike the process that parents often experience when their children write home or go off to college. Other members of the household start making plans for that person's room: "I can't wait to make Sally's room into a sewing room."

Many find the dead person's room comforting and will spend hours lying on the bed crying, talking, and remembering. This is usually helpful in expressing grief. If the room is comforting, it often takes much longer to be willing to let go of this environment.

Others cannot tolerate going into the room or house. When this is the case, we discuss the fears and attempt, very gradually, to desensitize the environment. One father, whose daughter was killed in a car accident, could not go near her room. It was not until much therapy was conducted, and he was into his second year of bereavement, that he could start entering her room and assist in rearranging it.

I was working with a beautiful person in her 80s whose husband had died after 65 years of marriage. Her daughters kept pushing her to get rid of "dad's things." She was not ready, but she was not strong enough to fight with her daughters. Often, others think they know what is best for the survivors, without considering their needs or history. We finally were able to get one of the daughters to understand her mother's need. Finally, Betty was ready. With many tears she packed up a life of memories. I suggested she keep a few things of which she was especially fond. In her own time she called the Salvation Army to pick up the remaining articles of clothing. We had planned that she would ask her granddaughter, of whom she was very fond, to come sit with her while she waited. She had his favorite sweater around her as she heard the clothing boxes being taken from the garage. Although it was sad for her, she felt good that she had done it in her own way and time.

Suicidal Thoughts and Plans

During anniversary times, as well as during the first year of bereavement, there is an increase in symptom formation, along with the increased realization that the person is really dead. Often this leads to an increase in suicidal thoughts and plans. This happens frequently, and the therapist, as well as the family, must always be alert that active or passive suicide may occur (see Chapter 3, Suicide). Ask your clients if they are experiencing thoughts or feelings of suicide and if they have a plan. They will usually tell you. If they do, a professional assessment needs to be made regarding the seriousness of the intent. If they will not say whether they have a plan, an assessment must be made to determine if, in fact, they do not, or whether they are "playing games" with you because they have decided to attempt suicide.

A suicide attempt or thought does not necessarily come on the anniversary itself. Often it is before, because they "can't bear to live to that date." Or it may occur after, since they are feeling that the "pain will never get better" and they just cannot go on living. A woman whose daughter died could not face life without her any longer and attempted suicide a week after the 1-year anniversary. A man whose son was hit by a train attempted suicide a month before the 1-year anniversary.

In many cases, the families are able to listen to the clues, which stem from desperate pain with the result that they seek help. Other times families do not hear, or do not know how to listen, thus avoiding the cries for help. Still, some know that if they are going to succeed at a suicide, they need to act "normal" and plan very well. In addition, there are so many who passively attempt, or succeed at, suicide that we do not label as such; for example, getting into a car accident, falling in the bathtub or "accidentally" shooting their gun.

It is often difficult to diagnose what is "normal" grieving behavior and when a "clinical depression" is being exhibited. Suicidal thoughts are very normal in a grieving person at any age. As mentioned above, suicidal thoughts or plans must always be assessed for potential harm. Some helpful areas to assess between normal grieving and potential suicide include the following:

1. Is there a change in sleeping patterns, especially early morning awakening? This symptom may also reflect depression, which one will always exhibit if they are thinking of suicide. The grieving person may wake 1 to 4 hours earlier than normal, may have trouble falling asleep or sleeping at all. A change in sleeping patterns does not always mean that there is a strong suicidal drive: sleeping changes are normal in a grieving person. However, it is a sign for caution, especially if a sleep pattern change suddenly occurs, gets worse, or is near an anniversary.

2. If a clinical depression and suicidal thoughts are present, there is often a morning "ebb-tide of spirits." The person feels worse in the morning and better by afternoon or evening. A typical grieving person will probably feel "awful" most of the day, and only gradually, after months, will they have positive feelings and thoughts.

3. Usually the level of interest in things and activities is a striking

indication that a person is depressed and may be suicidal. There is loss of interest in all kinds of things and activities. A clinically depressed person will probably not attempt new or usual daily activities. The lack of interest usually reflects the depth of the depression.

I was treating a woman because her son died. She had a grief response that developed into a clinical depression. Gradually she dropped out of every activity until she was spending most of the day in bed, without bathing or eating. There was nothing to get up for and achieve. She did attempt suicide when she had more energy, which often is the case.

A person with a "normal" grief response also has a lack of interest in unusual or new activities. This often occurs with or without having suicidal thoughts. It is normal to have the suicidal thoughts without acting upon them during this first year of bereavement. There is often a gradual increase in interest, however, although the person may not be aware of the change. Often they may have to force themselves to knit, watch television, or go to church. The difference between a person with clinical depression and a normal grief response is that the latter will initially try, even though they may not enjoy it, to participate in life activities.

4. Another means to assess if a person is suicidal is to ask them directly if they have suicidal thoughts or plans. Usually people are so shocked that one would be so direct that they will answer honestly without trying to cover their answers. This is especially true if the person is feeling ambivalent and "crying for help."

Active and passive suicides may occur in grieving people, as well as clinically depressed people. If the person has thoughts and plans, an assessment needs to be made regarding actual danger. Hospitalization may be needed. For people who do not need hospitalization, I have them sign an antisuicide contract for whatever amount of time they are willing—hours/days: "I, _____ , promise I will not actively or passively attempt suicide. If I find that I want to hurt myself, I will call Dr. Johnson (and other caretakers)." This contract is written, signed, and dated by the individual. Family members may also sign a support contract.

5. *Beware of initial or sudden improvements*. This is a strong indication that a suicide is planned. If a person, who had been seriously depressed, suddenly shows signs of lifted spirits, accompanied by expressed future plans and goals, and improved affect, do not believe that these are signs of health. The person may have come to a personal "solution": "I am going to take my life and you can't stop me. You will think I'm better because I am acting 'normal,' but I am just fooling you." This most often occurs after a person has sunk

to the lowest level of the depression and has begun to improve, which gives them more energy to think, plan, and act. This is an indicator for both a clinically depressed or grieving person.

6. Withdrawal is another symptom that is closely related to loss of interest. The potentially suicidal person will withdraw from contacts with friends, family, and associates. The more distance that is created with people and the less communicative they are, the poorer the chances are that the person will or can confide in another how desperate he or she feels. The normal grieving person may withdraw, but remain communicative with a small group of family members or friends. Their withdrawal often increases because they have no energy to give to others or to activities. To determine this, an assessment of the withdrawal and its reasons needs to be made.

7. A suicidal person will stop communicating about his thoughts and feelings. A person who can discuss how hopeless and helpless he feels is less likely to attempt suicide, because he is talking, releasing, and searching for an answer. It is important for both the depressed and grieving person to keep talking, or expressing thoughts and feelings in ways appropriate for that individual. If not, there is great concern for suicide.

8. If a person attempts suicide, the presence and expression of remorse and guilt has prognostic significance. The greater the remorse displayed and the sooner it appears, the more favorable the person's outlook; if this occurs, a second attempt is not likely immediately. In addition, if the attempt was well planned and they recover, a second attempt is probably not imminent, as long as remorse is also present. Conversely, a well-planned attempt, coupled with lack of remorse, increases the likelihood of a future attempt.

If a person wants to commit suicide there is not much one can do to stop them. It is important, however, to be aware of clues and cries for help that a person at high risk may present, either directly or indirectly. These clues may be very subtle; they may also relate to movement toward health.

For example, I was once a passenger in the car of one of my depressed, suicidal, and grieving clients. She had to park on a downward slant, very close to the edge of a high hill. When it came to backing out, she became extremely concerned that the car would move forward, carrying both of us over the cliff. This was the first glimmer of hope that she may have some want or need to protect herself, and me, from harm.

The grieving person may often express suicidal thoughts and plans, but never intend to carry them to action. The thoughts come from

;y, hopeless, and powerless: "Why go on?" Until there
;ion to life, there seems to be little reason to carry on

Sexual Intercourse

Another "task" in the reorganization of a survivor's life is the
resumption of sexual intercourse. This decision is based upon an
individual's and couple's need. Clinically, I often find that a person
will have a strong need to have intercourse, especially right after the
death of an adult significant other, although this may also occur after
the death of a child. This may or may not be with his/her partner.
The reason most often relates to comfort, caring, and a reaffirmation
of life. One woman told me she had gone home for her father's
funeral and ended up calling her old boyfriend. She had such a strong
need to be close to him, or anyone, that they had intercourse, for
which she felt very guilty.

I have had parents who, after the death of their child, will come
home from the hospital, crawl into bed, and have intercourse. Most
often the reason is to become pregnant rather than for comfort
(Johnson, 1984) (see pp. 130–136). People who have intercourse
right after a death often express guilt, "How could I think of sex at a
time like that?"

Others, however, abstain from intercourse after a death. This is
especially true if their child has died. From my research, those parents who had a short preparation time for death tended to abstain
longer than those with a long preparation time (Johnson-Soderberg,
1982). The abstinence lasts anywhere from several weeks to a year.
In clinical practice, I have had parents who abstained for several
years.

The parents reported that their lack of sexual interest, no matter
how short, resulted from being "engulfed with grief," and, therefore,
they had no desire or energy for sex. Although sex was an un-
welcome activity for most of the parents, there was a desire to be held
and to be close to each other. Both the men and women agreed that
this behavior was out of the ordinary for the men. In men's past sex
lives, they could not be physically close without having sex. The
women were surprised by this change in behavior, and the men often
expressed the feeling that they now understood why their wives
enjoyed, and were comforted by, hugging.

This closeness was also reaffirmed by the couples who had had
intercourse right after their child's death. Sex was a reaffirmation of
life and supported the strong need to be close and take care of each

other. These couples felt that sexual intercourse was the closest they could get to one another.

There seem to be four factors that relate to the issue of a decrease in sexual intercourse after a death. First, a decrease in sexual activity may occur because sex has not been an important activity in the marriage prior to the death. This may be the result of a low sexual desire or sexual "hang-ups." A second factor that must be assessed is whether marital problems existed prior to the death. Sex may have been decreasing because of these problems. A third consideration is whether the woman is postpartum. Couples are frequently advised to abstain from sexual intercourse for at least 6 weeks after a birth, independent of the type of delivery or its outcome. The fourth factor relates to the preparation time for the death, and being able to fill the void that was left with other activities. When a death is sudden, many parents have little, if any, time to prepare themselves for the death of their child. Therefore, the "hole" or the "void" that the child's death creates has not been filled or reinvested. This was especially true for the mothers with a short preparation time; they felt that their life's work and activities were taken away when their child died so quickly.

In most cases, the parents with a longer preparation time had time to begin to fill the holes with other activities before the child died. Some of these parents, especially women, had gone back to school or work and had begun to reinvest their time and energy. Men usually did not verbalize the need to fill vacant time; their life tended to be organized with work, home, community activities, and recreation. However, if the parents with a long preparation time did not begin to utilize the anticipatory bereavement in order to start reorganizing their lives, their response was similar to that of the short preparation group.

For many of the women in both groups, the investment in time, energy, and attachment was almost totally with their children, rather than the spouse, outside activities, or work. When their child died, the loss produced a vast emptiness that caused much stress, guilt, and grief symptoms. Because they had invested all their time in childcare activities, they tended to be at high risk for survivor bereavement, since there was so much empty time that needed to be filled. The void took longer to fill and was more obvious. Although the attachment is different, its vastness could be related to a person who retires without any plans; because of the emptiness that results, they, too, are at high risk.

The emptiness was so overwhelming that, for many, daily activities were difficult to accomplish. This included sexual intercourse. There was no need or energy for it. In addition, sexual intercourse symbolized the creation of this now dead child. The hole that was created by the death, and the subsequent guilt and symptoms, made sex an unwelcomed act.

One way that this void could be filled was to have another child, or a "subsequent" child. Parents also believed another child would assist them in undoing their guilt. Once this decision was made, sex became a welcomed act not for pleasure or comfort, but for procreation. This decison was especially apparent when the parents were asked if they had made a "decision to go on living." In order to make the decision to begin living again, a reason or purpose had to be found. One reason was to have another child (Johnson, 1982, 1984).

Replacement and Subsequent Children

Parents who have had a child die often have a strong desire and need to have another child. Some go to great lengths to accomplish this. Often, children who are born after a death of a sibling develop emotional pathology. The issue of child development following a previous sibling's death is important, not only from research and clinical positions, but from a parental one as well.

The two terms, replacement and subsequent, have different meanings. *Replacement children* tend to be conceived because of pathological issues and grief with the parents. This pathology develops or is potentiated because of the previous death. There is then the possibility that the child develops emotional problems because of the previous death.

A *subsequent child,* on the other hand, is one who has also been born after the death of a sibling, but does not develop emotional problems because of the previous death. Although I am continuing to conduct research on the difference between the two types of children born following the death of a sibling, some interesting issues arise from the data suggesting that not all subsequent children develop into replacement children.

Most of the parents in my study group had another child as a means of not only "beginning to live again" in order to fill the void, but a means of undoing the guilt from their child's death. Parents would often make statements like: "We have another chance." or "We'll be better parents this time."

The need for a subsequent child and the guilt feelings associated with the creation of this child have been reported in other studies (Cain & Cain, 1964; Joseph & Tabor, 1961; Legg & Sherick, 1976:

Natterson & Knudson, 1960; Poznanski, 1972). These studies found that guilt may be transferred to and affect the subsequent child.

It appears from my research and practice that once the subsequent child learns there was a previous child, he or she may develop what Lifton termed "survivor guilt" (Johnson, 1982, 1984; Lifton, 1967). Frequently, the subsequent child learns that the previous child had to die before he or she could be wanted, conceived, or adopted. Therefore, he or she begin to express phases like, "Why am I alive while my sister had to die?" or "I feel guilty because I am alive and my brother is dead." Consequently, a child growing up after the death of a previous child has the potential to develop pathology. One of the first issues in the development of pathology seems to deal with how, when, and why the parents decide to have another child.

My research with 14 couples who had had a child die and were in their first year of bereavement, revealed differences between the short preparation group (SPG) and the long preparation group (LPG) in deciding to have another child. Of the 8 couples in the SPG, 4 couples had a child within the first year of bereavement, three were pregnant at the time of the interviews, and 1 became pregnant soon after the interviews. Two others had children early in the second year of bereavement. Therefore, 6 of the 8 couples were pregnant some time during the first year of bereavement (Johnson-Soderberg, 1982).

One woman in the SPG had physical problems and was advised not to become pregnant, although she and her husband talked about adoption. They also paid the burial expenses and donated a grave to a dead newborn who was found in a garbage can. Soon after, they assumed the care of a foster child diagnosed with apnea (their child had died of SIDS). This couple divorced soon after returning the foster child, in the second year of bereavement. The other couple had a remaining newborn twin and did not feel the need to have another child, although they had discussed it. Since the study two of these couples have had a second child.

The LPG couples were older than the SPG couples (see Table 4-1). Three LPG couples were no longer of childbearing age. One woman who was still of childbearing age had physical problems and believed she should not become pregnant again. She had a tubal ligation a year after the death of their son. One couple had a baby in the first year of bereavement, but divorced in the second year of bereavement (in addition, this woman had an abortion in the second year due to a pregnancy after a rape by her husband). The sixth couple had had a spina bifida child and were too frightened to have another baby.

TABLE 4-1. Mean Age of Parents

	Age (N=28)	SPG (N=16)	LPG (N=12)
Mothers	31.7	29.6	34.5
Fathers	33.8	31.5	36.8

In summary, two years after the death of their children, 7 of the 11 childbearing couples had a subsequent child, 1 had a remaining twin, 2 had physical problems, and 1 chose not to have another child because of the handicap of the one who died. Also in that second year, 2 couples were pregnant with their second child since the death.

Although these couples believed they could not "replace" their dead child, they wanted another child of the same sex, and as quickly as possible (see Table 4-2). One couple had intercourse as soon as they returned home from finding out their child had died of SIDS. Couples, both in this study and in my practice, have gone to great lengths to achieve a pregnancy. One father had a vasectomy reversed a month after his child died and their subsequent child was born prematurely, 9 months to the day after the reversal of the vasectomy!

TABLE 4-2. Replacement Births in First Year of Bereavement (by Preparation Time for Death and Parental Age)

	SPG (N=16)*	LPG (N=12)	Total (N=28)
Mother's age	29.6	34.5	31.7
Father's age	31.5	36.8	33.8
Pregnancies in first year of bereavement	6	1	7

*N = number of individuals. For instance, in the SPG group there were 16 individuals, making 8 couples, which had 6 pregnancies.

Parents mentioned that they would like to name the next child the same name as the one who died. No one actually did this, but the parents unconsciously used the same letter of the previous child (e.g., Sven-Sarah, Sally-Steve). An extreme example was a 50-year-old patient, Darah, who presented extreme grief and depression when her 24-year-old son moved out of the house. As we worked together, it was uncovered that she was a replacement child and also had a child who died. She always felt much survivor guilt and knew she was an unwanted child. The secrets about her childhood were slowly revealed: She had never been legally named. She was called Carrie. When she was in her 30s she asked to be legally named: Her mother named her Darah, the name of the dead sister.

In my study group, when the subsequent child was born and was the opposite sex of the dead child, parents were initially disappointed and upset. They often expressed much guilt for being upset. However, they usually would laugh, uncomfortably, and say they finally decided to "keep" the child.

Replacement children are very much a clinical concern. The previously mentioned research on replacement children used replacement children who were already in treatment for mental pathology. In the early 1960s, Albert and Barbara Cain (1964) worked with disturbed replacement children. They saw these children in treatment at least 8 to 13 years after the death of the previous child. They discovered two important things about the parents of these disturbed children. First, the mothers were predominantly guilt-ridden, depressive, phobic, compulsive, and had experienced large numbers of family losses in their own childhood. Second, the parents had an intense narcissistic investment in the dead child.

Lehrman (1956), Natterson and Knudson (1960), and Solnit and Green (1959) also reported personality "danger signs" in parents attempting to have a replacement child. These parents tended to have premorbid, phobic, obsessive, and depressive characteristics. Also, parents who are older find it difficult, if not impossible, to raise a young child. They also found that excessive idealization of the dead child, the suddenness of the child's death, and the death of an older child increases the danger in producing a replacement child.

Could there be a "normal" need for parents of childbearing age to want to continue to bear and parent another child? If parents "live" for their children and that goal is extinguished, can they "replace" a child without having a pathological outcome? How do we, the clinicians, counsel parents who want and "need" another child so that they become subsequent rather than replacement children? Exploration of others' research as well as my own may help answer some of these questions. There are some indicators that may help parents in this position make a responsible decision regarding another child.

In assessing and counseling parents regarding another child, it is imperative to assess the "completion of grief" and mental health of the parents. The Cains' study reported that the children were born into a world of mourning, of apathetic or withdrawn parents, and a world that was focused upon the past; worshipping the image of the dead child. In my research, all of the parents who had a baby, or were pregnant in the first and second year of bereavement, had made a decision to start living again. They did not exhibit apathetic or withdrawn behavior. Although they still missed and grieved their dead child, they had begun to fill the void that was left by the death. Although frightened about the unknown, all of them were extremely excited and pleased about the forthcoming child.

Another area to assess is the age of the parents. In the Cains' study all the parents were older (late 30s and early 40s) and were not prepared for the disruption of a new baby in the home. Although it is not said directly, it is implied that these parents chose not to have more children before the death occurred, and usually, the child that died had been of latency age or early adolescence.

All but one couple in my study who had another child were starting families, and the dead children were between 9 days to 3 years of age. Except for one couple, the parents were in their 20s and early 30s. This couple had two children, the youngest of which was 3 when he was killed. Previously, they had no intentions of having any more children and so the father had had a vastectomy. However, the accidental death of Sven encouraged them to reevaluate that decision.

A third area that I assess is whose decision it is to have another child. The Cains' study reported it was the mother's decision to have another baby, with little, if any, involvement from the father. In my study, all but one couple had mutually made the decision to have another baby. That couple divorced early in the second year of bereavement. All couples who decided to have a child believed they had discussed the issue thoroughly and were excited about the decision.

An important feeling to assess is the "amount" and "intensity" of parental guilt. The feeling of guilt, especially in the mothers, was concurrent in both studies. Since unresolved guilt may have an effect upon the emotional development of a subsequent child, it must be dealt with extensively in practice. Unresolved guilt can be "played out" by projection, identifying the new child with the dead child, overprotection, conspiracy of silence, detachment, negative scripting, and many other behaviors or motives.

Ultimately it is the parents' decision whether to have another child. It is not, and should not be, a clinician's decision. Ethically, however, I may assist parents to make a responsible "adult" decision, for we have enough casualties in our world already. I explore with them clinical and research experience, as well as their own level and intensity of grief. They come to realize they cannot, and should not, have another child in the hopes that their previous one will return.

They must be able to accept and love this child for who he is in and of himself. This is a very difficult and painful process because experiencing the death of a child sheds a completely different light on issues of life, death, children, parenting, protectiveness, and happiness. Many parents would do "anything" to regain that child.

What happens to the parents who are not able to become pregnant again or who are past childbearing years? Often, even older or menopausal couples will try very hard for several years to have another child, secretly knowing it is not possible. This often causes much pressure and pain in the marriage. The pressures and strain seem similar to that of young couples who are going through fertility testing. After much struggle, they will often come to a mutual understanding that another child will not be conceived. Even then there is often a secret wish that it will occur. Depression often results because much anger is repressed.

As with other grieving people, it is important for older adults who are unable to have another child to channel the pain into some useful purpose, which involves the whole "decision to live again." It is in this important reorganization process that bereavement outcomes are developed. This decision-making process with these parents, as with as other grieving people, seems to make the difference in the outcome. Those that can channel their energies and attachments into new arenas or previous interests, tend to do better physically and emotionally in the long term.

One example involves an older couple whose youngest child died of Reye's syndrome at age 11. They tried for two years to have another child. They were in their 40s and had two other children, one in high school and one in college. The man had his vasectomy reversed, but no pregnancy resulted. In much frustration they gave up trying for a pregnancy. The woman decided to start a much needed preschool, which would allow her to care for children "as if they were my own."

People who do not make that decision or follow through with their goals tend to develop into angry, bitter, and detached people. Their behavior often becomes passive-aggressive in nature, stabbing at people who have complete families, resisting any positive change in their lives, or hanging onto phrases like, "life isn't fair."

Granted, it is easy to become angry at life when your child has died. It is a very difficult and painful time. Many variables are involved, as we have seen, in the outcome of grief. Some may choose to be angry and bitter all their lives, thinking it is a way of "getting back" for what has happened to them; others will not know they are angry or channel it into unhealthy behaviors because of their own lack of insight; and still others will attempt to change their grief, with or without professional help.

SUMMARY

In summary, the first year of bereavement is a very potent, dangerous, and painful time for the survivors. There is not much pleasure or hope. The days are dark; some darker than others. It is important for the survivors to feel their grief. As Crowles said, "Grief is itself a med'cine" (Cowper, 1968). In addition, the tasks of the first year must be accomplished, although there is no timetable for grief, which may carry the tasks into the second year. One will always feel the pain, but one does have the opportunity to process the pain, "give sorrow words" and make good and healthy decisions for his or her life. These are not easy tasks, and often it is very healthy and advisable to receive professional help during this time.

REFERENCES

Bullfinch's Mythology. (1964). Fertham, Middlesex, England: The Hamlyn Publishing Group-Spring Books.

Cain, A., & Cain, B. (1964, July). On replacing a child. *Journal of American Academy of Child Psychiatry, 3,* 443–456.

Cowper, W. (1968). Charity, 1. 86. In *The Oxford dictionary of quotations.* London: Oxford University Press.

Johnson, M. (1963). Sex role learning in the nuclear family. *Child Development, 34,* 319–333.

Johnson, S. (1984). Sexual intimacy and replacement children after the death of a child. *Omega, 15,* (2), 109–118.

Johnson-Soderberg, S. (1982). The ethos of parental bereavement and guilt, (Doctoral dissertation, University of Michigan, 1982). *Dissertation Abstracts International* (University of Microfilm, Ann Arbor, Michigan, 1982).

Joseph, Edt., & Tabor, J. (1961). The simultaneous analysis of a pair of twins and the twinning reaction. *Psychoanalytic Study of the Child, 16,* 275–299.

Keirsey, D., & Bates, M. (1978). *Please understand me: Character and treatment types.* Del Mar, CA: Prometheus Nemesis Books.

Kübler-Ross, E. (1969). *On death and dying.* New York: MacMillan.

Legg, C., & Sherick, A. (1976, Winter) The replacement child—A developmental tragedy: Some preliminary comments. *Child Psychiatry and Human Development, 7,* 113–126.

Lehrman, S. R. (1956). Reactions to untimely death. *Psychiatric Quarterly, 30,* 546–578.

Lifton, R. J. (1967). *Death in life: Survivors of Hiroshima.* New York: Vintage Books Edition.

Natterson, J., & Knudson, A. (1960). Observations concerning fear of death in fatally ill children and their mothers. *Psychosomatic Medicine, 22,* 456–465.

Poznanski, E. (1972). The "replacement child": A saga of unresolved parental grief. *Journal of Pediatrics 81,* (6), 1190–1193.

Solnit, A. J., & Green, M. (1959, June). Psychological considerations in the management of deaths on pediatric hospital services: 1. The doctor and the child's family. *Pediatrics, 24,* 106–112.

Time, April 15, 1985, p. 83.

Worden, J. W. (1982). *Grief counseling and grief therapy: A handbook for the mental health practitioner.* New York: Springer.

CHAPTER V

The Second and Third Year of Bereavement

> in time my tears will diminish
> in time . . .
>   not now
>   not yet
>   in time . . .
>
>   elizabeth
>   (used with permission)

The pain of grief is not magically terminated at the end of the first year of bereavement. In fact, many of my patients say the second and third years are even worse. Very little attention is given in the literature or in our society to the second and subsequent years of bereavement. And yet, the grief continues.

These next several years are very important, since a number of issues need to be resolved. These years are crucial because if repression, avoidance, or the maintenance of unresolved issues of grief continue during this time, complicated grief will begin to emerge. There are several issues that are critical to the development of complicated versus uncomplicated grief: a decision to live again, along with a reorganization of one's life, should "begin" or continue; symptom formation should be decreasing, although there will be times during the years when it is increased; and themes and symptoms should be resolved. These topics, together with a discussion of indicators of complicated versus uncomplicated grief, the "ending" of mourning and appropriate candidates for grief therapy, will be discussed in this chapter.

THE DECISION TO LIVE ONCE AGAIN

Although the decision to live again was discussed in the "First Year of Bereavement," it is often not until the second or third year of bereavement that this process actively begins to take place. The length of time that it takes to make a decision to live again depends upon the factors discussed previously: preparation time for the death; relationship to the person; degree of attachment to the person; preventability of the death; "completion" of grief or unresolved grief from previous losses; personality type; and social, economic, religious, ethnic, and cultural factors. Therefore, it is not unusual, and may even be desirable because of the impact of the loss, for the process of restoring to begin sometime in the second or third year.

When this decision is made too quickly, it is often not a firm or committed decision. It is frequently made for the wrong reason, such as avoidance, denial, or escape: "I cannot stand the pain. I have to do something." It often takes several years to experience completely and "work out" the pain of grief before one is willing, able, and committed to make the decision to go on living.

In counseling, it is helpful to listen and assess aspects that indicate that the person "might" be starting to think about future ideas, hopes, and plans. Often the indicators are very subtle and involve short-term goals, such as buying a needlework project. (I do not mean even starting the project; just the thought, plan, and act of buying it takes tremendous effort!)

The person is not necessarily aware that behaviors are changing because of the subtleties of the process and lack of grief knowledge. Nor are these futuristic thoughts or plans necessarily related to what will eventually be the goal that will stimulate issues of change, hope, happiness, or excitement in life. These "small" predecisions and actions are a means to test the waters. Success at small goals may help produce confidence so that larger goals can be attempted. These small goals, however, may bring feelings of success and pleasure, which make the survivor uncomfortable, since there is often a belief that pleasure should no longer to be experienced by them.

Pleasure often stimulates guilt feelings, "I shouldn't be happy since my child died. That makes me feel guilty." Masochistic personalities in particular have difficulty feeling pleasure without guilt. It is helpful for grieving people with a major loss to be in therapy so that these feelings and thoughts can be explored. Often, I will say something like the following to my patients:

> If you can attempt to separate feelings (thoughts) of sadness about your child's death and other feelings (thoughts), it often helps you to understand the difference. You can begin to see that you can still feel (think) sadness about the death, while feeling (thinking) pleasure about your accomplishments. It is a separate issue.

As these small and large steps are made to "live again," I often see an increase in empathetic response toward others with a similar loss. My patients tell me that they find that they read the obituaries more frequently, for various reasons, and when they find a similar situation they often send a card or note to the grief stricken family. These efforts are often another way of getting close to a decision to start living by "getting out myself and beginning to see that others besides me have loss and pain. If I can help them a little by knowing they are not alone, I feel better."

The therapist or other health professional needs to be aware of these short-term plans, goals, successes, failures, and progression toward longer and more complicated goals. These changes support the decision-making and reorganizational process. This slow and quiet process is, I believe, the central focus of learning to live without one's loved one.

Once a healthy and committed decision is made, relief, peace, and a calmness emerge. In addition, there is usually a rapid decrease in symptom formation. These signs are excellent indicators that a decision to live again has been reached. That does not mean the pain is gone, which will never happen completely. The pain has changed from what I term a "torturing pain" to a "sweet sadness or sorrow."

SYMPTOM FORMATION

Separate from, but in addition to, the decision-making process, symptom formation usually decreases to some extent during the second and third year of bereavement. There may be several reasons for this decrease. First, hopefully the person has expressed their grief symptoms "enough" to "get it out" (recall Adam's story of "When will I stop crying?"). "Giving sorrow words" (in addition to tears, dreams, feelings, thoughts, and reactions) results in dissipation of symptoms. This is by all means the healthiest and most productive way to handle grief, although each must conduct this in his or her own way. If the loss has been significant, it takes 2, 3, or 4 years for the symptoms to be sufficiently expressed and for detachment to take place.

However, often the pain is so bad, or its anticipation is so bad, that avoidance is utilized. For example, many of my clients who are parents, especially the women, who have had an infant die, will avoid situations like baptisms. The avoided situations relate directly to intense memories of a celebration, ritual, or experience that centered on the now dead loved one. This may be a wedding after a spouse has died, returning to a favorite vacation place, or eating alone in a favorite restaurant. The situation or event is so painful in thought that one cannot tolerate the intensity, and thus the event is avoided.

Eventually the situational pain has to be confronted. The intense situations or events often cannot be confronted until the second or third year, since prior to this time there is little energy or ego-strength to accomplish it and any attempt is met with "failure." Consciously confronting or avoiding the pain is an individual decision. Whether one avoids the painful situation or not is in and of itself an initial confrontation of the pain. If the confrontation occurs, one is able to understand the decision-making process rather than just avoiding the issue or situation altogether.

One woman whose husband died 18 months prior to her therapy was very ambivalent about attending a church service where many of her husband's favorite hymns were to be sung. She had always avoided such situations in the past. As we discussed the ambivalence, she realized her hesitancy related to the anticipation of feeling intense grief pain and wishing to avoid pain. Yet, she really wanted to hear the hymns.

The need to experience and feel the pain was discussed and "exit behaviors," such as sitting in the back of the church by a door and asking a supportive friend to sit with her, were developed so that if the situation became intolerable she could leave. The pain was great, she cried quietly through the entire service, but much to her amazement she felt less pain the next day. She had confronted the situation, made it through the entire service (a tremendous accomplishment), and expressed her grief pain. All of this brought her relief, with additional side effects of feeling good about herself, and believing that the next time might not be as painful.

These avoidance behaviors are probably not new and are something that the survivor has been doing since the death. In the second and third year, however, these situations need confrontation or some physical or emotional pathology will probably develop, because of the avoidance and development of denial. Denial behaviors often become so intense that the person does not recognize them.

One reason that symptom formation tends to dissipate is because our culture assists in the production of denial. We have developed into "pleasure seekers" and are intolerant of any type of physical or emotional pain in ourselves or others. We want people to be "over their grief." We might tolerate others' grief pain during the first several weeks and perhaps as long as a year after the death. Certainly, after a year, avoidance of the topic is evident and a critical need develops for the nongriever to protect himself/herself from the survivor's pain.

The grieving person, however, continues to experience the grief pain, which is often more intense. But he/she has "learned" not to express it because it is usually not welcomed: "I have become very good at covering what I am really feeling. Everyone says to me, 'Oh, you look so good now. You must be all over your grief.' But on the inside, it's worse." Often, the nongrieving people want others to be over their grief so that it may support their myth that "everything is fine once again."

During the second and third year, grief symptoms should gradually decrease in intensity, duration, and potency if the person has done her grief work in the expression of pain. When symptoms increase or surface during this time and remain as potent as initially experienced, it is probably due to several factors. First and foremost, it means that they have not done their grief work and consequently there is no reason for the symptoms to dissipate.

At special times of the year, such as holidays, anniversaries, and birthdays, symptoms tend to increase temporarily. These will always be painful times because the memories—good and bad—are abundant. These are special times and are a celebration of life: "That is difficult to do when part of us is not here to celebrate the event." As difficult as the events remain, symptoms are usually not as intense or abundant.

In addition, many will indicate that there has been no expression or need to express symptoms for "long periods" of time. Then, often "out of the blue it just comes in waves." The unpredictability may or may not be related to a situation, event, or another loss. It just seems that there is a less frequent need to express symptoms if they have done their grief work in the past. Since grief is never really completed, however, some expression of symptoms may occur periodically.

An increase in symptoms often occurs if there is another loss. This may be true during the first several years or later. Unresolved grief themes are again brought to conscious levels with the subsequent loss or change. The loss does not even need to be significant for the "regrief" to occur. This is often confusing to the person, because he cannot figure out why he is reacting so vehemently to "losing a silly pen," "having my dog die," "a woman at work died whom I hardly knew," or "my great aunt died whom I had not seen since childhood."

Regrief is also common for children to exhibit. Children may grieve at their own level and when they get older or there is another loss, they will regrieve the childhood loss. Often this is confusing to the child and parents alike. A seemingly "normal" child may start to have extreme separation anxiety for no apparent reason. So it was with Eve, a fourth grader. She refused to go to school, although this had never been a problem in the past. Her mother brought her to me and it was uncovered that she was feeling very guilty for her grandmother's death, which occurred when she was 5. Her regrief was stimulated by the death of a close friend of her mother.

Often the regrief may get acted out in destructive adolescent behaviors, which may go unrecognized. This was evidenced by Sam, a 15-year-old, whom I counseled while he was in juvenile hall for multiple home robberies. When he was 5, he and three other siblings were playing with matches and started a fire from which Sam was the only survivor. He subsequently exhibited masochistic and destructive behavior during adolescence. He had such strong feelings that he needed to be punished that I was never able to change his guilt into constructive behaviors. Others may delay grief until adult years.

It is important to assess the reasons for an increase or decrease in symptoms during these years. An increase of symptoms for the "wrong reasons" can be just as destructive as a decrease in symptoms through denial. Therefore, the potency, duration, and intensity of symptom formation during this time are critical to the long-term emotional and physical health of the individual and family.

THEMES

The themes that have been utilized should be resolved during the second and third years. If themes like conspiracy of silence, scapegoating, detachment, masochism, or grief symptom formation continue to exist, physical or emotional pathology often results. This may develop into complicated bereavement. For example, I often see couples who have had a child die continue the detachment from each other with no wish, desire, or effort for it to redevelop. This continual process often results in separation and divorce.

A scapegoating theme may initially be a benign behavior however, it may progress and erupt into a destructive process toward a weak member of a family or even project into situations like malpractice law suits.

I have often seen, when a parent or child has died in a family, scapegoating or conspiracy of silence themes develop. After several years the scapegoated member, usually a child, has "learned" his or her role, and will begin acting out against himself or herself to continue the destructive process.

For example, Alden was 10 years old when his father died suddenly. His mother was very resentful that she had to be a single parent, find a job, and be responsible for three children. Her anger continually was projected onto Alden. He began to lose confidence, internalize guilt, and develop self-hatred: "I always felt like it was my fault my dad died and my mom had to go to work." Three and half years after his father's death the scapegoating process was accelerated and internalized by stealing and school problems. Adolescence is a difficult time in anyone's life, without having it complicated with unresolved grief themes.

Therefore, although these second and third years tend to be a quieting time for symptoms, it is important that the themes are resolved and not repressed or continued. If they are, additional cause for alarm exists because of the increased chance of pathology within the family system. Grief therapy is often needed because the person or family has become stuck and realize they are not progressing. In addition, resolution of the themes has often been avoided, not recognized, or repressed. Although it has already been stated, it is worth repeating: *It is easier to prevent pathology than to undo it later.*

COMPLICATED VERSUS UNCOMPLICATED GRIEF

I hope by this time the reader has some understanding of the complexity of *uncomplicated grief*. Complicated grief is even more ramified. Forgive me if I imply through my use of language, imagery, and examples in this section, that complicated grief is easily defined and diagnosed. It is not. The process is difficult, includes multiple variables, and definitely involves mind and body interactions, which are difficult to prove.

The most unscientific statement I could possibly make is this: Initially diagnosing complicated grief is often based upon experience and a clinical "intuition" that "something is wrong." I know what complicated grief "feels" like in interacting with a patient or family. It is difficult to define what it looks like, why it happens, how it is being expressed, and what the prognosis is. In addition, one must assess prolongation or avoidance of symptoms, unresolved themes, low level of functioning since the death, and no decision to go on living. The indicators of each will be discussed.

If grief is repressed or avoided, complicated grief can develop. Complicated grief involves physical or emotional pathology. The pathology displays itself in various symptom formations. Grief must be expressed—give sorrow words—or it will find its own expression. Just as water will find a course of least resistance, so will grief. Mind and body will unconsciously work together in a similar path of least resistance so that symptoms may be manifested even though symbolic and unconscious.

In complicated grief there is often a fine line between normal, exaggerated, and prolonged symptom formation. The symptoms that are expressed in the first several years of bereavement are normal, healthy, and need expression. When grief is repressed or avoided, symbolic symptoms often become "prolonged" or exaggerated and form the basis of complicated grief. During this evolutionary process of complicated grief, which often takes years, symptoms may either remain the same, although prolonged and severe, as they have been throughout grief or the grief symptoms become repressed and obtain symbolic and unconscious expression.

Therefore, if the grief continues without any evidence of resolution toward the end of the second and third year, pathology often develops from the expression of physical or emotional symptoms, such as asthma, arthritis, ulcers, ulcerative colitis, phobias, depression, anorexia, or bulemia. All of these diseases are a symbolic attempt either to keep the grief pain inside (depression, asthma, ulcers) or expel it (bulemia, colitis). The disease process continues because the underlying issue is not confronted.

Often it is difficult, if not impossible, for the survivor to see the need to uncover and understand the triggering source of the disease. This is usually because denial is so deeply rooted. In addition, since the pathology or disease can become life threatening, it becomes a priority to deal with the symptoms rather than the cause.

For example, a woman was being treated for a severe and prolonged case of ulcerative colitis. An ostomy was needed because of the threat to her life. Her physician insisted that she receive emotional help, but the woman did everything to sabotage her treatment with me. Although her physician tried and tried to convince her to be "compliant," she refused to see any connection between the past loss of two of her children and the colitis. The physician was frustrated because he was very much in support of holistic care. We in the health care professions, however, must always be reminded that we are not able to conduct treatment unless the patient is committed to that process.

Another issue to consider in complicated versus uncomplicated grief is that "pathology" rarely develops within the "first year" of bereavement unless other pathological issues have already existed or are triggered by the death. I use the term pathology here because the predisposing factors to the creation of problems have already existed, rather than develop from the death. In other words, the death stimulates the pathology rather than creates it.

It is difficult to diagnose pathology in the first year because symptoms are pronounced and severe anyway. It is helpful to take a good history to determine whether there have been emotional or physical problems in the past or previous losses that may result in regrief issues. Here the line gets foggier because there can be regrief issues without pathology. The most reliable clue indicating that there could be problems developing, or evidence that pathology is already present, is when the number and complexity of symptoms continues to increase rather than decrease over the first 6 to 12 months of bereavement, or are translated into physical symptoms. In other words, the symptoms are prolonged, pronounced, or exaggerated for that person; there has been no conscious decision to go on living; no goals have been developed; there is little if any hope; and the person appears to be "just existing" and exhibits a lower level of functioning.

As difficult as it is to diagnose pathology early in the bereavement process, it is more obvious with people with exaggerated symptom formation. Their hurt is often a "call for help." The ones who "fall down the crack," so to speak, are the "stoic," controlling, denying, and "thinking" (versus "feeling"-as in the Myers-Briggs study) people (Keirsey & Bates, 1978). These people tend to repress their grief and may eventually obtain symbolic and unconscious expression.

It is also difficult to evaluate complicated versus uncomplicated grief because no two people are really alike and no one experiences any type of death (loss, change, crisis) in the same manner, nor remains the same person after such an experience. Each gains and loses some level of emotional and physical health depending upon personality factors, such as strengths, weaknesses, and personality type; previous experiences with loss; type and circumstances of the present loss; support, such as groups or religion; previously learned coping mechanisms and themes; and helpful and hindering people.

People have similar experiences but never respond or "come out" the same. In crisis situations I see more and more that it is qualities within the person, supported by the "environment," which produce survivors as well as those who deteriorate. I see both types in treatment, so I believe the phrase "strong people never need help" is a myth. It is the process, energy, and effort on the part of both the therapist and the patient that make the difference in the end result. "Survivors" will make it, but so can the others; it just takes longer.

Symptoms of Complicated Grief

As mentioned above, there are definite symptoms and behaviors that reflect complicated grief. Many of these need careful probing and are only admitted after trust is developed between the therapist and patient. These symptoms and behaviors tend to be "secret," which the patient recognizes as "crazy" but does not want to "give them up." Others are more obvious and give the initial clinical indications that complicated grief is present or developing.

Worden (1982) provides an excellent discussion on abnormal grief reactions. Although our perceptions of complicated grief are similar, I included additional information.

Usually the survivor cannot talk about the dead person without "wearing her emotions on her sleeves." No matter what year of bereavement, there is always a freshness about the grief, as if it happened yesterday.

I was called to do a consultation on a woman who was having surgery for her peptic ulcers. There had been no apparent history of loss or death, but the physician believed "something was wrong." As I talked with her I noticed a picture, almost hidden, of a young boy. When I asked about him, the tears came. Her son had been run over by a car. The grief was abundant and fresh. I assumed it was recent, but clarified to find out that the death had occurred 8 years earlier. Although there is no "real time" when grief ends, discussing the dead person with a continual freshness in the sadness is a large clue that unresolved grief is present.

Another indication is when the person has an intense grief reaction to a relatively minor crisis. This may occur in response to breaking a dish, a minor traffic accident, or losing a personal article. There need not be a close attachment to the article that is lost or broken for a severe response to be experienced.

Often themes of loss may be discussed by the survivor. On the other hand, sometimes themes of loss are denied or a discomfort exists regarding discussion of the topic. A clinician with insight can pick up issues of denial or "overkill" in discussion.

The survivor often constructs a special area that is worshipped in secret. Shrining areas are usually not disturbed or verbally acknowledged by other members of the family. Often these areas contain clothing or articles that belonged to the dead person, memorabilia from the funeral, or an article that carries great attachment or significance, such as a family bible. As the shrining behaviors progress they develop into compulsive or ritualistic behaviors: "I can't start my day without first feeling the trunk with Mary's clothes in it." "Every time I walk pass my secret drawer, I have to stop, smell her clothes, and think—'this can never happen again.' "

Refusal to dispose of clothing and other belongings of the dead person is often connected with the shrining: "I kept her room just as it was the day she died; it still is that way (5 years later, the dirty clothes were still on the floor). Granted, cleaning out belongings usually takes a "long time" to accomplish, is very potent, and reflects the finality of the loss. Therefore, it is often the last task to be tackled because it is so painful, there is little energy in the first year to accomplish it, and the person or family does not want to believe "she is never coming back." It is not unusual to start cleaning out belongings sometime toward the end of the first, or into the second, year of bereavement. It becomes an indication of complicated grief when "many" years have passed without efforts to change the past environment.

Initially it is helpful to the grieving process not to relinquish the articles. The room becomes a comforting place where one can go, feel close to the dead person, and grieve. For others this is torture and is avoided. On the other hand, dispersal of the articles too early, either by oneself or by a so-called helpful person, often brings regrets and guilt. In therapy avoided areas, regrets, and guilts regarding clothing often become an issue that must be confronted or these, too, can add to the development of complicated grief.

Prolonged, continuous, compulsive, or avoided grave visiting is also a symptom of complicated grief. Guilt often develops when the person is not able to visit the grave. I do not want to imply that grave visiting should never occur after the second or third year. If issues are resolved, the grave should take on a new meaning and the behaviors at the grave becomes less potent: "I realized one day she really isn't there and doesn't know the flowers are for her. So I started bringing flowers to an elderly woman I love."

Another issue, which always accompanies complicated grief is an overwhelming, intense guilt. If these feelings are not resolved they tend to be expressed in masochistic ways. This may be either through physical or emotional problems. Guilt often holds the key to the production of complicated grief. I see it in so many of the symptoms and behaviors.

Along with guilt there is often much unresolved anger, which if internalized, presents itself in the form of depression. Usually there is a long history of depression, which may remain repressed or controllable until the next major loss. The opposite, however, may also occur. Often there is a "false euphoria" after the death (or future years of bereavement). This behavior is another way to avoid the pain of grief and may add to the process of complicated grief.

It is interesting that survivors often develop similar symptoms of the dead person's fatal illness. These physical or emotional symptoms tend to appear around anniversary times, especially on the anniversary of the death, holidays, or when they reach the age that the person became ill or died. Although this is not unusual during the first several years of bereavement, if it persists it is an indication of complicated grief.

The family practitioner often treats the survivor for similar symptoms. It is important, however, for health care providers to treat not only the symptoms but also the cause, which may be grief.

Phobias often develop regarding the illness of the deceased. For example, if a person died of cancer the survivor may develop a phobia about cancer: "I won't go by anyone who has cancer; you know it really may be catching." or "I am always reading and thinking about cancer. I am so frightened I have it too that I am doing breast exams every day."

In unresolved grief there is often a fantasy, particularly noted in men, that they should not outlive the person who died, such as their father. I had one family where every male child for at least the last five generations died at the age of 40. Although it is difficult to "get a handle on" this type of situation, certainly there is some unhealthy scripting and complicated grief occurring which is being passed on to other generations.

Radical changes in life style after a death imply that complicated grief may be developing. This is especially true if these changes are used to avoid or deny the death. These changes, or "escape cures," may take many forms, such as remarrying "immediately;" involve activities or behaviors that have not been typical for that person in the past, like use of alcohol or drugs; socializing when before the death he or she was introverted; taking a cruise when he or she has always been a "homebody"; or having a subsequent child after the death of another child late in life.

Another indication of complicated grief is the need to imitate the dead person by use of speech, mannerism, by changing body shape or hair color, or by wearing the dead person's clothing. These behaviors are typical in the first year and are utilized as a means to regain or feel closer to the loved one. Others use such behaviors as a means to undo an ambivalent or painful relationship. I had a patient who had lost 25 pounds so that she could fit into the clothing of her dead daughter. Even though she was in her third year of bereavement and the clothes were out of style, she continued to wear them.

Self-destructive behaviors are another indication of unresolved grief. This may either take the form of passive or active attempts to hurt oneself or in suicide ideas, plans, or actions.

Sadness will probably always occur at certain times of the year, such as holidays or anniversaries. If the sadness is always torturing rather than a "sweet sadness," it is an indicator of complicated grief. This is a symptom that must be evaluated with much information. There may be times when the "torturing sadness" reappears temporarily, such as the birth of a grandchild: "Oh, how I wish my dad were here to see this." It becomes a symptom of complicated grief when the response is consistent over time.

Not understanding or knowing the story surrounding the death can lead to the development of complicated grief. When the necessary information is not available, the grief can lead to fantasies, which are often worse than the reality. Constant searching occurs because the truth is not known.

WHEN IS GRIEF THERAPY APPROPRIATE?

I believe that anyone who has had a significant person die should be in therapy because of the changes, feelings, and reactions the death produces in his or her life. I know that this is not possible or realistic. However, I am convinced that grief is so complicated that it should not be taken as lightly as it is in our culture.

Those who would benefit most from therapy are: those who have had a short preparation time for death; those who have had a long preparation time but did not use the anticipatory period to work; those who have been very attached to or have had a strong "hatred" or ambivalence toward the dead individual; cases in which the death could have been prevented; the death involved issues of suicide, homicide, or murder; cases that involved the death of a child.

It is helpful if these issues can be confronted during the first year of bereavement rather than waiting until complicated grief has firmly developed. Like any disease process, it is best to treat it early in its course. It is very important for a person or family to seek treatment if they become "stuck" in their theme resolution or have prolonged or exaggerated grief symptoms after several years.

The therapist, family member, or friend must always remember that one cannot force someone into therapy. It can only be suggested. It must be the person or family's decision or it will not work.

WHEN IS MOURNING FINISHED?

The question of when mourning is finished is similar to a question such as, "How long is a piece of string?" Mourning is never really completed. There is no answer to this question, only indications of the resolution of the process. The sadness, loss, and memories will always be with the survivor. Time does not heal; hard work does. The grief work brings about a resolution of themes, including symptoms. Then a firm decision to begin living again can occur.

The pain of grief will always be there, but it should change to a "gentle" or sweeter sadness. The reorganization of life is an important issue in how one lives without the person. In addition, one needs to evaluate what the survivors have learned, what behaviors have changed, and what altruistic responses have developed as a result of the tragic experience.

SUMMARY

This chapter explored aspects involved in the second and third years of bereavement. There are several important processes that occur during this time: the decision to live (or not to) again, and the resolution of symptoms and themes. Complicated versus uncomplicated grief was discussed, as well as when grief therapy is appropriate and when mourning is finished.

The process of grief is probably the most difficult and painful journey one will ever have to make. The pain should not be avoided or denied. We will never be the same people because of our losses and attachments. We take with us the good and the bad, the joyful and the sad, and the hard and the easy times. But in order to come through grief in the healthiest manner possible—*give sorrow words!*

> listen to and perhaps identify with
> these words of sorrow . . .
> for only then will they have meaning.
>
>   elizabeth
>   (used with permission)

REFERENCES

Keirsey, D., & Bates, M. (1978). *Please understand me: Character and treatment types.* Del Mar, CA: Prometheus Nemesis Books.
Worden, J. (1982). *Grief counseling and grief therapy: A handbook for the mental health practitioner.* New York: Springer.

CHAPTER VI

Interventions

Interventions are based on the problems and themes the patient or family is presenting. In addition to talking, expressing feelings, and sharing thoughts, I use a wide variety of approaches, depending upon personality, personal problems, support systems, strengths, individual and family themes, and type and preparation time for death.

I would like to share specific interventions as they relate to practice, rather than vice versa. By presenting them in this way, as compared to a case by case approach, the reader may better understand the range and specific interventions.

Please do not think that these interventions are "quick and dirty" formulas for grief therapy. Grief is far too complicated to address with a basic recipe or cookbook approach. However, help is available whether you are a therapist who needs to learn more about grief therapy, or are confronted with death in your profession (an ICU nurse, physician, or clergy).

I have a warning: if you are a counselor or professional who encounters clients in grief, do not think that because you have read this book you can conduct grief therapy. That would be very dangerous. Much study and clinical training needs to be undertaken to conduct this type of therapy. A grief therapist should have a minimum of a masters degree in psychiatric nursing, social work, psychology, or pastoral counseling and specialized education and training in the area of thanatology. Grief therapy is very specialized and complicated. Grief *counseling*, on the other hand, does not necessarily mean in-depth therapy. If you can utilize the information in this book in your practice to be more sensitive to your clients and their

After a Child Dies

ily's needs and problems, then you help prevent more serious
omplications of grief.

With this warning, we may proceed with interventions. Many
interventions can be done without being in therapy. If, however, you
the caretaker, find that the "simple" ones are not helpful to the
survivors, it may be a warning that they need some in-depth therapy
to help sort through their themes and problems and develop appropriate interventions.

STORYTELLING

Stories tend to be memorized scripts of the who, what, when, how,
and where aspects of the death. The client or family is usually not
aware that they have structured such a script. Storytelling is very
helpful, both to the therapist and the client. For the therapist, it is a
means of assessing areas that may lead, or have led, to complicated
grief: missing aspects, affect and guilt, areas that may be blocked, or
never having said good-bye to the dead person. A goal in the therapy
becomes to construct and complete the story as much as possible. For
the patient it is a way to structure the tragic situation. By telling their
story over and over it becomes a means to work through and understand their grief, which will make it less potent.

A completed or well-constructed story will eventually bring relief
and peace. The story must be the survivor's; ownership of it brings
feelings of peace and "power." Often they feel some sense of relief in
sharing it with a person who will actively LISTEN.

When initially seeing patients, I find it especially important for me
to hear and assess their story. It is a means for me to gain trust,
because they are the talkers and I primarily listen. I listen to the
following aspects of their story: how it is constructed; how and when
the story started; who tells the story; its length; what is included;
what is excluded (saying good-bye, seeing the body, support); what is
the affect during the storytelling; where in the story is it potent; when
do the tears come (or do not come); nonverbal messages; and themes
that emerge. Interventions are based upon these, as well as other
information.

As therapy progresses and the story becomes more complete, I
have them tell it again. I have the patient frequently retell the story, in
whole or in part. First, just to me and then, as they become more
comfortable, to "helpful" people. Often the more the story is told,
the more organized the script becomes, which decreases the potency
and increases the resolution and peace. A sign that grief is healing
occurs when the story can be told without total breakdown and the

script changes slightly to include positive affect about the dead person or the survivor.

In addition, I have my clients either write or tape-record their story so that in the future when memories begin to fade, they will always have a record of what happened; not only their story, but also including who the person was, what they miss about him or her, who were the special and helpful people, and a description of their own grief and how it changed.

Women seem to tell the stories more frequently than men. Men usually add information and are careful listeners to the story. This trend also seems to be consistent with who is most verbal in the family, which could be either sex. The telling seems to depend upon who is more expressive. The silent ones will often tell me it is too painful to verbalize it themselves, but it helps them vicariously when their spouse tells it. As the story is more complete and one is feeling stronger, the nonverbal person often tells the story. This is also true with the "Ping-Pong" effect: the one who is up usually tells the story.

The following are two examples of stories. Note as you read them their organization, the sequencing of events, potent areas, affect, who tells, etc. The first is Trudy and John's story.

Before we began the session, I noticed Trudy had been crying. I handed her some Kleenex. She said, "I am prepared," and pulled out a box of Kleenex, keeping it very close to her throughout the interview. John did not shed any tears, but did talk about how sad he was and how he had cried. Trudy described her crying:

> When I talk about it, like at work, I still cry. Whenever I discuss it, I cry. They say it's healthy to cry—I should be the healthiest person around [all of us laugh, then crying again]. I think I have probably shed more tears in the last 4 months that I have in my entire life.

Trudy then gave this short and concise initial story:

> TRUDY: [crying, it is very hard for her to talk] We were expecting our second child, and I am a diabetic and so he (the physician) was keeping a close check on my pregnancy. I had had some abnormalities and so he put me in the hospital to do a stress test and it was o.k., and while I was there, I went into labor. I was there on a Wednesday but I never went into active labor until the next day. Then he did an amniocentesis to make sure that the baby wasn't premature since I was three and a half weeks early . . .
> . . . He (the physician) got in there and he got to the point where he wanted me to push because the baby was up too far and he was going to use forceps so he wanted me to push. They got to the point where he could use the forceps, so he put the forceps on and he told me one more push and the baby would be out. As far as I can remember, the nurse who was checking the fetal heart tones, said "I don't hear any fetal heart

tones"—the baby was o.k. up until that point. But they had been having trouble hearing the fetal heart tones with just a regular stethoscope without the Doptone®. The baby's head was crowning, and he said one more push and the baby will be out. So I was pushing and nothing was happening, and he was pulling with the forceps and nothing was happening. [crying again] So both the nurse and the doctor got up on my stomach and tried to push the baby out, and nothing happened. So he called the nurse and said she better get an anesthesiologist right away. And that is the last thing I remember until I woke up . . .

. . . So they transferred the baby to City E, and he lived for 10 days and then he died. When the baby was born, he did not have a heartbeat nor was he breathing. They had to resuscitate him. What happened to him was that the baby weighed 12 lb, 6 oz, and during the delivery his shoulders got stuck. So when he had gotten the anesthesiologist, the baby was stuck and the cord was part way out so the cord had been compressed. The baby was without oxygen so when he was born he had been without oxygen for a long period of time. At that point, they didn't know how long the baby had been without oxygen so they resuscitated him. In the 10 days when he was in City E [crying] he never cried, he didn't move. Sometimes he would open his eyes, but they said it was just a reflex [crying very hard].

Because of having a C-section, Trudy was not released from the hospital for a week.

TRUDY: I was dismissed on [July] the 4th, and I asked the doctor if I could go to City E at that point to see the baby [crying]. We didn't know if he was going to live or not and if he did live, if he would be totally incapacitated [crying]. We were willing to bring him home and take care of him. So Saturday we went into City E and stayed overnight in a hotel and then went back to see the baby on Sunday. We were unable to go Monday or Tuesday because my husband had meetings in the evening and so we were going to go on Wednesday, and Tuesday night around 5:00, no, 6:00, we got a call from the doctor in City E who was taking care of Erik. He said that Erik had died. (This is the first time that she used his name.)

Trudy mentioned that she had intuitive feelings that something was "wrong" with the fetus and did everything she could to persuade people. Her guilt was created because she felt she could not convince people to listen to her concerns.

With Greg the pregnancy was essentially normal. I delivered him 5 weeks early and he weighed 7 lbs, 6 oz. So the doctor didn't realize when I went into labor with Erik that the baby was going to be that big [starting to cry]. I was concerned a lot of my pregnancy because I knew I was diabetic, and diabetics have big babies. I thought that he was bigger—just his movement and I had had constant heartburn. I really felt he was just too big and I never had that (feeling) when I carried Greg. On the visit that I made to the doctor, I made some comment that Erik or the baby was much bigger than Greg was. So when I was in the hospital on Wednesday I asked him about a pelvimetry to make sure that the baby was small enough for delivery [crying again]. And he told me that I sounded like a worried old woman, that I shouldn't worry about that. He did order the x-ray and told me I could go down for the pelvimetry. When I got done with the x-ray, the technician came out [crying really hard] and said to me "you have a small enough baby here to deliver" [silence]. So I thought maybe it's not as big as I thought . . . and I would be able to deliver the baby [crying, silence].

I really felt the baby was too big to deliver. I was in the hospital the first week of June for some tests and there was a diabetic up there and she had just had a baby by C-section and that baby was like 11 lbs. She was 3 weeks early and by that time I was 5 or 6 weeks early and I looked like I was ready to deliver. I kept thinking that my baby is getting too big, too. At that point I didn't know if I would have a C-section or a normal delivery . . . [starting to cry again]. I see that x-ray technician around the hospital, and everytime I see her I think that she told me I had a small enough baby to deliver. I don't really know if she knows that I lost the baby. I have never talked to her.

They were presented with the decision to transfer Erik back to City A.

TRUDY: And another hard thing was that Dr. W had called Tuesday—Erik died Tuesday [crying]. He had said that if we wanted to, we could start making the arrangements to transfer him back to City A, that he could either go back to Hospital N's pediatric unit or to Hospital R's pediatric unit. I said we will be going in on Wednesday; he said he would be off on Wednesday and to call him on Thursday and let him know how we felt about transferring him back. At the time [crying] I was in limbo. I didn't know if pediatrics could deal with all the problems that he had even though they were not doing that much for him anymore. I wasn't sure that they could handle it, but we were going to take a look at it when we went in there. This was on Tuesday afternoon about 2:30 and we got the call at 6:00 that in fact [crying] he had already died. They were saying that he was having some respiratory difficulty. They used to call in when I was in the hospital. I would hear from them about three times a day, at least once a shift. But not during the night. They would call once in the morning, once in the afternoon, and then once in late evening. They told me before that he was maybe having some respiratory difficulties, and when the nurse called me Tuesday, she told me the same thing. It didn't mean anything because I had heard that before. Evidently, late Tuesday afternoon he stopped breathing. They stimulated him to breathe. We had asked them not to do any sort of heroics. In fact, his heart stopped beating, he stopped breathing and then they didn't resuscitate him again. But at first it didn't take too much to start stimulating him again and he did start breathing but they didn't realize that the end was quite so soon, otherwise they would have called us. We could have come in. I guess he died around 5:00 or a little after 5:00. I really don't remember now.

JOHN: It was 5:45, because they called us right after; it was 6:00.

TRUDY: Oh, o.k. He went into an attack where his heart started beating very fast [crying], and then he stopped breathing. They didn't do anything to him to resuscitate him at that point.

DR. JOHNSON (S. J.): Did you have expectations when you heard that phone ring constantly?

TRUDY AND JOHN [*simultaneously*]: No, we really didn't expect . . .

TRUDY: They called at 6:00, and I just expected a progress report even though someone had called in the afternoon. Greg was being fussy, and my mom took him outside right away, and John had answered the phone. By the time I got to the phone . . . [crying] and by that time he was explaining how the heart rate had gone so fast and that he had been experiencing difficulties and stuff during the day—I did not realize that he had died.

JOHN: [*at the same time*] She did not realize he had died.

TRUDY: I asked, "Should we come right in?" He (doctor) said "it's too late."

JOHN: We had talked to them about transferring him to City A, so when they called we expected that they were talking about transferring him here. They said it could last for months, so we had no idea this would happen.

It appeared that Trudy was the storyteller and that the process was important in expressing her sadness, coming to terms with what happened, and trying to resolve her guilt. The story was well developed and did not exhibit issues of unfinished business. From the story an initial plan of action could be developed: to deal with sadness and to explore and resolve guilt.

Another example is Jane and Mark, whose 3-year-old, Sven, was run over by a car on a busy street. Jane began the concise, well-organized story:

The accident occurred Friday, July 11th, of this year [Jane was sitting up next to Mark on the couch and the dog was sitting behind her. Mark was constantly rubbing her leg with his foot.] My husband and I were two blocks from our house when the accident occurred. We were at Mark's folks mowing the lawn. I left to come down here [home] and thought he [Sven] was inside with Mark's mother and father. Mark was mowing the lawn and Sally (their 6-year-old daughter) was not with us. She was in

Ohio with her cousins. Sven came out of the house, asked his dad [Mark] where I was, and he told him.

MARK: That you had gone to get a tool that we had forgotten down here.

JANE: Mark started to mow again. He (Sven) had never walked down these two blocks by himself but on that particular day he decided to follow me. There is just one main street between that house and ours and it is rather a busy street. This happened about quarter to twelve on a Friday morning. As I was going back to Mark's folks, I saw the "white car" at this intersection, and saw people gathered around, and saw a little boy on the street. I immediately recognized it was Sven and had enough presence of mind to stop the vehicle and get out and kind of screamed helplessly and numbly "that is my little Sven." At that point, he was already unconscious. He never responded again. He had all the symptoms—as I could visually see—of having a lifeless look and I just felt already immediately that he was gone. People were gathering and I told one of the neighbors to go run and get Mark and tell him that Sven has been in a very bad accident. I think others were coming down because they heard the sirens.

MARK: I was on my way down because I noticed—even though I had the lawnmower on. Then I looked down there and I saw the truck and I thought, oh boy, Jane has been in an accident. So I started walking down and that is when the neighbor came up and said "come quick, Sven has been in a bad accident and it is really bad." So that is when I came upon the scene.

Although Jane is a nurse, she said that she chose not to participate in the resuscitation. At this point in the interview, she described his physical condition and said she believed he was not being effectively resuscitated. However, she described herself as "too numb" to help. Both Jane's and Mark's response was "Oh, God, he is gone." A friend drove them to the emergency room.

JANE: Well, we really didn't even want to (go to the hospital). I didn't anyway. I felt that way. I felt he wasn't responding. If he was (responding) at all then I would have wanted to have been there. It may sound strange, cold, for a parent but, I felt too strongly about that; he was already being caressed in the arms of Jesus. I just felt that so strongly that, it could have been me of small faith, but I really didn't think anything miraculous could have occurred. I felt so strong already that he was gone. Gone for good, and I just kind of felt we had to help each other. During those next 9 hours, we had people that took care of us and fed us. Even when we went to the emergency room, one of our pastoral staff was there and we didn't even go and see Sven in the emergency room. They indicated that they were working on him and that he arrested and they were transferring him to intensive care.

Jane and Mark had no desire to be with Sven during those 9 hours.

> MARK: Had he been responding in any way I would have wanted to be there. I think that would have changed our perspective of what needed to be done. But because he was unconscious and totally unresponsive, maybe again because of our background, we didn't feel that there was anything that we would be able to do. So I really didn't feel any particular desire to be there.
>
> JANE: I didn't either.

When Sven's condition worsened, they were offered the opportunity by the hospital staff to be with him.

> MARK: They (friends) answered the phone for us. The hospital finally called and said Sven has gone into heart block. "Do you want to be here?" And we decided that he was totally unconscious that it would not be necessary and we just said let us know when he has died.
>
> JANE: We both felt very at ease about that, and I don't know if there was just a lack of interest there or we both felt it is not going to make any difference. As soon as he died, we knew we would have to go back to the hospital.

There is much thought detail in this story and not much expression of feelings. My assessment was that these people were primarily "thinking" people and processing information was important in their grief. The story was well organized and may have given a sense of power in a powerless situation.

It was interesting that they made the decision not be be with Sven at the hospital. They had evaluated the situation and decided he was already dead. This may have been an area where guilt might have developed, but never did. The storytelling allowed me to make initial assessments of their coping process, values, and needs.

The health professional may feel in value conflict when the client chooses to handle a situation differently than they themselves might. It must be remembered that people respond and react because of their own needs and coping mechanisms. There is no one right way to respond—and for Jane and Mark it was more necessary to be home than at the hospital.

The stories are usually extremely sad. I often find it helpful to spend time being sad after a session. The pains are so deep for my clients, as are their expression. Yet the stories need to be told and heard over and over. After listening to hundreds of stories, I can understand why people initiate the conspiracy of silence: It hurts too much to hear them. It is important for the health professional to experience a "mini-grief" to allow sad feelings to be expressed in whatever ways are helpful to the person. Otherwise, they are just as liable to develop a conspiracy of silence, and the silence in denial of one's own feelings may become a variable in one's professional burnout.

USE OF PICTURES

I use two types of pictures in grief therapy. First, I always have my clients bring recent and past pictures of their family and important people in their lives. This is done in an early therapy session. I can gather much information from these pictures: family relationships, who stands by whom and how close, what affects are expressed, what were they doing together, how has the client changed over the years, how do they show the pictures to you (do they give them to you or do they "own" them and explain them to you while they hold them), and how do they organize or not organize the pictures.

This information tells me much about the family dynamics, as well as the patient's place and role within the family. For example, in viewing pictures of a family where the father and son had conflicts and the son died in a car accident, it became evident how in many pictures the son would "look up" to his father. I was then able to use this information, which was confirmed by the wife, that although there was conflict, there was also admiration. Guilt feelings were decreased for the man. I must be able to gather as much information as possible, and when this cannot be done directly, tools like pictures are of great vicarious assistance.

The pictures are also helpful in observing changes over the years. I was treating a woman who had developed a conspiracy of silence over the death of her infant. She continually denied that the death 13 years ago had any impact upon her present depression. She refused for months to bring pictures in to show me. When she finally did, it became apparent to her that since that death she had changed physically and emotionally: She had gained 50 pounds, increasingly looked older than her age, stood farther away from her husband and then her family, and increasingly looked more depressed. The pictures allowed her to confront the reality of the present depression.

This process also allows me the opportunity to see whom and what we are discussing. For me it is helpful, because I am then able to be more involved in the process. It is always helpful for me to put a face with a name, and the pictures tell a great deal about who the person was and confirm what the family is saying: "Yes, Kelly was very beautiful and vivacious, I bet you miss her for those qualities " or "Your mother doesn't look that mean."

For the patient or family, it is a means to talk about their family; their joys and pains. It is also a means to express their grief. Donna, whose daughter, Kate, died of leukemia at 4 years of age, had chronological pictures of her through the illness. It was a helpful means for Donna to share her pain and helplessness in Kate's illness and death.

Second, I use pictures to help the patient vicariously say good-bye. These pictures may be from someone who took pictures at the funeral. In addition, I encourage funeral directors to take pictures, with or without a closed casket. If they keep them on file it is helpful if the person has needs or desires in the future.

Looking at the pictures is, of course, a very stressful and difficult task for the client. I will never show them to the clients unless I have their permission, and we both determine that they are ready to view them. It takes a great deal of preparation.

If need be, I will obtain pictures from the coroner or police. These are usually detailed pictures of the death scene. Because these pictures are usually very descriptive, they should only be used if the persons have denial or doubts that their loved one is dead, or if they were never able to say good-bye because they did not see, or were not allowed to see, the body.

Although the coroner's and police's intent in picture taking is for investigation, I encourage them to keep in mind also that they may be used for grief therapy in the future. Keeping that in mind, the pictures of the environment, specific articles, the condition of vehicles, or other inanimate objects that were involved, and the body or parts of the body, are important.

Although painful, the pictures are extremely helpful because they allow for the confrontation of reality. I had a family who was so tortured because they had never seen their daughter dead because of her injuries. They couldn't believe then that she was dead and buried. There were no pictures. They finally decided to reopen her casket after she had been buried for a year. There are less traumatic ways to determine this, and this need can be anticipated. Again, it is easier to prevent a problem than to have to undo it later. Although families think it is "gross" to take pictures at the funeral, for questions and concerns longitudinally, they can serve a very helpful purpose and they need not be taken obtrusively.

Over the years I have developed techniques for viewing the coroner's pictures. First, it is important to determine if there is really a need to view them, or whether less stressful methods can be utilized (e.g., writing a letter to the dead person, talking to an empty chair, or "pretending" with a doll).

The need usually is apparent when the patient presents symptoms of denial of the death, prolonged and exaggerated grief symptoms, or relationship problems, especially with other children or the spouse. The patient most likely never saw their loved one dead and although there was probably a funeral, never really said good-bye face to face or in his mind. Consequently, the first task of mourning, to accept the reality of loss, is arrested (Worden, 1982). Even though they may feel the pain of grief (second task of mourning), it is not yet a reality because of the denial.

Such was the case with an 8-year-old that I was treating. Both of her parents were killed in a plane crash. There were four children, who were split between the mother's siblings. Because of the crash, they were told they could not see the bodies. Kristen did not, and would not, believe they were dead. She began acting out, became paranoid that her aunt and uncle were stealing all of her parents' money, and became violent. Her behavior was causing difficulties between her aunt and uncle, as well as their children. She was convinced that her parents were not dead, but had gone away on a trip and would return shortly. Consequently, she was projecting anger onto her new family.

I was able to obtain the coroner's pictures of the accident. Although many would have been inappropriate to share with Kristen because of her age and the degree of bodily destruction, there were some of her parents' hands and legs that were easily identifiable. Kristen was aware that I had the pictures, which only increased her pathological behaviors. That was a sign that it would have been totally inappropriate to show them to her; she was not ready. The behaviors became so extreme she needed to be hospitalized in a distant city. There were other issues that dealt with her own growth and development that needed resolution before the problem of her grief could be addressed.

Although the client may express denial, there is "a force" inside that wants to come to peace with the reality; "I want to know, but I don't want to know." By facing the reality it will mean a change in perception and behavior regarding the loss. Therefore, in preparing someone to see the pictures, much work needs to be done with the ambivalence. In working through the ambivalence the person has to be able to understand the impact of maintaining either position: continuing to believe the person is alive versus coming to realize the person is dead. They must begin to see the value in letting go of the fantasy, although a painful process. The pictures then are not such a threat to them because the pain of maintaining the delusion becomes less than the reality.

Such was the case with Christy, whose son had died accidentally of carbon monoxide poisoning in a car with his girlfriend. The parents, Christy and Bill, were not allowed to see him because the funeral director said the bodies were too decomposed. However, Christy later found that the young woman's parents were allowed to see her and the coroner's pictures did not resemble deteriorated bodies. Because the death happened suddenly, and not seeing him, she never believed Moses was dead:

> He's gone off on a trip. But how can he play such a horrible trick on his mother. He never did that before. He'll be back soon; I know he will. There is a young man in town that dresses and looks like Moses and I keep trying to find him, because it might be him. I know he is coming back.

Christy was so convinced that Moses was coming back that she could not even utter the word "dead." She would talk about him in the present tense, yet she was experiencing the pain of grief by exaggerating grief symptoms and grave visiting, which were regular and compulsive (taking pictures of each bouquet of flowers she placed on the grave). She needed to see that he was dead in order to confirm his death; the coroner's pictures were less stressful to use here than disinterring the body.

After the ambivalence is worked through, then it is helpful to have the patient fantasize about what they think the pictures will look like. Christy could not even conjure up an image in her mind, even though she was a visual person and could fantasize about other things. This is an important aspect to assess—is the patient able to fantasize or are they auditory in their learning and experiencing? When Christy could not fantasize, I asked her permission to describe the first picture that I would eventually show her. She agreed, but still could not develop an image in her head. The denial remained intact.

In addition to fantasy, I encourage people to keep and write in their journals about their fears, concerns, fantasies, and questions about seeing the pictures. When people are able to fantasize about the pictures, they are beginning to break the denial and blocks. Often they find that they are finally dreaming about the death, which is very helpful in uncovering issues.

It is important to arrange the pictures in a helpful and nonthreatening order. This process may also help develop the missing aspects of the story if the pictures could somehow represent a chronological order. I start with the least potent, or so I assume, to the most potent, although they will all be potent. With the pictures of Moses, I arranged them from pictures outside of the car, with no bodies, to pictures of the front seat, which included things like the steering wheel and dashboard, jackets and shoes. The last set of pictures began with the feet to the entire bodies. I find it best to start with environment or inanimate object pictures. In addition, it is often helpful for the family to bring some of their favorite and "healthy" pictures of the dead person. These can be used during the sessions to keep focused both on the loss and on who the person was to them.

For Christy any picture was going to be extremely frightening because she would have to admit "something"—that Moses was dead; she still could not say the word. As the denial began breaking and the ambivalence decreased, she began to develop many questions: "Why did something happen *that* night when he used to park there all the time?" "What did the car look like inside?" Once the questions were verbalized we could go about developing some answers, which helps in the reality and the completion of the story. She was finally ready, although very frightened to see the first picture.

Because of Christy's extreme denial, the presentation of the pictures took a very long time. I had begun to desensitize her by placing the whole unopened packet of pictures on my desk. She avoided any eye contact or verbalization of them during the whole session, but she was well aware that they were there. I chose not to mention it, so as not to push the issue. In the second session I had them out again and this time she said, "We aren't really going to look at those today." I said, "No, but it would be helpful if you could touch the packet," but she couldn't. These small interventions were attempts to get her to accept that the pictures were real and her son was dead.

Although she never missed an appointment prior to looking at the pictures, her anxiety level became extremely high, to the point of hyperventilating and feeling extremely nauseated. This is not uncommon and, in fact, I have had people who have vomited while they looked at pictures. All of those who have vomited have felt a great relief. "There was this pain in the pit of my stomach that had to come out," which probably is connected with sadness.

It is imperative that the client work through the ambivalence, confront the reality, and want to work through the grief rather than maintain the delusion. I must have the full support of the client and of any involved family members. They must also trust that I will do them no intentional harm. This process is very critical and needs appropriate assessment and clinical decision making. As a therapist, however, I always question if the pain and anxiety is worth it. I ask myself if I am "torturing" my clients. Although these and other questions are always helpful and necessary to ask and assess, this experience is like surgery; on an inflamed appendix: one has to go through the pain to feel better.

When it came time to look at the first picture I had Christy get as comfortable as possible. I explained that she may feel nauseated and placed a wastepaper basket by her. She chose to have her husband sit by her. (I had shown him the pictures several sessions prior to her viewing, so that he may help prepare her for the experience at home. He was extremely supportive of her and the situation.) I described what the first picture would be in great detail and then held it up to show it. It was a picture of the outside of the car. Her eyes would look at it and then turn away. She continued that process until she could look at it for longer periods of time. She did not hold the picture yet. This process continued until she could look, hold, ask questions, and feel as we began to put the story together.

When she was finally able to look at the pictures of Moses, she still could not believe that it was he, and she could not say he *was* dead. At this point, she could not hold the pictures of him. There was one picture of him lying nude on the coronor's blanket. That was extremely offensive to her. She finally was able to take the picture. She wrapped a Kleenex around this picture, as if to cover him. It was at that point that she began, very slowly, to say he was D . . . E . . . A . . . D. *She said it!!* (I don't remember ever working so hard in my life.) I would have her repeat this statement over and over: "This is Moses and he is dead." Because of the strong denial it took almost 2 months to get through the three groups of pictures for the first time.

Although the experience was painful for all of us, the denial, pathology, and symptom formation began to dissipate. The story could then be completed: The conditions were right for the death to occur; they were parked in a gully, it was foggy, they had a full tank of gas, the windows were shut, the car was an old model with the exhaust pipe extending that became blocked by the hill, and there were tall weeds.

The pictures allowed for the breakdown of the denial. She was finally able to hold him vicariously and say good-bye to her dead son. All of this could probably have been prevented if she had been able to see him at the time of his death. Through this process she had slowly been able to make a decision to live again. In this decision, one of her "missions" or goals is to remind young people that if they are going to "park" to make sure the windows are open and be aware of conditions that may lead to carbon monoxide poisoning.

In another case we used pictures of the one car accident to see if we could determine any insight as to whether Sheri's son, Kevin, had committed suicide or just fallen asleep at the wheel. Again, she was not allowed to see him, but did know he was dead. The torturing question she had concerned the circumstances surrounding the death. There was a total conspiracy of silence within the family, and therefore she could not express her concerns and questions.

She went through the first year of bereavement without taking steps to gather more information. As is often the case, the next loss triggered all of the unfinished business from the previous loss; her husband wanted a divorce, which precipitated a clinical depression.

The pictures became a helpful, though painful, tool to piece together the accident. In addition to using the pictures, I asked the emergency room physician to reread his report to see if he could remember if there was a question regarding suicide; he had remembered the case and strongly felt that Kevin had fallen asleep at the wheel. A year after viewing the pictures, Sheri still felt they were helpful and that, although painful, they allowed her to come to a resolution and peace about Kevin's death.

USE OF JOURNALS

Journaling, either writing or talking into a tape recorder, is a helpful tool for patients. It is helpful for the patient to keep track of feelings and ideas between therapy sessions. This also allows me to discover problems, as well as improvements. Although patients generally keep their journal to themselves, most feel comfortable sharing them with me.

I was seeing a physician whose daughter had an acute infection and died quickly. During the hospitalization, I suggested that he keep a journal. He used his computer to write something every day about what was happening to their little Heather and to themselves. After her death he realized he had written over 300 pages, which were extremely helpful to him.

Many of my patients keep a journal and eventually share it with their children and grandchildren. Some have used it to write short articles for the newspaper, church journals, and magazines. If it is kept faithfully, it is an excellent history of the death and one's grief journey.

USE OF LITERATURE, STORY INVENTION, PUPPETS, DRAWINGS, AND DOLLS

The arts have always been a medium for addressing the issues of death, dying, and mourning. No matter what mode, literature, music, or other forms of art, the artist has always attempted to find answers to difficult questions, express pain, or take the audience on a journey in hopes of understanding this mystery. Joan Hagan Arnold and Penelope Buschman Gemma (1983), in their recent book, *A Child Dies: A Portrait of Family Grief,* include excellent examples of art-work and poetry that related to death and mourning.

If this creative process has helped the artist, as well as the viewer, it seems it is a very appropriate intervention with the survivor. I encourage my patients to use their own creativity, both in and out of therapy, as well as to explore the classics in art, music, and literature, which may be helpful to them.

Although drawing pictures is extremely helpful in expressing grief, understanding, and saying good-bye, I find that children are the most comfortable with this medium. That does not mean adults cannot utilize it, it just takes more permission-giving and encouragement. My niece, who is an art major, tells me that most people stop drawing and doodling by the age of 10! Consequently, it is often difficult for adults to "get into" this type of intervention. However, it is usually so beneficial that it is worth the effort.

I have in my office a collection of markers, papers, puppets, and dolls—ranging from infant boy and girl dolls to a large "Raggedy Ann." (Our daughter says it's not her that we should be concerned about in a toy shop; it's Mom!) They are there for ANYONE to use. I will share with you some classic examples of how these types of interventions can be helpful with both adults and children.

Literature

Literature has always been a creative way for authors to express the pain of death. Mary Jane Moffat (1982) has edited a wonderful book of literature on mourning. In fact, most poets and writers have dealt with grief and mourning as they attempted to make sense out of their world and culture. Many knew the pain of bereavement.

If my clients enjoy poetry or literature, I encourage them to explore these areas and find poems, stories, or Bible passages that relate to them or are comforting to them. Often a single poem or verse can bring great relief and can be used for meditation and quiet escape from grief sometime during the day.

My first article on grief themes was very enjoyable to write because it utilized Ibsen's play *Little Eyolf* to help depict the various family themes (1981). Little Eyolf had drowned and the parents continued to reenact the themes that had been previously utilized by them, such as detachment, conspiracy of silence, guilt, and scapegoating (Johnson-Soderberg, 1981). Literature can also be helpful to the therapist.

Children's Literature. Children's books are not just for children anymore! In fact, I believe that children are much too young to understand them. One must have "years of experience" to comprehend the humor, sorrow, and joy of this special type of literature. Take for example, Judith Viorst's (1972) book, *Alexander and the Terrible, Horrible, No Good, Very Bad Day.* No one really knows what a bad day is until the bank goes bankrupt, three of your clients have committed suicide in one day, or your house burns down and you've lost everything. But then you can put it all in perspective by reading this book, or *Could Be Worse,* by James Stevenson (1977).

Not only do children's books stimulate adult issues, they often trigger memories that were painful or unresolved as a child. I recommend these books for both adults and children. Many times I will read my clients a book during a session, if there is a particular theme that we are discussing that might be made clearer by a children's book. For example, in dealing with a woman who was not allowing her family to care for her after the death of their son. We got into a 2-year old issue: YOU CAN'T MAKE ME DO IT! This issue is often played out in adult situations. *Smile for Auntie,* by Diane Paterson (1976), is a fun little book that deals with this very issue. For those of us who have ever tried running away from home, Joan Hanson's book entitled *I'm Going to Run Away From Home* is an excellent triggering book. Or for those experiencing the masochistic theme, Cathy Guisewite's (1983) book, *How to Get Rich, Fall in Love, Lose Weight, and Solve all your Problems by Saying "No,"* may be helpful.

I will often read my clients a story that relates to current issues in therapy. I will ask them to assume their "child" position, not to read the words and only look at the pictures. Then we will discuss it. Often they will take the book home to read for homework. Even though it is a simplistic method, there is great depth to the meanings in the books (e.g., Remy Charlip's (1967) little book *I Love You* says over and over I Love You, which the "child" wants to hear so desperately). Another book, which is beautifully illustrated, is Charlotte Zolotow's (1980) book *Say It!* In their grief and loneliness, people often feel unloved.

If feelings are an issue—in not understanding how one feels—Aliki's (1984) book *Feelings* is wonderful. Also, *Sometimes I Like to Cry* by Elizabeth and Henry Stanton (1978) gives permission to adults and children to express their sadness through tears.

Other issues relate to separation anxiety, which adults also experience. Dorothy Corey's (1976) book *You Go Away* shows very simply that people go away and come back. As shown in the chapter on the development of a concept of death in children, I strongly believe that the child has to understand that concept, before he or she can understand that people go away and *don't* come back. This is a helpful book for adults as well as children.

There are also many good books on death that can be helpful to adults and children. Although I have included in the Appendix a lengthy list of books and articles that may be of interest, there are several that are worth mentioning by name. Judith Viorst's (1971) *The Tenth Good Thing About Barney* is an excellent book about a cat that dies and the sad feelings described by a little boy—the child is so sad he can't even watch television. Earl Grollman's (1970) dialogue between parent and child in *Talking About Death* discusses death and teaches us to call it by the right and proper name, rather than developing euphemisms like "kicked the bucket" or "expired."

The Two of Them by Aliki (1979), is a beautiful story of the love between a grandfather and granddaughter. He has a stroke and dies. Her sadness and grief are expressed beautifully, both in words and illustrations. For the older child, Katherine Paterson's book *Bridge to Terabithia* is very helpful (1977). Many of my adult patients find *The Fall of Freddie the Leaf* by Leo Buscaglia very meaningful (1982).

There are, of course, many classics that can be utilized (see Appendix), but I find it so very helpful to have simple and short, yet poignant, books I can pull off the shelf to help emphasize a point, develop a concept, or support an idea.

STORIES, PUPPETS, AND DRAWINGS

Story Invention Using Puppets and Drawing

Stories are helpful in that the issues can be addressed symbolically and often indirectly. I have the person develop a theme either with or without props. With small children it is often helpful to "play the game" where one person starts the story and the other then adds a sentence, and so on. Children, and adults, tend to lead the story into unresolved issues. This is helpful information for me, as well as the patient.

Often a child will develop a story and then add props. Heather, a 7-year-old whose father died when she was 3, had been "protected" from her father's death. She found out he had died only when a cleaning lady at the hospital said to her mother, several days after the death, that she was sorry her husband had died. Her family participated in the conspiracy of silence. Heather's mother noticed that her school work was decreasing, she wouldn't go out to play, complained of nightmares, and was withdrawn. The issue for Heather was that she believed she had caused her father's death by saying in anger one day that she hated him and hoped he would die.

She drew a picture of her father in the hospital bed and proceeded to get the puppets and play out her resolved story of his death:

> This rabbit is very sick. He is in the hospital, but he is scared because no one is with him. He doesn't like to be alone. He likes his little bunnies around him (taking more puppets and placing them around the "father"). Now, with every one around he can tell them how much he loves them and doesn't want to leave them, but he had to go to be with Jesus.

In her wishful thinking, she was seeing the need to break the conspiracy and then she didn't have to pretend that she killed him because, indirectly, he told her how he felt.

After she played out the story, she looked up to me and with her big brown eyes full of tears said, "You know, my daddy really loved me." On her own level, she began to see that she hadn't, nor could have, killed him.

Adam, whose sister fell off the extension ladder, was feeling that he could have prevented Sundai's death. His play and drawings reinacted the day she died. He acted out their tennis game, then the ball going up on the roof and finally getting the extension ladder. As the ladder would start to fall, he continued to believe he could hold it. Since Adam was a very intelligent child he needed more concrete information than merely playing it out, although the play and stories were helpful in confronting the issues. Adam had to actually see the extension ladder and understand the principles of physics for himself.

Adam's other problem was that he was grieving very differently from his mother. It made him extremely uncomfortable to see her cry. He was attempting to understand the differences in their grieving and also answer the question of when this pain would be over. He made up the following story with the use of puppets. He set the stage and told me I could be his mother; he would play himself and the other characters. I took my cues from him and he told me initially what to say. He essentially played out the story and I wrote it down later; later, he agreed to what I had written. In reading this you may find it to be long, but he was working very hard at coming up with answers to two difficult questions: Why do people grieve differently? and How long does grief last?

When Will I Stop Crying
dedicated to Sundai Marie Peters

One afternoon, Adam was watching TV, as he and his sister, Sundai, always did. They enjoyed playing together so much. But one day several months ago Sundai died in a sad accident. Then, Sundai was not there to be with Adam to watch TV or his mom and dad. It was really sad for Adam and his mom and dad not to have Sundai with them. Sometimes Adam was so sad he didn't even like to watch TV, play tennis, or go out and ride his bike. His mom and dad were very sad too. Each in his own way.

Today, Mom was crying very hard in the kitchen while she was trying to make dinner. She would cry a lot. Adam said, "Here we go again," and went to hug her.

Mom said, "I am so sad and it hurts so bad now that we don't have Sundai. Oh Adam, when will the tears ever stop?" Adam said, "I don't know, why don't you ask Dad. He'll know."

So Mom asked Dad. Mom said, "I miss Sundai so much and it is so painful for me. When will the tears ever stop? Adam thought maybe you would know." Dad said, "I don't know, why don't you ask Grandpa? He'll know."

So Mom asked Grandpa. Mom said, "Oh Grandpa, I miss Sundai so much and it is so painful for me. When will the tears ever stop? Phil thought maybe you would know." Grandpa said, "I don't know, why don't you ask Grandma. She will know."

So Mom asked Grandma. Mom said, "Oh Grandma, I miss Sundai so much and it is so painful for me. When will the tears ever stop? Grandpa thought maybe you would know." Grandma said, "I don't know, why don't you ask Great Grandpa, he'll know."

So Mom asked Great Grandpa. Mom said, "Oh Great Grandpa, I miss Sundai so much and it is so painful for me. When will the tears ever stop? Grandma thought maybe you would know." Great Grandpa said, "I don't know, why don't you ask Great Grandma, she'll know."

So Mom asked Great Grandma. Mom said, "Oh Great Grandma, I miss Sundai so much and it is so painful for me. When will the tears ever stop? Great Grandpa though maybe you would know." Great Grandma said, "I don't know, why don't you ask Great-Great Grandpa."

So Mom asked Great-Great Grandpa. Mom said, "Oh Great-Great Grandpa, I miss Sundai so much, and it is so painful for me. When will the tears ever stop? Great Grandma thought maybe you would know." Great-Great Grandpa said, "I don't know, why don't you ask Great-Great Grandma. She will know."

So Mom asked Great-Great Grandma. Mom said, "Oh Great-Great Grandma, I miss Sundai so much and it is so painful for me. When will the tears ever stop? Great-Great Grandpa thought maybe you would know." Great-Great Grandma said, "I don't know, why don't you ask Great-Great-Great Grandpa? He will know."

So Mom asked Great-Great-Great Grandpa. Mom said, "Oh Great-Great-Great Grandpa, I miss Sundai so much, and it is so painful for me. When will the tears ever stop? Great-Great Grandma thought maybe you would know." Great-Great-Great Grandpa said, "I don't know, why don't you ask Great-Great-Great Grandma. She will know."

So Mom asked Great-Great-Great Grandma. Mom said, "Oh Great-

Great-Great Grandma, I miss Sundai so much, and it is so painful for me. When will the tears ever stop? Great-Great-Great Grandpa thought maybe you would know." Great-Great-Great Grandma said, "I don't know, why don't you ask Great-Great-Great-Great Grandpa? He will know."

So Mom asked Great-Great-Great-Great Grandpa. Mom said, "Oh Great-Great-Great-Great Grandpa, I miss Sundai so much, and it is so painful for me. When will the tears ever stop? Great-Great-Great Grandma thought maybe you would know." Great-Great-Great-Great Grandpa said, "I *don't* know. *Nobody* knows when they are going to stop crying." Mom said "I'm so glad, to hear that. My tears just have to get out of my body, but I wanted to know when they will stop. But you are probably right. You've made me feel better because no one does know when we will stop crying. Can I give you a hug?" Great-Great-Great-Great Grandpa said, "Sure, but be very careful. I am a thousand and three." The end.

(used with permission)

He had found his answer: There is no time when we can say we will be able to stop crying from our grief. Adam learned this from his story, which many adults also need to learn. Even those of us in the health professions are not always as tolerant of the length of people's grief. I hear frequently statements like: "You're just feeling sorry for yourself " "Stop crying in your beer " or "Just get going." We need to assess ourselves to see if we really believe that there is no time when grief ends, or if we are giving subtle or direct messages that we believe there is a magic time when it should be finished.

Adam felt great relief after playing this out. He was a very special boy, who at least for this time in his life, has come to some understanding of his sister's accidental death. The children who usually have problems with grief are the intelligent and creative ones. They are attempting to find answers but they often do not have the needed cognitive and emotional skills. They tend to make up their own answers, which often deal with self-incrimination. If this is not changed in the first several years of bereavement, destructive behaviors can occur, especially during adolescence. Through symptom formation the child is asking for help, but doesn't know how to ask directly.

Another example, one of using pictures or drawings in therapy comes from one of my favorite patients, 3-year-old Jeremy. His grandmother had died after a long battle with cancer 6 weeks before I saw him. During her illness, as she became sicker and sicker Jeremy was separated from her. She had been a primary caretaker for him, but his parents had only briefly explained what had happened to "Nannie" and where she had "finally gone."

Jeremy's mother, Marcia, was having an extremely difficult time with her mother's death and projected her need for a conspiracy of silence onto Jeremy. He became confused, but knew something "terrible" had happened to Nannie. Prior to this, Jeremy was a confident child who loved to be with people. The conspiracy resulted in a slow regression of behaviors: He became frightened of animals and insects; would not be alone in his room when it was time to sleep; had to have the windows in his room shut, even though it was summer, because the "ghost" may get him; would not let his mom and dad out of his sight; utilized much testing behavior; forgot his numbers and letters; would not play with others, and; protested violently about attending preschool.

His parents decided it was "one of those stages," and tried to ignore his behaviors. However, the behaviors became more intense. One night, while being put to bed by his dad, Tim, Jeremy became very upset. Tim grew angry because friends were over to help build a deck. Jeremy was holding onto his father so tightly that it hurt him. He wanted Tim to stay with him. Tim began to yell, he spanked Jeremy, and took away his favorite toys, but Jeremy would not release him. They knew he needed some help. They called their pediatrician, who referred them to me.

I was able to break the conspiracy and Jeremy was allowed to express his grief and fears in direct, symbolic, and appropriate ways. He was such a creative and intelligent little boy that he knew what he needed in therapy. The expression of Jeremy's grief had been blocked because of the conspiracy, as well as the myth that children are too young to understand about death and grief. However, this 3-year-old knew that he needed expression and was desperately crying for the opportunity to have it.

Initially, trust needed to be developed. Because of the conspiracy over Nannie's illness and death, he was not sure if he should or could trust adults. For example, the day of his first appointment, his parents told him they were going to visit a "friend." However, his parents said that he started screaming as soon as he walked into my building. He knew something was "up," and I was "no friend" of his family. During the first session he would not come into my office, so I talked to his parents and spent my time with Jeremy in the hall. He was able to draw a picture. It was characterized by very light nonaggressive lines (see Figure 6-1a).

This medium seemed to be of interest, so I continued to utilize it as an intervention. I asked him if he would like to tape it to my door, which he did. This was one way to show him he could trust me since I would keep his pictures there. He continued to tape all of his drawings to the door. In this session he was also able to tell me that his grandmother had died and he missed her very much; his parents were amazed that he seemed to understand and could verbalize his loss. At the close of the session, I asked him to bring his favorite puppets and told him I had puppets too, that we would play with them and draw next time.

In the second session he brought what he called "Hairy Monster," which symbolized death to him. He was able to express much anger and "ate me up." He began to experience control over the "monsters." He'd often lead me in his expression of grief. He knew what he needed.

He was able to draw two more pictures. One had a more aggressive line with dark purple dots, and hairy monsters around it (see Figure 6-1b). The third drawing was of Nannie, who was in green (see Figure 6-1c). There were "lots of scary monsters around her." Jeremy had a well-developed body concept for a 3-year-old. He was able to talk to me about her, but not to his parents. Jeremy was becoming more aggressive and verbal in our sessions. I also read him a story about monsters (see Appendix).

In the third session he felt safe enough to express his fears more directly. He took out the puppets and acted out this story: The other puppets did not like the Hairy Monster and were scared of him. I asked what the other puppets should do about it. Jeremy said they should beat Hairy Monster up and I asked him to show me. He had a puppet in one hand and Hairy Monster in the other. Hairy was hit, pounded upon, and thrown across the room, while Jeremy beamed. Then he became frightened of his power.

He started to become withdrawn but then asked if he could draw. He drew a picture of hairy monsters (see Figure 6-1d). The picture is more aggressive and violent and has more color. He continued to tape his pictures on my door, but now more tape was used "to keep the monsters in their cage."

Drawing 6-1e was very aggressive with distinct green markings. I believe this symbolized Nannie again (see 6-1c) since he said the green part was being "eaten up" by the hairy monster (Nannie's cancer and death). He then taped another piece of paper on top of the hairy monsters and began stabbing it with an orange marker. He was going to destroy the hairy monsters (see Figure 6-1f). He smiled and appeared very relieved when he was finished. I suggested that maybe he could lock the Hairy Monster away, showing how powerful he was. He took the puppet and locked it in the file cabinet. He felt confident and bolder.

Although his grief expression was mostly symbolic, he was

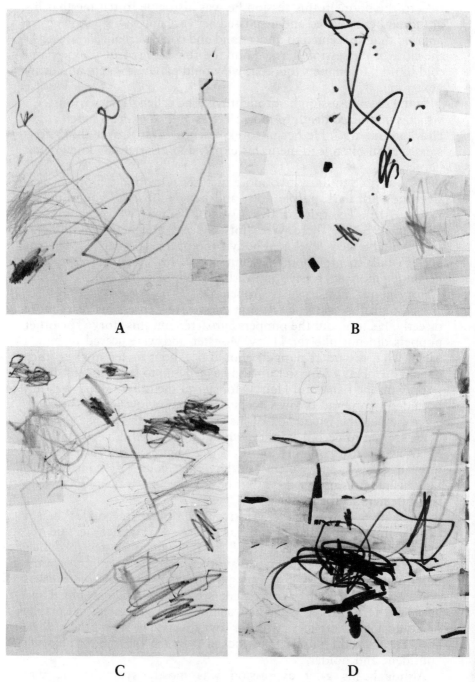

A

B

C

D

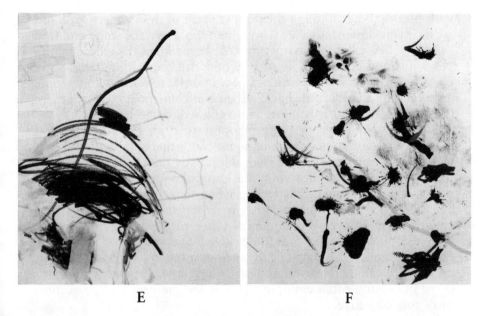

E   F

FIGURE 6-1. A: Jeremy's initial drawing. B: Drawing from second session. C: Drawing from second session; Grandmother surrounded by "hairy monsters." D: Third session drawing. E: More aggressive drawing. Notice the lighter, longer lines (Grandmother) being overtaken by the bolder strokes (hairy monsters). F: Destroying hairy monsters.

attempting to understand what happened to Nannie and express his feelings about it (he was angry). He was also secretly wondering if "it" would happen to him or his parents. Little Jeremy was feeling powerless with all these frightening and mysterious forces infringing on his secure world.

His parents began to see changes in his behavior after this session. Several days later a bee flew by and Jeremy was not even scared (insects had previously frightened him). His parents were amazed. He was gaining confidence again and was, on his own level, able to understand that even though Hairy Monster got Nannie, he was healthy and so were his parents. He began to talk about the positive aspects of Nannie. Using appropriate past tenses he would say how much he missed "her cookies, her hugs, and their play time."

Although the behaviors were decreasing he still was very frightened to be alone. The Hairy Monsters were "locked away," but issues of separation anxiety still remained. To reteach him this concept we took a puppet and threw it over the railing. I would discuss with him that even though the puppet was not there where he could see it, it was downstairs. We would then run down the stairs and find the puppet. We did this many times. At home I had the whole family play hide-and-go-seek. This is a wonderful game that I have my children, as well as adult patients, play in order to relearn that people go away but usually come back. When confronted with a death there is always testing in trusting that people will come back.

I have my adults go to a large shopping center. The rules are that they need to find their spouse or significant others many times. First they start in one store on one floor. Gradually they are to expand the territory until they are searching the entire shopping center. They are to notice how their body is feeling when they are alone and how it changes when they find the person; what are their thoughts and changes in their level of confidence? Often people will express panic and become frightened that their loved one will also "not come back." Although it may feel silly at first, it always works. People at all age levels must relearn that people don't always go away and not come back, and often children's games are the best tool to accomplish this objective.

For Jeremy, these games were very helpful. He also played peek-a-boo with his younger sister. Jeremy became a happy and confident child once again. His parents said he was not "their same Jeremy," but one never goes through a situation like this without changing. The whole family had learned about healthy ways to handle death and the need for expression by everyone.

Jeremy and I have a special fondness for each other. Periodically he needed to come to see if I was still around and give me a hug. He will always be a special person to me because he taught me so very much about young children's needs for grief expression. He cried so loud with his behaviors in hopes that someone might help him. I am thankful his parents were willing to listen.

Dolls. Dolls have a very special place in the interventions. They are particularly helpful when used to say good-bye to a child who has died, or to the child that never was. I have a wide variety of dolls—from small infants to large ones, including both boys and girls. Often people will bring their own doll or one of their children's dolls.

This intervention has been very successful with women. I have only had one man who was comfortable enough with himself to hold and touch a doll. The expressive roles and saying good-bye seems to be much more of an issue for women. Females are socialized to be the "expressive" people in our culture (Johnson, 1963). The female role is focused on giving and receiving affection, being responsive to the needs and feelings of others, and keeping harmony. Males are socialized toward playing the instrumental role; they have traditionally been the family's link or liaison to the larger society. This doesn't mean that there is not overlapping of roles or even changes in our culture, but when a crisis, like death, arises, I see people *experiencing more of the issues connected with the "traditional" role-socializations.*

For those people who are experiencing expressive conflicts and guilts, the use of dolls can be extremely helpful to reenact the needs they were unable to fulfill. Women will complain that one of their grief symptoms is aching arms; holding the doll allows a vicarious experience. They may need to tell their child something, like "I love you so much." Again, they can say it to the doll. The most potent issues surround saying good-bye to that child, which they usually have not been able to accomplish. They will hold, touch, undress, redress, and talk to the doll. The expression of grief comes abundantly. Relief is often felt immediately, although for others it may not come for days.

For example, Nina, whose son was killed in the farm accident, brought her own doll to our therapy session. This was after *much therapy* regarding Oliver's death. She was able to cry and talk to "Oliver" (doll) about her pain and helplessness at the time of death, the conspiracy of silence, how much she missed him, and the family problems that developed after his death. After 18 years, the story had been pieced together and she was able to let go of him and remember the good and fun times she shared with him and the family. It was an extremely difficult experience for both of us, but the benefits were great.

Another woman, Susan, whose adopted son Hugh, had died, used the doll to grieve the child she was never able to bear. She had so wanted her own children, and had not realized that she had never allowed herself to grieve for what she couldn't have. She chose a girl doll, realizing as we progressed that she probably chose her because boys and men are so threatening to her. Susan talked about what she would have wanted her child to become, what she had learned from Hugh's death, and about herself and life. She had locked these feelings away for 22 years. It was no coincidence that over the years she developed pain during intercourse. There was nothing physically wrong with her. Although the pain was a good excuse not to have intercourse, she had also placed her sadness and unresolved grief in her vagina. This caused her great physical and emotional pain.

Homework

It is helpful if specific tasks can be assigned at the end of the therapy session. The goal is for the person to work between sessions on issues that we are developing in therapy. The activity must be meaningful to the client, otherwise she will not do it. In addition, she must be committed to homework.

Homework may involve writing in a journal, playing hide-and-seek at the shopping center, punching a punching bag, talking to someone about the unfinished business, experiencing how he feels, or writing a letter to the dead person. The clients find these assignments helpful. I am always very clear that therapy just doesn't occur an hour a week; the patient must make daily attempts to understand, resolve issues, and change behaviors.

For example, Nina and I had finally put the story together about Oliver's death. This was especially difficult because many of the family members continued to maintain the conspiracy of silence. Because of their need, she was unable to share the story with them. We agreed that there were several safe people at work to whom she could talk, thinking they did not know about the accident (of course they did). She had some good experiences and support in sharing. She was also willing to develop a short speech about her grief and pain, which she presented to the medical students I was teaching. She worked very hard on her assignments; it was healthy for her to share her experiences and it was also helpful to the students (there was not a dry eye in the auditorium). This experience also gave permission to many of the students who were dealing with their own grief to ask for help.

The more Nina was able to risk telling her story, the more comfortable she became with it and the more peaceful she felt about Oliver's death. It was a long and painful process for her, but the homework assignments allowed her to continue in-between sessions.

Some find that homework is not helpful. In that case, I attempt to assess if it is really *not helpful* or whether the client is *not committed* to treatment. More often than not, resistance is present.

For example, Elizabeth was a teenager referred to me for a school phobia. I had a very difficult time with the reason for the phobia and, in fact, never really uncovered it. We had agreed on a behavior modification approach. She would give all of her treasured Beatle records and paraphernalia to her parents. For appropriate behavior she would receive back a portion of her things, depending upon the behavior accomplished. Elizabeth decided she didn't like this, so one day she found the hiding place of her Beatle records and took them all back. She also refused to come back to treatment. (She wrote me a letter some months later, which included her report card showing high marks, and told of the many activities with which she was involved. What made the difference?) One cannot, or should not, "make" their clients do homework, or even remain in treatment, but for those who are committed it helps in one's therapy.

GRAVE VISITING

It is often necessary to make a trip to the grave with the person or family. There are a variety of reasons for this: to break down a conspiracy of silence, to assess the potent meanings of the grave, or to say good-bye once again.

In assessing survivors who utilize a conspiracy of silence, there is often a denial and silence regarding the grave. Many have refused to visit and may not know where it is located. As conspiracy begins breaking down, it is often helpful for the therapist and client to visit the grave. This visit may also take place with just the client, with a family member, or with a helpful friend.

The client must be willing to make the visit and should never be forced to do so. Some form of agenda is helpful. It may involve finding the grave, looking at the stone, saying a few words, or talking out the story of the death. Even a task that seems small, like finding the grave, will probably consume much energy and cause anxiety.

After completing the task, it is helpful if the client does something positive, allows time to rest, and strokes himself for his accomplishments. There is often a feeling of release when the issues are confronted. If the therapist does not accompany the client, it may be helpful to have an appointment shortly after the visit.

When the grave has very potent meanings, or is attached to complicated grief, I will often request that we both make a visit to the grave. This is most effectively done when the person is ready to make her decision to go on living, has realized she does not need to live continuously in the past, and is strong enough to share her secret behaviors and let them go. These mutual visits are structured to say good-bye once again. Often he or she will bring flowers, a toy, a picture, or even a balloon. He or she may choose to write a letter and burn it, or place it in a balloon and let it "fly" while we are there. Several times I have asked clergy to come and reenact the graveside service, emphasizing "ashes to ashes; dust to dust." This is often very helpful since at the original funeral service the patient was either in shock or not ready to say good-bye.

One young woman, whose father died when she was 14, had

avoided the cemetery, and her grief, for 10 years. She had had a bilateral mastectomy for fibrocystic disease at the young age of 25. Her therapy not only dealt with her breasts and body-image change, but with her ability to regrieve her father's death, since that grief was repressed during her adolescence. She had much unfinished business with him and his death. We planned how she would say her final good-bye to him on his birthday, thank him for all he had given her, share her own pain, and talk about the years and the conspiracy of silence that developed after his death. She wanted to do this alone, but had an appointment scheduled for after the visit. That gave us an opportunity to process the visit. She felt great relief and peace—much deserved.

A grave is often a very potent and important place in one's grief, especially in the first year of bereavement. Interventions are often needed because of the conspiracy of silence, the grave visiting becoming a compulsion, or the need to say a final good-bye.

RELAXATION, EXERCISE, AND FOOD

Because grief takes so very much energy, survivors must have time away from their pain. Some people attempt to escape their pain by excessive use of drugs or alcohol. Instead, I teach and encourage my patients to do relaxation exercises, yoga, meditation, imagery, or to have quiet time at least three times a day. These times do not need to be long, maybe only 5 minutes, but it is helpful to renew and prevent deterioration of physical and emotional health. Since concentration is usually poor, it is not helpful to read complicated literature for long periods of time. Short verses, listening to a record or song, or listening to a short piece into which one can "escape," is extremely helpful.

Initially, the grief pain is very intense, and it is difficult to escape from. The goal is not to avoid the pain, but to obtain some renewing time so that the pain can be confronted. Often people feel guilty when they aren't grieving, or when they are feeling better, especially at first. I try to encourage my clients that it is a "break," just like one takes a break from a difficult or tedious task, and it is okay to feel better.

Survivors usually do not have energy to accomplish vigorous exercise, but some form of exercise every day assists in maintaining health. Those who will not exercise are assigned homework that encourages some form of physical activity. For some it may be as minimal as walking around the outside of the house, then a little further, and finally around the block. These are small steps, but very important: they maintain health, encourage them to take care of themselves, and in a small way, says their life can continue.

Although I am not a nutritionist, I have found that diet is also important in one's recovery. What people eat tends to effect the intensity of grief feelings. If one is depressed, alcohol or large amounts of carbohydrates will potentiate that depression. I encourage my people to eat well-balanced meals, which are high in fruits and vegetables and low in carbohydrates, sugars, and alcohol (especially red wines). In addition, grieving people do not need large quantities of food.

Soon after the death people usually do not feel like eating. This is especially true with a tranquil shock. Because of body "shutdown" it is not necessary to eat a great deal, if at all. But I do encourage people to drink fruit juices and water to maintain their electrolyte balance. One must also remember that a weight gain or loss of 10 to 15 pounds is not unusual. Because people can often become very dehydrated, as well as suffer other effects from lowered electrolytes, it is important to maintain a fluid balance.

My families are often relieved when I tell them they don't need to eat everything that is presented to them. Food becomes a symbolic healing force when a death occurs. Food is immediately brought by well-wishers. Nothing is wrong with that; in fact, it is a beautiful gift showing that others care. Survivors, however, are often not hungry. In fact, the sight of food nauseates many. Food means different things to different people. We often try to "make things better" or "all right" by eating (my family always knows when I've had a "terrible, horrible, no good, very bad, day" because I want mashed potatoes). Therefore, survivors often feel forced to eat when they don't want to, in order to satisfy others' needs. Giving them permission not to eat great quantities, or not to eat at all, brings relief.

Of course, this should not go on indefinitely. People do need food. The body is wonderful, however, because it tells us in ways like hunger pains, thoughts of food, or cravings that it needs fuel. When food is needed I encourage people to start slowly with bland foods. I explore with my patients comforting foods and encourage them to eat those, if appropriate. I had one woman who could not eat because her husband died. She finally had a craving for strawberries. Unfortunately, it was late fall and strawberries were difficult to find. Her son was sent on a "mission" and finally found some. They were much appreciated and, for the woman, were a symbol that she could take "things" in once again.

HUMOR

Norman Cousins (1979) is right in believing that humor and laughter are good tonics. People feel better when they can laugh and feel some joy in a dark, lonely, and sad world. I, too, encourage my people to laugh, and not feel guilty about it. Often the fact that a person starts to laugh again shows progress.

A young woman who had experienced multiple changes over several months (her husband was killed, her mother died, a daughter was born, and she moved into a new house), remembers the first time she laughed. She finally decided to sell her husband's snowmobile. A man came to look at it, and she started to tell him of her plight and how difficult it was to sell this. He said he knew exactly what she was talking about. She said, "You mean your wife died too?" He said, "Oh no, I'm trying to sell my snowmobile!" She burst out in laughter for the first time!

To be able to laugh at oneself, one's environment, and one's situation, allows relief of tension and makes way for a little joy. It is difficult to do when the world looks so black, especially for a person who tends to be depressed anyway, or for someone who does not have a strong survivor instinct. But one should encourage trying— and then praise the effort.

SUMMARY

This chapter explored interventions that are helpful to clients experiencing grief. The use of storytelling; pictures; journals; literature, stories, puppets, drawings, and dolls; children's literature; homework; grave visits; relaxations; and humor. Interventions should relate to the problems the client is presenting.

REFERENCES

Aliki. (1979). *The two of them*. New York: Greenwillow Books, 1979.
Aliki. (1984). *Feelings*. New York: Greenwillow Books.
Arnold, J. H., & Gemma, P. B. 1983). *A child dies: A portrait of family grief*. Rockville, MD: Aspen Systems Corporation.
Buscaglia, L. (1982). *The fall of Freddie the leaf*. Thorofare, NJ: Charles B. Slack.
Charlip, R. (1967). *I love you*. New York: Avon Books.
Corey, D. *You go away*. (1976). Niles, IL: Albert Whitman & Company.
Cousins, N. (1979). *Anatomy of an illness as perceived by the patient: Reflections on healing and regeneration*. New York: Norton.

Grollman, E. A. (1970). *Talking about death.* Boston: Beacon Press.

Guisewite, C. (1983). *How to get rich, fall in love, lose weight, and solve all your problems by saying "No."* Fairway, KS: Universal Press Syndicate.

Hanson, J. *I'm going to run away.* New York: Platt & Munk.

Johnson, M. (1963). Sex role learning in the nuclear family. *Child Development, 34,* 319–333.

Johnson-Soderberg, S. (1981). Ibsen's *Little Eyolf:* A study of grief themes. *Advances in Nursing Science, 3,* (4), 15–26.

Moffat, M. (Ed.). (1982). *In the midst of winter: Selections from the literature of mourning.* New York: Vintage Books.

Paterson, D. (1976). *Smile for Auntie.* New York: The Dial Press.

Paterson, K. (1977). *Bridge to Terabithia.* New York: Thomas Y. Crowell.

Stanton, E., & Stanton, H. (1978). *Sometimes I like to cry.* Chicago: Albert Whitman & Company.

Stevenson, J. (1977). *Could be worse.* New York: Penguin Books.

Viorst, J. (1971). *The tenth good thing about Barney.* Hartford, CT: Aladdin Books.

Viorst, J. (1972). *Alexander and the terrible, horrible, no good, very bad day.* Hartford, CT: Aladdin Books.

Worden, J. W. (1982). *Grief counseling and grief therapy: A handbook for the mental health practitioner.* New York: Springer.

Zolotow, C. (1980). *Say it!.* New York: Greenwillow Books.

CHAPTER VII

Taking Care of the Caretaker: Professional Burnout

I am often asked how I survive in such a sad and high-stress area as thanatology. At times it has not been easy. I hear many sad stories and have seen, heard, and felt the pain of my clients and their families. I see how many people take destructive paths because of their loss, and I can do very little unless they accept help. However, I also see how most of my clients have come to terms with the pain of their grief, reorganized their life to live without their loved one, and gone on to develop new interests as a result of their experience with death. This is very gratifying.

Just like my clients, I have had to learn how to care for myself. I know there is prolific literature in the field of stress and burnout. Dealing with dying and death is often very painful and stressful. Accordingly, in this chapter I would like to cover some symptoms of burnout and characteristics of a stress-prone person, as well as address some of the problems in taking care of oneself while working or practicing in a high-stress situation.

BURNOUT SYMPTOMS

Who takes care of the caretaker? Usually, we have difficulty letting others help us, yet we help many. Who helps you when you have had a bad day? Have you noticed that every day begins to feel like Monday? Have you felt overwhelmed by all the demands and obligations both at work and home? Have you come home exhausted, knowing you are yelling at the kids just because you have had a hard day? Have you begun to feel there is too much week left at the end of the weekend? If responses to these questions are consistently "yes," you may have symptoms of what has come to be known as "burnout." (Truthfully, I am "burned out" by that term.)

This process has long been a problem in the caretaking professions such as nursing, medicine, dentistry, psychology, and the ministry. Burnout, however, is a term that has only recently been designated as a syndrome and expounded on by many (Freudenberger, 1974; Maslach, 1976, 1978; Hall, 1979; Edelmich, & Brodsky, 1980; Shubin, 1978). Burnout is emotional exhaustion: The person has given tremendously of himself or herself and there is little left. It tends to be a progressive condition causing a loss of idealism, energy, and purpose. It involves a process of giving and giving, without much taking, healing, or reviving. It is "bankrupting" one's emotional reserves.

The lesson we must learn is to manage our stress in "healthy" ways, or we will burn out. Burnout occurs when our reserve adaptation energy is depleted. Selye (1974, 1976) believes that we inherit our adaptation energy and that we can make "withdrawals," but has no proof that we can make "deposits." He believes we are not able to return to our prior level of adaptability. However, we are probably all aware that we are able to "restore" our emotional energy by getting some good rest, exercising, taking a vacation, or obtaining some professional help. According to Holmes and Rahe (1967), the longer we are exposed to multiple stressors the longer it takes us to recover, if recovery is at all possible.

I was counseling a member of the clergy who had given and given to his congregation. Although his religion was against drinking, he found himself drinking too much from hidden liquor bottles both at church and home. Gradually, he became verbally abusive to his wife and children. Being a "good minister's wife" she took the abuse and also insisted the children do the same. A quiet and secret war began to rage in their household and a "together, loving, and warm family" exposed themselves to the church. Over a period of several years the war gradually became worse and he began to abuse his wife physically, which again she covered. At no point in time did he think he was in trouble, and he continually avoided the subtle as well as the disastrous warning signs. It was not until his father died, ending a very ambivalent relationship, that he realized he needed help. The process of burnout was gradual and involved somatic, psychological, and interpersonal symptoms.

Somatic Symptoms

As with grief, many somatic symptoms are exhibited with burnout. There is exhaustion and fatigue. Freudenberger (1974) said this is the first distress signal. The person finds that there is weariness, fatigue, and a lack of energy. Usually the person has a difficult time accepting that they are tired because they have always had a high energy level. The vicious cycle begins because they believe if they try harder they will be able to meet the present demands, as they did in the past.

People often complain of physical symptoms like headaches, gastrointestinal disturbances, shortness of breath, or twitches. Usually there is insomnia, which tends to be exhibited by early morning awakening. In addition, the person usually finds that there is an increase in physical illness: "I never get sick, and now I have had a cold for 6 weeks." Although there may be multiple symptoms, it is important that the somatic and psychological symptoms not be seen in isolation, but that they be viewed as interrelated.

Psychological Symptoms

As with somatic symptoms, psychological symptoms tend to be progressive in nature. There is irritability and intolerance toward others. Often the person has habitual difficulty being tolerant and this is now compounded with a burnout situation. In addition to the irritability, there is an increase in rigidity. The person becomes more inflexible, which is often a means to control the uncontrollable. This behavior results in difficulties with co-workers, as the burned out person projects the problems back to the co-workers. Eventually, the burnout victim constructs a concept that it is "everyone else's fault," that there are problems, and begins to dislike everyone with whom he or she works.

As the projection increases, negativism and cynicism toward others develop, which may be accompanied by displaced and inappropriate anger. One often hears derogatory comments regarding co-workers or patient/clients. "Black humor" often accompanies the negativism. For example, a state's attorney continued to speak of his clients as the "cream of the crap." In addition, the person may become extremely pessimistic in their negativism and continually play, "Ain't it awful."

The person developing burnout will always experience symptoms of depression such as inability to concentrate, sleep and eating disorders, nightmares, and low energy. The depression tends, however, to be situational: Once the person is removed from the environment that is producing the burnout, the depression tends to dissipate. This is different from other types of depression where the person is depressed no matter what the situation or environment.

Burnout victims also begin to deny their feelings, especially if they feel threatened or hurt. When this happens, they attempt to distance themselves as a protection. This in turn causes more problems, since distancing from others increases the progression of burnout. Finally, caregivers who were once energetic, caring, empathetic, and excited about their work begin to deny their feelings, withdraw from people and situations, and detach from important people in their lives. In addition, they are unable to invest in new relationships.

As these behaviors increase, a feeling of paranoia develops. This is usually due to both withdrawal and distancing as well as the appearance of nonacceptance. Usually they are unaware that the nonacceptance has developed from their own negative and cynical behaviors. This in turn leads to intellectualization and labeling, "Oh, they are so dumb here and that is why none of my ideas ever get through."

I was treating a physician, Dr. W., for multiple losses and changes in his life over the past several years. As we reworked the history it became evident that he had been "burning out" emotionally for some time, but was not aware of the symptoms. He began yelling at the nurses on the floor when his orders were not carried out to his liking. He discounted his patients for their problems, treated them impersonally, and dehumanized his contact. He began "hating" his wife for anything she did. This projecting behavior was a symptom: When there are many unresolved needs in one's own life, it is difficult, if not impossible, to minister to patients.

His decision-making abilities began to fail and he chose coping mechanisms like "I'll have four drinks instead of two to relax," and "I was secretly so angry with my wife that I found another woman who I thought would be better." His "quick-and-dirty" cures did not help the situation; rather, they served to increase his depression and negativism. The problem was still present: He did not want to be a physician. He was able to take steps to change his profession, but it was too late to recapture the relationships that had been destroyed.

Intrapersonal and Interpersonal Symptoms

There can be many ways through which a person can begin to detach from people. Nonverbal distancing maneuvers are often used, such as continually standing with arms crossed, standing farther from people than is normally acceptable, decreasing eye contact, or turning the body away. Often people will avoid situations, events, or specific people all together. It becomes safer to isolate oneself.

This detachment causes less concern with self and others and this often results in taking foolhardy risks. This can frequently be interpreted as passive suicide attempts. For example, although it was totally unlike Dr. Ws personality, he started to take skydiving lessons as the burnout progressed.

In an attempt to rectify the intrapersonal and interpersonal problems, a person may often begin to work longer hours and attempt to say, "I'll show you I am o.k. You'll have to appreciate me." The distancing, however, only becomes more pronounced. The whole process becomes circular in nature: something is wrong, so they try harder. They try to adapt, but the adaptations tend to be harmful, and often expressed in such ways as affairs, excessive drug use, gambling, drinking, or excessive physical activity. Everything is done in the extreme in an effort to prove to oneself and the world that "I'm o.k." There is a continual search for meaning through sensory experiences. Freudenberger (1974) stressed that disengaging, distancing, dulling, or deadening will not solve the problem or halt the progression. My work shows that it is helpful to assess the burnout situation, keep attachments, and treat the problem(s).

Burnout is a resignation. It is personal surrender to unconfronted problems either with the position, profession, or private life. It is giving up without much effort to change oneself or the situation. Often the person will believe he or she has a solution, such as changing positions, divorcing, or increasing already inadequate coping mechanisms. In reality, however, such changes are not solutions, but rather resolutions. The problem will remain and, as with grief, wait to raise its ugly head once again in the future.

CHARACTERISTICS OF A STRESS-PRONE PERSON

There has been much research done on the stress-prone personality, leading to such labels as "Type A" personality or workaholic (Friedman & Rosenman, 1973; Friedman & Ulmer, 1984). I will briefly summarize the research, in addition to clinical indices from my practice, which relate to stress-prone people. These factors tend to place people at high risk for burnout. As you review these characteristics you may say to yourself, "Oh, my goodness, she is talking right to me." That may be true and all the more reason to learn to care for oneself. As mentioned in an earlier chapter, it is difficult, if not impossible, to change our "true personality," but we can certainly learn to change behaviors.

People who enter the helping professions, such as physicians, nurses, dentists, psychologists, attorneys, or teachers have a strong tendency to burnout. They have direct and intensive interpersonal contact with others and it is "expected" that they give and give to the population they serve. Because of their commitment, dedication, productivity, and achievements, these professionals are valued by our society. Yet, these people often believe the myth that they can give and give without receiving. That is because they often have strong needs to rescue people, and do not allow themselves the opportunity to be taken care of by someone else. In addition, they have a very idealistic view of the world.

People who have an idealistic approach to their position have the greatest tendency for burnout. They need everything to be perfect and when they discover it is not, it causes them great emotional pain. It is very easy for them to get into the circular pattern of "trying hard" to make everything all right and then once again be disappointed.

Most often, recognition is the primary motivator for these people—usually more so than money. They want to feel needed and appreciated. Many will go to extremes to receive that recognition.

I often see burnout in professionals when there is much role ambiguity or conflict. This may be due to entering a profession or marrying a certain person because their parents scripted them to be "something" ("my son the doctor," or "he is more our type, dear") rather than making their own decision. In addition to the family pressures in deciding upon a spouse or profession, one also receives messages from our society. This is especially true of professional women. I have heard many times of the guilt instillers who add to their own role conflicts: "How could you leave your infant and go back to work?" "You must be a terrible parent not to be home." or "You shouldn't be a physician/attorney/clergy? That is a man's job."

People who possess the qualities of being hard-driving, competitive, time-urgent, impatient, hostile, aggressive, polyphasic thinkers, need to win at any task (even when playing a game with their children), and need control, are susceptible to stress. These are the people who overplan each day with unrealistic goals. They drive themselves toward completing them and have difficulty saying "no." They continually attempt to prove to themselves that they "can do it." In their efforts to succeed they are often seen involved in multiple projects. There is a strong drive to work. Work becomes their life and becomes a means to hide from all other problems.

It is difficult for these people to relax without feeling guilty. If they do relax it often becomes a source of stress. Their hobbies tend to be stress inducing or hard-driving (e.g., jogging 26 miles, riding a bike cross-country, or swimming 10 miles).

Perhaps many of you possess these qualities. There is nothing wrong with them. Much of the "work" in our country gets done by people with such qualities. It must be recognized, however, that possessing these qualities has side effects, some of which are dangerous to our health. Burnout is a syndrome of energetic, intelligent, and educated people. Therefore, it is important that they learn how to take care of themselves so that they may continue their work in efficient and healthy ways.

TAKING CARE OF ONESELF

There is no cookbook recipe for taking care of oneself. It is a personal issue and what will work for one will not work for another. With my clients, we attempt to develop a "total" approach to dealing with stress and make an individual plan. The goal is to learn to cope better and prevent or halt the burnout process.

It is helpful to have a meaningful life away from work. How that develops is an individual issue. Hobbies, relaxation, and vacations are essential. However, hobbies need to be assessed, since often the hobbies themselves are stressful. For example, the hard-driving person should not take up running the 4-minute mile; day-sailing may be better than racing.

Often it is helpful to take some time each week to set some realistic goals for the next week. I always encourage my patients to add rewarding and fun goals to the list. Recognition should be given to yourself when these goals are accomplished. I have always loved the bumper sticker that says "Have you hugged your kid today?" That should not only mean our children, but also the "child" inside us, which must be stroked and cared for so we can care for others.

In our work situation, it is important to attempt to be supportive of each other. It is helpful to sit down weekly, or biweekly, to talk about work-related problems, give feedback, and support each other. Since detachment does not work, attachment does—at work, home, and socially. One does not need many intimate friends, but several who can be supportive. Those who hinder rather than support are not needed in our busy life space.

After work it is useful to have some decompression time on the way home. For many it is helpful to go for a walk, workout, meditate, use other relaxation techniques or take quiet time. If the day has been somewhat stressful or if there have already been many changes in recent times, do not add to the stress by taking a new way home, going to a new store, or changing a routine. At those times, life should be as consistent as possible. Life may be stressful, but at least you are not adding to the stress by placing yourself in new situations.

Take mental health days and PLAY!! (Cousins, 1974). That is so important in reviving oneself. In addition, sabbaticals and vacations present the opportunity to renew one's body and mind. Our summer neighbors in northern Michigan take long periods of time every summer to relax, play, read, and think. It is time for both of them to review the previous year's goals and tasks, as well as plan for the coming year. It is important to have some uninterrupted time every day. There is a boat on our lake called "Company Business." I think that is a wonderful name for when one needs uninterrupted time: One can always say they are on Company Business!!

One of the most difficult things for a hardworking person to do is to learn to say NO and then not feel guilty for saying it. This is an important lesson that can take a lifetime to learn. It is always important to evaluate one's level of stress and recognize one's best functioning level. When you feel or think you are getting into "hyperstress", it is time to say NO. Few hardworking people have problems with being understressed.

In assessing stresses it is often helpful to categorize it (see Table 7-1).

The catagories in Table 7-1 are important areas in evaluating how we care for our needs; all of these things can add stress to our lives. For example, a client is going blind (physical). Because of that he cannot carry out his normal work functions (performance) and is very bored being retired (boredom). He is grieving his loss (bereavement) and is extremely frustrated (frustration) because of all the changes. However, stress does not always have to appear to be negative. Winning a million dollars in the lottery may change one's whole life-style and that is also stressful.

It is unrealistic to expect a stress-free life—and that would be boring!! Stress is real. It affects us both positively and negatively. Stress is really an "inside job," because much of our stress we cause ourselves. Burnout is also real. Since we each are important in our own way, we owe it to ourselves to take care of ourselves. We can do this either by noncognitive or cognitive behaviors.

We can seek relief without really clarifying the nature of the

TABLE 7-1. Categorizing Stresses

Emotional:	within self or in confronting others
Spiritual:	conflicts with one's beliefs
Financial:	problems with too much or too little money
Environmental:	difficulties with one's immediate or global surroundings (smoking or "acid rain" and threat of nuclear war)
Social:	who are your helpful and hindering friends and situations
Sexual:	how, when, and where are these needs experienced or met—or not
Threats:	actual and perceived
Boredom:	from understimulation
Performance:	when present skills or knowledge are less than needed for the job at hand
Loss and bereavement:	single or multiple changes or losses
Frustration:	cannot do anything correctly, behind or delayed in work; lack of appreciation for work achieved; lack of recognition by myopic management
Fear:	actual or imagined threats
Physical:	physical stressors such as noise, pollution, diet, sleep, aging, heat, cold, or lack of exercise—physical stresses affect other forms of stress.
Diet and exercise:	how, when, why, what, and with whom we eat; the type and amount (too much, too little) exercise

problem, such as "taking a drink to relax after a stressful phone call" or "yelling at a co-worker" when you are not sure why you are yelling. If these behaviors are consistent, burnout may be in progress.

If one cognitively evaluates stresses, activities, and personality types, it tends to be more productive in preventing or solving problems. It is helpful to identify logically the stress areas; the supportive people, such as helpful health care professionals, family, and friends; the hindering people; to explore ways of taking care of needs; and to ask for help when it is needed (which is very difficult for people of this type). Continually evaluate what makes you happy and what you want out of life. Problems and issues can then be placed in perspective.

By all means, do not forget to have fun and socialize. Humor is so important. One must be able to laugh not just at situations, but also at ourselves. I often encourage professionals to utilize children's books, like Judith Viorst's (1972), *Alexander and the Terrible, Horrible, No Good, Very Bad Day*, in order to help put one's day into perspective. No matter where you go, even if you move to Australia, there will be bad days and stress; but the bad days help us appreciate the good ones.

Learn to take care of yourself. You are worth it. It is essential if you are to continue to care for your family, friends, and clients . . . because they are worth it also.

SUMMARY

This chapter explored burnout symptoms and the characteristics of a stress-prone person. Burnout is emotional exhaustion. Steps to take care of oneself in high-stress positions were discussed.

REFERENCES

Cousins, N. (1974). *The celebration of life: A dialogue on immortality and infinity*. New York: Harper & Row.

Edelmich, J., & Brodsky, A. (1980). *Burn-out: Stages of disillusionment in the helping professions*. New York: Sherman Services Press.

Freudenberger, H. J. (1974). Staff burn-out. *Journal of Social Issues, 30*, (1), 159–165.

Friedman, M., & Rosenman, R. (1973). *Type A behavior and your heart*. New York: Knopf.

Friedman, M., & Ulmer, D. (1984). *Treating type A behavior and your heart*. New York: Knopf.

Hall, R. C. W., Gardner, E. R., Gerl, M., Stickney, S. K., & Pfefferbaum, B. (1979, April). The professional burn-out syndrome. *Opinion*, 12–17.

Holmes, T. H., & Rahe, R. H. (1976). The social readjustment rating scale. *Journal of Psychosomatic Research, 11*, 213–218.

Maslach, C. (1976, September), Burnout. *Human behavior*, 16–22.

Maslach, C. (1978, Spring). Job burnout: How people cope. *Public Welfare*. Spring, 1978.

Selye, H. (1974). *Stress without distress*. Philadelphia: J. B. Lippincott.

Selye, H. (1976). *The stress of life*. New York: McGraw-Hill.

Shubin, S. (1978, July). Burnout: The professional hazard you face in nursing. *Nursing 78*, 22–27.

Viorst, J. (1972). *Alexander and the terrible, horrible, no good, very bad day*. Hartford, CT: Aladdin Books.

Appendix:
Selected Children's Books
on Death and Dying

PRESCHOOL CHILDREN

Brown, M. W. (1958). *The dead bird*. New York: Young Scott Books.
Stein, S. B. (1974). *About dying*. New York: Walker & Company.

CHILDREN'S LITERATURE

Abbott, S. (1972). *Old dog*. New York: Coward, McCann and Geoghegen.
Aliki. (1979). *The two of them*. New York: Greenwillow Books.
Aliki. (1984). *Feelings*. New York: Greenwillow Books.
Anders, R. (1978). *A look at death*. Minneapolis, MN: Lerner.
Bartoli, J. (1975). *Nonna*. Irvington-on-Hudson, NY: Howey House.
Buscaglia, L. (1982). *The fall of Freddie the leaf*. Thorofare, NJ: Charles B. Slack.
Carrick, C. (1976). *Accident*. New York: Seabury Press.
Charlip, R. (1967). *I love you*. New York: Avon Books.
Cohen, M. (1984). *Jim's dog muffins*. New York: Greenwillow Books.
Corey, D. (1976). *You go away*. Niles, IL: Albert Whitman & Company.
DeFord, F. (1983). *Alex: The life of a child*. New York: The Viking Press.
De Paola, T. (1981). *Now one foot, now the other*. New York: G. P. Putnam Books.
Dobrin, A. (1971). *Scat!* New York: Scholastic Book Services.
Grollman, E. A. (1970). *Talking about death*. Boston: Beacon Press.
Hanson, J. *I'm going to run away*. New York: Platt & Munk Publishers.
Miles, M. (1971). *Annie and the old one*. Boston: Little Brown.
Paterson, D. (1976). *Smile for Auntie*. New York: The Dial Press.

Viorst, J. (1972). *The tenth good thing about Barney*. Hartford, CT: Aladdin Books.
Viorst, J. (1972). *Alexander and the terrible, horrible, no good, very bad day*. Hartford, CT: Aladdin Books.
Warburg, S. S. (1969). *Growing time*. Boston: Houghton Mifflin.
Zolotow, C. (1980). *Say it!*. New York: Greenwillow Books.

LIFE CYCLES IN NATURE

Anglund, J. W. (1963). *Spring is a new beginning*. New York: Harcourt Brace Jovanovich.
Anglund, J. W. (1966). *Morning is a little child*. New York: Harcourt Brace Jovanovich.
Birnbaum, A. (1973). *Green eyes*. Racine, WI: Western Publishing.
Brenner, B. (1974). *Baltimore Orioles*. New York: Harper and Row.
Carrick, C., & Carrick, D. (1969). *Swamp spring*. New York: Macmillan.
Coutant, H. (1974). *First snow*. New York: Knopf.
Craig, J. (1965). *Spring is like the morning*. New York: Putnam.
De Paola, T. (1973). *Nana upstairs and Nana downstairs*. New ed. New York: Putnam.
Holl, A. (1974). *The wonderful tree*. Racine, WI: Western Publishing.
Krauss, R. (1947). *Growing story*. New York: Harper & Row.
Parker, B. M. (1974). *The wonders of the seasons*. Racine, WI: Western Publishing.
McNulty, F. (1974). *Woodchuck*. New York: Harper & Row.
Tresselt, A. (1972). *The dead tree*. New York: Parents' Magazine Press.

BODY CHANGES IN DEATH

Borack, B. (1969). *Someone small*. New York: Harper & Row.
Brenner, B. (1973). *Bodies*. New York: Dutton.
Kantrowitz, M. (1973). *When violet died*. New York: Parents' Magazine Press.
Pringle, L. (1977). *Death is natural*. New York: Scholastic Book Service.
Zim, H. S., & Blecker, S. (1970). *Life and death*. New York: Morrow.

OLDER SCHOOL CHILD

Brooks, J. (1973). *Uncle Mike's boy*. New York: Harper & Row.
Coburn, J. B. (1964). *Anne and the sand dobbies*. New York: Seabury Press.
Cohen, B. (1974). *Thank you, Jack Robinson*. New York: Lothrop, Lee & Shepard.
Klein, N. (1974). *Confessions of an only child*. New York: Pantheon Books.
Lee, V. (1972). *The magic moth*. New York: Seabury Press.
Rock, G. (1974). *The House Without a Christmas Tree*. New York: Knopf.
Rock, G. (1974). *The Thanksgiving Treasure*. New York: Knopf.
Sawyer, R. (1936). *Roller skates*. New York: Viking Press.
Smith, D. B. (1973). *A taste of blackberries*. New York: Thomas Y. Crowell.
White, E. B. (1952). *Charlotte's web*. New York: Harper & Row.
Wiggin, K. D. (1941). *The bird's Christmas carol*. Boston: Houghton Mifflin.

YOUNG ADOLESCENTS

Alcott, L. M. (1962). *Little women*. New York: Macmillan.
Armstrong, W. H. (1969). *Sounder*. New York: Harper & Row.
Bawden, N. (1971). *Squib*. Philadelphia: Lippincott.
Brenner, B. (1971). *Year in the life of Rosie Bernard*. New York: Harper & Row.
Buck, P. S. (1973). *The big wave*. New York: John Day.
Cleaver, V., & Cleaver, B. (1975). *Grover*. New York: New American Library.
Eunson, D. (1946). *The day they gave babies away*. New York: Farrar, Straus & Giroux.
Fitzgerald, J. D. (1971). *Me and my little brain*. New York: Dial Press.
Greenfield, E. (1974). *Sister*. New York: Thomas Y. Crowell.
Grollman, E. A. (1976). *Talking about death: A dialogue between parent and child*. Boston: Beacon Press.
Harnden, R. (1964). *High Pasture*. Boston: Houghton Mifflin.
Harvis, A. (1965). *Why did he die?* Minneapolis: Lerner Publications.
Molloy, A. S. (1967). *The girl from two miles high*. New York: Hastings House Publishers.
Orgell, D. (1971). *Mulberry music*. New York: Harper & Row.
Paterson, K. (1977). *Bridge to Terabithia*. New York: Thomas Y. Crowell Company.
Shecter, B. (1971). *Someplace else*. New York: Harper & Row.

AWARENESS OF FEELINGS

Berger, T. (1971). *I have feelings*. New York: Human Science Press.
Dunn, P. (1971). *Feelings*. Mankoto, MN: Creative Education Society.
Simon, N. (1970). *How do I feel?* Chicago: Albert Whitman.

Bibliography

Abrams, R., & Finesinger, J. E. (1953). Guilt reactions in patients with cancer. *Cancer, 6,* 474–482.

Ainsworth, M. D. (1964). Patterns of attachment behavior shown by the infant in interaction with his mother. *Merrill-Palmer Quarterly, 10,* 51–58.

Allinsmith, W., & Greening, T. C. (1955). Guilt over anger as predicted from parental discipline: A study of superego development. *American Psychologist, 10,* 320.

American Psychiatric Association. (1980). *Diagnostic and statistical manual of mental disorders,* (3rd ed.). Washington, D.C.: Author.

Anthony, S. (1940). *The child's discovery of death.* New York: Harcourt, Brace .

Arnold, J. H., & Gemma, P. B. (1983). *A child dies: A portrait of family grief.* Rockville, MD: Aspen Systems.

Aronfreed, J. (1963). The effect of experimental socialization paradigms upon two moral responses to transgression. *Journal of Abnormal and Social Psychology, 66,* 437–448.

Aronfreed, J. (1964). The origins of self-criticism. *Psychological Review, 71,* 193–218.

Aronfreed, J., Cutick, R. A., & Fagen, S. A. (1963). Cognitive structure, punishment, and nurturance in the experimental induction of self-criticism. *Child Development, 34,* 281–294.

Bachmann, C. C. (1964). *Ministering to the grief sufferers.* Englewood Cliffs, NJ: Prentice-Hall.

Barry, M. J., Jr. (1973). The prolonged grief reaction. *Mayo Clinic Proceedings, 48,* 329–335.

Barry, M. J., Jr. (1981). Therapeutic experience with patients referred for "prolonged grief reaction"—Some second thoughts. *Mayo Clinic Proceedings, 56,* 744–748.

Beable, W. H. (1971). *Epitaphs: Graveyard humor and eulogy.* New York: Thomas Y. Crowell.

Beck, A. T., et. al. (1963). Childhood bereavement and adult depression. *Archives of General Psychiatry, 9,* 295–302.

Becker, E., (1973). *The denial of death.* New York: The Free Press.

Becker, H., Gees, B., Hughes, E. C., & Strauss, A. M. (1961). *Boys in white.* Chicago and London: The University of Chicago Press.

Bendiksen, R., & Fulton, R. (1975). Childhood bereavement and later behavior disorders. *Omega, 6,* 45–60.

Benfield, D., Leib, S., & Reuther, J. (1976). Grief response of parents after referral of the critically ill newborn to a regional center. *The New England Journal of Medicine, 294,* 975–978.

Benfield, D., Leib, S., & Vollman, J. (1978, August). Grief response of parents to neonatal death and parent participation in deciding care. *Pediatrics, 62,* 171–177.

Benoliel, J. Q. (1975). Research related to death and the dying patient. In P. J. Verhonick (Ed.), *Nursing research I* (pp. 189–227). Boston: Little, Brown.

Berman, L. (1978). Sibling loss as an organizer of unconscious guilt: A case study. *Psychoanalytic Quarterly, 47,* 568–587.

Bermann, E. (1973a). Death terror: Observations of interaction patterns in an american family. *Omega, 4,* 275–291.

Bermann, E. (1973b) *Scapegoat: The impact of death-fear on an american family.* Ann Arbor: The University of Michigan Press.

The Holy Bible. Revised standard version (1952). New York: Harper and Brothers.

Bibring, G. L., Dwyer, T. F., and Huntington, D. S. (1961). A study of the psychological processes in pregnancy and of the earliest mother-child relationship: 1. Some propositions and comments. *Psychoanalytic Study of the Child, 16,* 9–72.

Binger, C. N., Albin, A. R., Feuerstein, R. C., Kushner, J., Zoger, S., & Mikkelson, C. (1969). Childhood-leukemia: Emotional impact on patient and family. *The New England Journal of Medicine, 280,* 414–418.

Birtchnell, J. (1970). Depression in relation to early and recent parent death. *British Journal of Psychiatry, 116,* 299–306.

Birtchnell, J. (1970). Recent parent death and mental illness. *British Journal of Psychiatry, 116,* 289–297.

Birtchnell, J. (1970). The relationship between attempted suicide, depression and parent death. *British Journal of Psychiatry, 116,* 307–313.

Bluebond-Langner, M. (1977). Meanings of death to children. In Feifel, H. (Ed.), *New meanings of death* (pp. 47–66). New York: McGraw-Hill.

Bornstein, P. E., et al. (1973). The depression of widowhood after thirteen months. *British Journal of Psychiatry, 122,* 561–566.

Bowlby, J. (1960). Grief and mourning in infancy and early childhood. *Psychoanalytic Study of the Child, 15,* 9–52.

Bowlby, J. (1960). Separation anxiety. *International Journal of Psychoanalysis, 41,* 89–113.

Bowlby, J. (1961). Process of mourning. *The International Journal of Psychoanalysis, 42,* 317–340.

Bowlby, J. (1969). *Attachment and loss: Attachment* (Vol. I). New York: Basic Books.

Bowlby, J. (1972). The child's tie to his mother: Attachment behavior. In C. S. Lavatelli and F. Stendler (Eds.), *Readings in child behavior and development* (3rd ed.,) pp. 317–333. New York: Harcourt Brace Jovanovitch.

Bowlby, J. (1973). *Attachment and loss: Separation* (Vol. II). New York: Basic Books.

Bowlby, J. (1980). *Attachment and loss: Loss, sadness, and depression* (Vol. III). New York: Basic Books.

Bozeman, M., Orgach, C. E., & Sutherland, A. (1955). Psychological impact of cancer and its treatment: III. The adaptation of mothers to the threatened loss of their children through leukemia: Part I. *Cancer, 8,* 1–19.

Brown, R. L. (1968). *A book of epitaphs.* New York: Taplinger.

Bugen, L. A. (1977). Human grief: A model for prediction and intervention. *American Journal of Orthopsychiatry, 47,* 196–206.

Bulfinch's Mythology. (1964). Feltham, Middlesex, England: Homlyn Publishing Group–Spring Books.

Cain, A., & Cain, B. (1964). On replacing a child. *Journal of American Academy of Child Psychiatry, 3,* 443–456.

Cain, A. C. (Ed.). (1972). *Survivors of suicide.* Springfield, IL: Thomas.

Cain, A. C., Fast, I., & Erickson, M. (1964). Children's disturbed reactions to the death of a sibling. *American Journal of Orthopsychiatry, 34,* 741–752.

Clayton, P. (1975). Weight loss and sleep disturbance. In B. Schoenberg, I. Gerber, A. Weiner, A. Kutscher, D. Peretz, & A. Carr (Eds.), *Bereavement: It's psychosocial aspects* (pp. 72–77). New York: Columbia University Press.

Clayton, P. J. (1973). The clinical morbidity of the first year of bereavement: A review. *Comprehensive Psychiatry, 14,* 151–157.

Clayton, P. J. (1974). Mortality and morbidity in the first year of widowhood. *Archives of General Psychiatry, 30,* 747–750.

Clayton, P. J. (1975). The effect of living alone on bereavement symptoms. *American Journal of Psychiatry, 132,* 133–137.

Clayton, P. J. (1979). The sequelae and nonsequelae of conjugal bereavement. *Psychiatry, 136,* 1530–1534.

Clyman, R., Green, C., Rowe, J., & Mikkelsen, C. (1980, April). Issues concerning parents after the death of their newborn. *Critical Care Medicine, 8,* 215–218.

Coddington, M. N. (1976, Spring). A mother struggles to cope with her child's deteriorating illness. *Maternal Child Nursing Journal, 5,* 39–44.

Coolidge, & Fish (1983–1984). Dreams of the dying. *Omega, 14,* (1), 1–8.

Cousinet, R. (1939). L'idee de la mort chez uns enfants. *Journal of Psychiatrie les Normale et Pathologique, 36,* 65–76.

Cousins, N. (1979). *Anatomy of an illness as perceived by the patient: Reflections on healing and regeneration.* New York: Norton.

Crisp, A. H., & Priest, R. G. (1972). Psychoneurotic status during the year following bereavement. *Journal of Psychosomatic Research, 16,* 351–355.

David, C. J. (1975). Grief, mourning, and pathological mourning. *Primary Care, 2,* 81–82.

Deutsch, H. (1937). Absence of grief. *Psychoanalytic Quarterly, 6,* 12–22.

Deutsch, H. (1959). A two-year-old boy's first love comes to grief. In L. Jessner & E. Pavenstedt (Eds.), *Dynamics of Psychopathology in Childhood.* New York: Grune and Stratton.

DeVaul, R., & Zisook, S. (1976). Unresolved grief: Clinical observations. *Postgraduate Medicine, 59,* 267–270.

Doka, K. J., & Schwarz, E. (1978). Author. Assigning blame: The restoration of sentimental order following accidental death. *Omega, 9,* 287–292.

Edelmich, J., & Brodsky, A. (1980). *Burn-out: Stages of disillusionment in the helping professions.* New York: Sherman Services Press.

Engel, G. L. (1961). Is grief a disease? A challenge for medical research. *Psychosomatic Medicine, 23,* 18–22.

Engel, G. L. (1964). Grief and grieving. *American Journal of Nursing, 9,* 93–98.

Engel, G. L. (1980–1981). A group dynamic approach to teaching and learning about grief. *Omega, 11,* 45–59.

Evans, A. E., & Edin, S. (1968). If a child must die. *The New England Journal of Medicine, 278,* 138–142.

Freedman, J. L., Wallington, S. A., & Bless, E. (1967). Compliance without pressure: The effect of guilt. *Journal of Personality and Social Psychology, 7,* 117–124.

Freud, S. (1933). *New introductory lectures on psychoanalysis.* New York: Norton.

Freud, S. (1947). *The ego and the id.* London: Hogarth Press. (Original work published 1923).

Freud, S. (1957a). *Totem and taboo,* Standard Edition (Vol. XIII). London: Hogarth Press. (Original work published 1912).

Freud, S. (1957b). *Mourning and melancholia,* Standard Edition (Vol. XIV). London: Hogarth Press. (Original work published 1917).

Freud, S. (1961). Some psychological consequences of the anatomical distinction between the sexes. In J. Strachey (Ed. and Trans.). *The complete works of Sigmund Freud* (Vol. 19, pp. 257–258). London: Hogarth Press. (Original work published 1923).

Freudenberger, H. J. (1974). Staff burn-out. *Journal of Social Issues, 30,* (1), 159–165.

Frey, W. H. (1980). Not-so-idle tears. *Psychology Today, 13,* 91–92.

Friedman, J. J. (1973, June). Depression, failure, and guilt. *New York State Journal of Medicine,* 1700–1704.

Friedman, M., & Rosenman, R. H. (1973). *Type A behavior and your heart.* New York: Knopf.

Friedman, M., & Ulmer, D. (1984). *Treating type A behavior and your heart.* New York: Knopf.

Friedman, S. B. (1967). Care of the family of the child with cancer. *Pediatrics, 40,* 498–519.

Fulton, R., & Fulton, J. (1971). A psychosocial aspect of terminal care: Anticipatory grief. *Omega, 2,* 91–100.

Fulton, R. (1977). *Death, grief, and bereavement: A bibliography* (pp. 1845–1975). New York: Arno Press.

Furman, E. (1974). *A child's parent dies: Studies in childhood bereavement.* New Haven: Yale.

Furman, R. A. (1964). Death and the young child. *Psychoanalytic Study of the Child,* (Vol. 19, p. 321). New York: International Universities Press.

Futterman, E. H., Hoffman, I., & Sabshin, M. (1972). Parental anticipatory mourning. In B. Schoenberg, A. Carr, D. Peretz, & A. Kutscher (Eds.), *Psychosocial aspects of terminal care* (pp. 243–272). New York: Columbia University Press.

Gardner, R. A. (1969, November). The guilt reaction of parents of children with severe physical disease. *American Journal of Psychiatry, 126,* 636–644.

Garfield, C. A., & Jenkins, G. J. (1981–1982). Stress and coping of volunteers counseling the dying and bereaved. *Omega, 12,* 1–13.

Glaser, B., & Strauss, A. (1964). The social loss of dying patients. *American Journal of Nursing, 6,* 119–121.

Glaser, B., & Strauss, A. (1965). *Awareness of dying.* Chicago: Aldine

Glaser, B., & Strauss, A. (1967). *The discovery of grounded theory: Strategies for qualitative research.* Chicago: Aldine.

Glaser, B., & Strauss, A. (1976). Initial definitions of dying trajectory. In E. Shneidman (Ed.), *Death: Current perspectives* (pp. 210–218). Palo Alto, CA: Mayfield.

Glick, I. O., Weiss, R. S., & Parkes, C. M. (1974). *The first year of bereavement.* New York: Wiley.

Green, R. G., & Quanty, M. B. (1977). The catharsis of aggression: An evaluation of a hypothesis. In. L. Berkowitz (Ed.), *Advances in experimental social psychology* (Vol. 10, pp. 1–37). New York: Academic Press.

Gould, R. K., & Rothenberg, M. B. (1973, July). The chronically ill child facing death—How can the pediatrician help? *Clinical Pediatrics,* 447–449.

Green, M. (1967, March). Care of the child with a long-term life-threatening illness: Some principles of management. *Pediatrics, 39,* 441–445.

Greenblatt, M. (1978). The grieving spouse. *American Journal of Psychiatry, 135,* 43–47.

Greene, W. A. (1958). Role of a vicarious object in the adaptation to object loss: I. Use of a vicarious object as a means of adjustment to separation from a significant person. *Psychosomatic Medicine, 20,* 344–350.

Grigson, G. (1977). *The Faber book of epigrams and epitaphs.* London: Faber and Faber.

Grinberg, L. (1964). Two kinds of guilt—Their relations with normal and pathological aspects of mourning. *International Journal of Psychoanalysis, 65,* 366–371.

Gross, A. E. (1972, September). *Sex and helping: Intrinsic glow and extrinsic show.* Paper presented at meeting of the American Psychological Association, Honolulu.

Grusec, J. (1966). Some antecedents of self-criticism. *Journal of Personality and Social Psychology, 4,* 244–252.

Guisewite, C. (1983). *How to get rich, fall in love, lose weight, and solve all your problems by saying 'No'.* Fairway, KS: Universal Press Syndicate.

Gut, E. (1975). Some aspects of adult mourning. *Omega, 5,* 323–342.

Hagan, J. M. (1974). Infant death: Nursing interaction and intervention with grieving families. *Nursing Forum, 13,* 371–385.

Hall, R. C. W., Gardner, E. R., Gerl, M., Stickney, S. K., & Pfefferbaum, B. (1979, April). The professional burn-out syndrome. *Opinion,* 12–17.

Hamovitch, M. B. (1964). *The parent and the fatally ill child.* Duarte, CA: City of Hope Medical Center.

Hare-Mustin, R. (1979, April). Family therapy following the death of a child. *Journal of Marital and Family Therapy, 5,* 51–59.

Harman, W. V. (1981, January). Death of my baby. *British Medical Journal, 282,* 35–37.

Heffron, W. A., Bommelaere, J., & Masters, R. (1973, December). Group discussions with the parents of leukemic children. *Pediatrics, 52,* 831–840.

Heimler, E. (1975). *Survival in society.* New York: A Halsted Press Book.

Hildebrand, W., & Schreiner, R. (1980, November). Helping parents cope with perinatal death. *AFP, 22,* 121–125.

Hinton, A., Shirby, L., & Tenbusth, L. (1982). *Getting free.* New York: Grove Press.

Hoffman, M. L., & Saltzstein, H. D. (1967). Parent discipline and the child's moral development. *Journal of Personality and Social Psychology, 5,* 45–57.

Hoffman, M. L. (1970). Moral development. In P. H. Mussen (Ed.), *Carmichael's manual of child development* (Vol. 2, pp. 261–317). New York: Wiley.

Hoffman, M. L. (1970). Conscious, personality and socialization techniques. *Human Development, 13,* 90–126.

Hoffman, M. L. (1974). Developmental synthesis of affect and cognition and its implications for altruistic motivation. *Developmental Psychology, 11,* 607–622.

Hoffman, M. L. (1975). Sex differences in moral internalization and values. *Journal of Personality and Social Psychology, 32,* 720–729.

Hoffman, M. L. (1976). Empathy, role taking, guilt, and development of altruistic motives. In T. Lickona (Ed.), *Moral development and behavior: Theory, research, and social issues* (pp. 124–143). New York: Holt, Rinehart and Winston.

Hoffman, M. L. (1977). Moral internalization: Current theory and research. In L. Berkowitz (Ed.), *Advances in experimental social psychology* (p. 18). New York: Academic Press.

Holmes, T. H., & Rahe, R. H. (1967). Social readjustment rating scale. *Journal of Psychosomatic Research, 11,* 213–218.

Holmes, T. S., & Holmes, T. H. (1970). Short-term intrusions into the life style routine. *Journal of Psychosomatic Research, 14,* 121–132.

Holmes, T. H., & Masuda, M. (1973). Life change and illness susceptibility. In J. P. Scott & E. C. Senay (Eds.), *Separation and depression: Clinical and research aspects.* Washington, DC: American Association for the Advancement of Science, *94,* 161–186.

Ingles, T. (1974). St. Christopher's hospice. *Nursing Outlook, 22,* 759–763.

Jackson, E. N. (1957). *Understanding grief.* New York: Abingdon Press.

Jackson, E. N. (1961). *You and your grief.* New York: Hawthorn Books.

Jackson, E. N. (1963). Guilt and grief. *Journal of Pastoral Counseling, 1.*

Jackson, E. N. (1970). *When someone dies.* Philadelphia: Fortress Press.

Jackson, P. L. (1974). Chronic grief. *American Journal of Nursing, 74,* 1290–1291.

Jagan, J. M. (1974). Infant death: Nursing interaction and intervention with grieving families. *Nursing Forum, 13,* 371–385.

Jersild, A. (1978). *The psychology of adolescence* (3rd ed.). New York: Macmillan, 260–261.

Johnson, M. (1963). Sex role learning in the nuclear family. *Child Development, 34,* 319–333.

Johnson, R. C., & Kalafat, J. D. (1969). Projective and sociometric measures of conscious development. *Child Development, 40,* 651–655.

Johnson-Soderberg, S. (1977). Theory and practice of scapegoating. *Perspective in Psychiatric Care, 15,* 153–159.

Johnson-Soderberg, S. (1981). The development of a child's concept of death. *Oncology Nursing Forum, 8,* 23–26.

Johnson-Soderberg, S. (1981). Ibsen's *Little Eyolf:* A study of grief themes. *Advances in Nursing Science, 3:4,* 15–26.

Johnson-Soderberg, S. (1982). *The ethos of parental bereavement and guilt.* (Doctoral dissertation, University of Michigan, 1982). *University Microfilm International, 1,* 222-502.

Johnson-Soderberg, S. (1983a). Parents who have lost a child by death. In R. Hoekelman, (Ed.), *A round table on minimizing high-risk parenting* (pp. 55–61). New Brunswick, NJ: Monograph sponsored by Johnson & Johnson Baby Products.

Johnson-Soderberg, S. (1983b). Minimizing high-risk parenting: A review of what is known and considerative of appropriate preventive intervention. In V. Sasserath & R. Hoekelman (Eds.), *Pediatric Round Table: 7.* New Brunswick, NJ: Monograph sponsored by Johnson and Johnson Baby Products, 55–61.

Johnson, S. (1983). Guiding adults through bereavement. *Nursing Life,* 34–39.

Johnson, S. (1981). Counseling families experiencing guilt. *Dimensions of Critical Care Nursing, 3,* (4), 238–244.

Johnson, S. (1984). Sexual intimacy and replacement children after the death of a child. *Omega, 15,* (2), 109–118.

Johnson, S. (1986). The patient experiencing grief. *The Nurse Psychotherapist in Private Practice.* New York: Springer Publishing Co.

Joseph, E., & Tabor, J. (1961). The simultaneous analysis of a pair of twins and the twinning reaction. *Psychoanalytic Study of the Child, 16,* 275–299.

Kastenbaum, R. (1967). The child's understanding of death: How does it develop? In E. Grollman (Ed.), *Explaining Death to Children* (p. 105). Boston: Beacon Press.

Keddie, K. M. G. (1977). Pathological mourning after the death of a domestic pet. *British Journal of Psychiatry, 131,* 21–25.

Keirsey, D., & Bates, M. (1978). *Please understand me: Character and treatment types.* Del Mar, CA: Prometheus Nemesis Books.

Kennell, J. H., & Klaus, M. H. (1976). Caring for parents of an infant who dies. In J. H. Kennell & M. H. Klaus (Eds.), *Maternal-infant bonding* (pp. 209–239). St. Louis: Mosby.

Kennell, J. H., Slyter, H., & Klaus, M. (1970, August). The mourning response of parents to the death of a newborn infant. *The New England Journal of Medicine, 283,* 344–349.

Kibec, H. D. (1980). Ending human relationships: Problems and potentials. *Journal of Religion and Health, 19,* 18–23.

Kilham, W., & Mann, L. (1974). Level of destructive obedience as a function of transmitter and executant roles in the Milgram obedience paradigm. *Journal of Personality and Social Psychology, 29,* 696–702

Kippax, J. (1969). *Churchyard literature: A choice selection of American epitaphs.* Detroit: Singing Tree Press, Book Tower. (Original work published 1877).

Kitson, G. C., et al. (1980). Divorcees and widows: Similarity and differences. *American Journal of Orthopsychiatry, 50,* 291–301.

Klein, M. (1948). Mourning and its relation to manic-depressive states. In M. Klein (Ed.), *Contribution to psycho-analysis.* London: Hogarth Press.

Knudson, A. G., & Natterson, J. M. (1960). Participation of parents in the hospital care of their fatally ill children. *Pediatrics, 26,* 482–490.

Kohlberg, L. (1976). Moral stages and moralization: The cognitive-developmental approach. In T. Lickona (Ed.), *Moral development and behavior* (pp. 31–53). New York: Holt, Rinehart and Winston.

Konaske, P., Staple, S., & Graf, R. G. (1979). Compliant reactions to guilt: Self-esteem of self-punishment. *Journal of Social Psychology, 108,* 207–211.

Koocher, G. (1974). Talking with children about death. *American Journal of Ortho-Psychiatry, 44,* (3), 404.

Kübler-Ross, E. (1969). *On death and dying.* New York: MacMillan.

Kushner, H. S. (1981). *When bad things happen to good people.* New York: Avon Books.

Kutscher, A. H. (Ed.). (1969). *Death and bereavement.* Springfield, IL: Thomas.

Lamers, W. M., Jr. (1969). Funerals are good for people—M.D.s included. *Medical Economics, 46,* 1–4.

Lascari, A. D., & Stehbens, J. A. (1973, April). The reactions of families to childhood leukemia: An evaluation of a program of emotional management. *Clinical Pediatrics, 12,* 210–214.

LaVoie, J. C. (1973, January). Individual differences in resistance-to-temptation behavior in adolescents: An Eysenck analysis. *Journal of Clinical Psychology, 29,* 20–22.

Legg, C., & Sherick, A. (1976, Winter). The replacement child—A developmental tragedy: Some preliminary comments. *Child Psychiatry and Human Development, 7,* 113–126.

Lehrman, S. R. (1956). Reactions to untimely death. *Psychiatric Quarterly 30,* 546–578.

LeShan, E. (1976). *Learning to say good-by.* New York: Macmillan.

Leukemia strains emotional ties. (1973, April). *Medical World News,* p. 23.

Lewis, C. S. (1961). *A grief observed.* London: Faber & Faber.

Lifton, R. J. (1967). *Death in life: Survivors of Hiroshima.* New York: Vintage Books Edition.

Lindemann, E. (1944). Symptomatology and management of acute grief. *American Journal of Psychiatry, 101,* 141–148.

Lowman, J. (1979, December). Grief intervention and sudden infant death syndrome. *American Journal of Community Psychology, 7,* 665–677.

Mandelbaum, D. (1959). Social uses of funeral rites. In H. Feifel (Ed.), *The meaning of death* (pp. 39–63). New York: McGraw-Hill.

Mandell, F., & Wolfe, L. C. (1975). Sudden infant death syndrome and subsequent pregnancy. *Pediatrics, 56,* 774–776.

Mann, S. A. (1974, March). Coping with a child's fatal illness, A parent's dilemma. *Nursing Clinics of North America, 9,* 81–87.

Margolis, O. S., et al (Eds.). (1981). *Acute grief: Counseling the bereaved.* New York: Columbia University Press.

Maslach, C. (1976, September). Burnout. *Human behavior,* 16–22.

Maslach, C. (1978, Spring). Job burnout: How people cope. *Public Welfare.*

Matchett, W. F. (1972). Repeated hallucinatory experiences as a part of the mourning process among Hopi Indian women. *Psychiatry, 35,* 185–194.

McDonald, M. (1964). A study of the reactions of nursery school children to the death of a child's mother. *Psychoanalytic Study of a Child,* (Vol. 19, p. 358). New York: International Universities Press.

McIntire, M., Angle, C., & Struempler, L. (1972, June). The concept of death in midwestern children and youth. *American Journal of the Diseases of Children, 123,* 527–532.

Melges, F. T., & DeMaso, D. R. (1980). Grief-resolution therapy: Reliving, revising, and revisiting. *American Journal of Psychotherapy, 34,* 51–61.

Milgram, S. (1963). Behavioral study of obedience. *Journal of Abnormal and Social Psychology, 67,* 371–378.

Miller, D. R., & Swanson, G. E. (Ed.). (1960). *Inner conflict and defense.* New York: Henry Holt and Company.

Miller, J. B. M. (1961). Children's reactions to the death of a parent: A review of psychoanalytic literature. *Journal of the American Psychoanalytic Association, 19,* 697–719.

Morgan, J. H., & Goering, R. (1978). Caring for parents who have lost an infant. *Journal of Religion and Health, 17,* 290–298.

Morris, P. (1958). *Widows and their families.* London: Routledge and Kegan Paul.

Nagera, H. (1967). *Vincent van Gogh, a psychological study.* London: George Allen and Unwin.

Nagy, M. H. (1948, September). The child's theory concerning death. *Journal of Genetics and Psychology, 73,* 3–27.

Natterson, J., & Knudson, A. (1960). Observations concerning fear of death in fatally ill children and their mothers. *Psychosomatic Medicine, 22,* 456–465.

Nolfi, M. (1967, October). Families in grief: The question of casework intervention. *Social Worker*, 40–45.

Orbach, C. E., Sutherland, A. M., & Bozeman, M. E. (1955, January–February). Psychological impact of cancer and its treatment: III. The adaptation of mothers to the threatened loss of their children through leukemia: Part II. *Cancer, 8*, 20–33.

Parkes, C. M. (1964). Effects of bereavement on physical and mental health— A study of the medical records of widows. *British Medical Journal, 2*, 274–279.

Parkes, C. M. (1964). Recent bereavement as a cause of mental illness. *British Journal of Psychiatry, 110*, 198–204.

Parkes, C. M. (1965). Bereavement and mental illness: Part I. A clinical study of the grief of bereaved psychiatric patients. *British Journal of Medical Psychology, 38*, 1–12.

Parkes, C. M. (1965). Bereavement and mental illness: Part II. A classification of bereavement reaction. *British Journal of Medical Psychology, 38*, 13–25.

Parkes, C. M. (1970). The first year of bereavement: A longitudinal study of the reaction of London widows to the death of their husbands. *Psychiatry, 33*, 444–467.

Parkes, C. M. (1972). *Bereavement: Studies of grief in adult life.* New York: International Universities Press.

Parkes, C. M. (1975). Unexpected and untimely bereavement: A statistical study of young Boston widows and widowers. In B. Schoenberg, I. Gerber, A. Wiener, A. Kutscher, D. Peretz, & A. Carr (Eds.), *Bereavement: Its psychological aspects* (pp. 119–138). New York: Columbia University Press.

Parkes, C. M. (1975). Determinants of outcome following bereavement. *Omega, 6*, 303–323.

Parkes, C. M. (1980). Bereavement counseling: Does it work? *British Medical Journal, 281*, 3–6.

Parkes, C. M., Benjamin, B., & Fitzgerald, R. G. (1969). Broken heart: A statistical study of increased mortality among widowers. *British Medical Journal, 1*, 740–743.

Peck, M. (1983–1984). Official documentation of the black suicide experience. *Omega, 14*, (1), 21–31.

Petrich, J., & Holmes, T. H. (1977, July). Life change and onset of illness. *Medical Clinics of North America, 61*, 825–838.

Piaget, J. (1965). *The moral judgment of the child.* New York: Free Press.

Piers, G., & Singer, M. (1953). *Shame and guilt: A psychoanalytic and cultural study.* Springfield, IL: C. H. Thomas.

Pollock, G. H. (1970). Anniversary reactions, trauma, and mourning. *Psychoanalytic Quarterly, 39*, 347–371.

Pollock, G. H. (1972). Bertha Pappenheim's pathological mourning: Possible effects of childhood sibling loss. *Journal of the American Psychoanalytic Association, 20*, 476.

Poznanski, E. O. (1972). The "replacement child"—A saga of unresolved parental grief. *Journal of Pediatrics, 81*, 1190–1193.

Priest, R. G., & Crisp, A. H. (1973). Bereavement and psychiatric symptoms: An item analysis. *Psychotherapy and Psychosomatics, 22*, 166–171.

Prilook, M. E. (Ed.). (1977). When caring is all that's left to give: A patient care roundtable on dying and death. *Patient Care*, 18–126.

Quint, J. (1967). *The nurse and the dying patient.* New York: Macmillan.

Quint, J., & Strauss, A. (1964). Nursing students, assignments, and dying patients. *Nursing Outlook, 12,* 24–27.

Rahe, R. H. (1972). Subjects recent life change and their near future illness susceptibility. *Advances in Psychosomatic Medicine, 8,* 2–19.

Rahe, R. H., & Lind, E. (1971). Psychosocial factors and sudden cardiac death: A pilot study. *Journal of Psychosomatic Research, 15,* 19–24.

Rees, W. D. (1971). The hallucinations of widowhood. *British Medical Journal, 4,* 37–41.

Rees, W. D. (1972). Bereavement and illness. In B. Schoenberg, A. Carr, D. Peretz, & A. Kutscher (Eds.), *Psychosocial aspects of terminal care* (pp. 210–220). New York: Columbia University Press.

Rees, W. D. (1975). The bereaved and their hallucinations. In B. Schoenberg, I. Gerber, A. Wiener, A. Kutscher, D. Peretz, & A. Carr (Eds.), *Bereavement: Its psychosocial aspects* (pp. 66–71). New York: Columbia University Press.

Regan, D. T., Williams, M., & Sparling, S. (1972). Voluntary expiation of guilt: A field experiment. *Journal of Personality and Social Psychology, 24,* 42–45.

Regan, J. W. (1971). Guilt, perceived injustice, and altruistic behavior. *Journal of Personality and Social Psychology, 18,* 124–132.

Rest, J. R. (1973, March). The hierarchical nature of moral judgment: A study of patterns of comprehension and preference of moral stages. *Journal of Personality, 41,* 86–109.

Richmond, J. B., & Waisman, H. H. (1955). Psychological aspects of management of children and malignant diseases. *American Journal of the Diseases of Children, 89,* 42–47.

Rogers, J., & Vachon, M. L. S. (1975). Nurses can help the bereaved. *The Canadian Nurse, 71,* 1–4.

Rogers, J., et al. (1980). A self-help program for widows as an independent community service. *Hospital and Community Psychiatry, 31,* 844–847.

Rowe, J., Clyman, R., Green, C., Mikkelsen, C., & Height, J., et al. (1978, August). Follow-up of families who experience a perinatal death. *Pediatrics, 62,* 167–170.

Schaffer, H., Rudolph, & Emerson, P. (1964). The development of social attachment in infancy. *Monographs of the Society for Research in Child Development, 29,* (3), 5–77. (Serial No. 94).

Schmale, A. H. (1971). Psychic trauma during bereavement. *International Psychiatric Clinics, 8,* 147–168.

Schoenberg, B., Carr, A., Peretz, D., & Kutscher, A. (1970). *Loss and grief: Psychological management in medical practice.* New York: Columbia University Press.

Schoenberg, B., Carr, A., Kutscher, A., Peretz, D., & Goldberg, I. (1974). *Anticipatory grief.* New York: Columbia University Press.

Sears, R. S., Maccoby, E. E., & Levin, H. (1957). *Patterns of child rearing.* Evanston, IL: Row, Peterson.

Sears, R. S., Rau, L., & Alpert, R. (1965). *Identification and child rearing.* Stanford, CA: Stanford University Press.

Selye, H. (1974). *Stress without distress.* Philadelphia: J. B. Lippincott.

Selye, H. (1976). *The stress of life.* New York: McGraw Hill.

Shainess, N. (1984). *Sweet suffering: Women as victim.* New York: Bobb-Merrill.

Silverman, P. R. (1969). The widow-to-widow program: An experiment in preventive intervention. *Mental Hygiene, 53,* 333–337.

Silverman, P. R. (1973). *Helping each other in widowhood.* New York: Health Services Publishing.

Simos, B. G. (1977). Grief therapy to facilitate healthy restitution. *Social Casework, 58,* 337–342.

Simos, B. G. (1979). *A time to grieve.* New York: Family Service Association.

Simpson, E. L. (1974). Moral development research: A case study of scientific cultural bias. *Human Development, 17,* 81–106.

Singher, L. J. (1974, October). The slowly dying child. *Clinical Pediatrics, 13,* 861–867.

Smialek, Z. (1978). Observations on intermediate reactions of families to sudden infant death. *Pediatrics, 62,* 160–165.

Smith, A. G., & Schneider, L. T. (1969, March). The dying child: Helping the family cope with impending death. *Clinical Pediatrics, 8,* 131–134.

Solnit, A. J., & Green, M. (1959). Psychological considerations in the management of deaths on pediatric hospital services: I. The doctor and the child's family. *Pediatrics, 24,* 106–112.

Spinetta, J. J., Rigler, D., & Karon, M. (1973, December). Anxiety in the dying child. *Pediatrics, 52,* (6), 841–845.

Staub, E. (1971). Helping a person in distress: The influence of implicit and explicit "rules" of conduct on children and adults. *Journal of Personality and Social Psychology, 17,* 137–144.

Steiner, G. L. (1965). *Children's concepts of life and death: A developmental study.* (Doctoral dissertation, Columbia University, New York, 1965).

Stoddard, S. (1978). *The hospice movement.* New York: Vintage.

Stroebe, M. S., et al. (1981–1982). The broken heart: Reality or myth? *Omega, 12,* 87–106.

Sudnow, D. (1967). *Passing on: The social organization of dying.* New Jersey: Prentice-Hall.

Switzer, D. (1970). *The dynamics of grief.* Abingdon.

Time, April 15, 1985, p. 83.

Vachon, M. L. S. (1976). Stress reactions to bereavement. *Essence, 1,* 23–33.

Vachon, M. L. S., et al. (1977). The final illness in cancer: The widow's perspective. *Canadian Medical Association Journal, 117,* 1151–1154.

Vachon, M. L. S. (1979). Staff stress in care of the terminally ill. *Quality Review Bulletin,* 13–17.

Vachon, M. L. S., et al. (1980). A controlled study of self-help intervention of widows. *American Journal of Psychiatry, 137,* 1380–1384.

Vachon, M. L. S. (1981). Type of death as a determinant in acute grief. In O. S. Margolis, et al. (Eds.), *Acute grief counseling the bereaved.* New York: Columbia University Press.

Vernick, J. (1973). Meaningful communication with the fatally ill child. In J. Anthony & C. Kaupernik (Eds.), *The child in his family: The impact of disease and death* (Vol. 2, p. 105). New York: Wiley.

Verwoerdt, A. (1966). *Communication with the fatally ill.* Springfield: Charles C. Thomas.

Volkart, E. H., & Michael, S. T. (1957). Bereavement and mental health. In A. H. Leighton, J. A. Clausen, & R. N. Wilson (Eds.), *Explanations in social psychiatry* (pp. 281–307). New York: Basic Books.

Waechter, E. Y. (1971, June). Children's awareness of fatal illness. *American Journal of Nursing, 71,* (6), 1168–1172.

Weisman, A. D. (1974). Is mourning necessary? In B. Schoenberg, et al. (Eds.), *Anticipatory grief* (pp. 14–18). New York: Columbia University Press.

Westberg, G. E. (1961). *Good grief—A constructive approach to the problem of loss.* Philadelphia: Fortress Press.

Westphal, M. (1984). *God, guilt and death: An existential phenomenology of religion.* Bloomington, IN: University Press.

Wiener, A., Gerber, I., Battin, D., & Arkin, A. M. (1974). The process and phenomenology of bereavement. In B. Schoenberg, I. Gerber, A. Wiener, A. Kutscher, D. Peretz, & A. Carr (Eds.), *Bereavement: It's psychosocial aspects* (pp. 53–65). New York: Columbia University Press.

Worden, J. W. (1976). *Personal death awareness.* Englewood Cliffs, NJ: Prentice-Hall.

Worden, J. W. (1982). *Grief counseling and grief therapy: A handbook for the mental health practitioner.* New York: Springer.

Yarrow, L. J., & Pedersen, F. A. (1972). Attachment: Its origins and course. In W. Hartup (Ed.), *The young child.* Washington, D.C.: N.A.E.Y.C., 2, 54–66.

Index